Theatre

Theatre

Its Art and Craft

Seventh Edition

CYNTHIA M. GENDRICH
STEPHEN ARCHER

ROWMAN & LITTLEFIELD
Lanham • Boulder • New York • London

Published by Rowman & Littlefield
A wholly owned subsidiary of The Rowman & Littlefield Publishing Group, Inc.
4501 Forbes Boulevard, Suite 200, Lanham, Maryland 20706
www.rowman.com

Unit A, Whitacre Mews, 26-34 Stannary Street, London SE11 4AB

British Library Cataloguing in Publication Information Available

Library of Congress Cataloging-in-Publication Data

Names: Gendrich, Cynthia M., 1952– author. | Archer, Stephen M. author.
Title: Theatre : its art and craft / Cynthia M. Gendrich, Stephen Archer.
Description: Seventh edition. | Lanham : Rowman & Littlefield, 2017. | On the
   previous edition, Stephen Archer's name appears first on the t.p. |
   Includes bibliographical references and index.
Identifiers: LCCN 2016041765 (print) | LCCN 2016057336 (ebook) | ISBN
   9781442278028 (hardback : alk. paper) | ISBN 9781442277748 (pbk. : alk.
   paper) | ISBN 9781442277755 (electronic)
Subjects: LCSH: Theater.
Classification: LCC PN2037 .A63 2017 (print) | LCC PN2037 (ebook) | DDC
   792—dc23
LC record available at https://lccn.loc.gov/2016041765

♾️™ The paper used in this publication meets the minimum requirements of
American National Standard for Information Sciences—Permanence of Paper
for Printed Library Materials, ANSI/NISO Z39.48-1992.

Printed in the United States of America

Contents

Introduction

Theatre: Its Art and Craft is an introductory theatre text focusing on theatre practitioners and their processes.

For the seventh edition the book has been thoroughly revised. It contains new statistics, updated references and photos, and a fair amount of condensing in chapters 1 and 5. New sidebars have been added throughout, including one on cultural appropriation, another on lighting technology, and more and better discussions of what carpenters, technical directors, stage managers, and others do. This reflects our ongoing commitment to exploring how all theatre practitioners work.

We have also interspersed new content about devised theatre, attempted to regularize a few formatting oddities from earlier editions, and throughout have worked to keep the text relatable without ever talking down to our readers. With the explosion of youthful involvement in theatre—as well as interest in plays like *Hamilton* and *The Book of Mormon*—we feel confident in the next generation's passionate involvement in this living, breathing art form.

Not everything in the book has been changed, of course. We continue to cover critics, playwrights, directors, actors, historians, theorists, and all types of designers. Our design chapters remain split into two halves: one on the tactile elements of design (chapter 7: sets, props, costumes, makeup, and hair) and one on the temporal elements (chapter 8). You will note that, grouped with lighting and sound, we have written an expanded section on projections design. With the explosion of their use in live theatre, and with the advent of MFA programs in this area at places like Yale and Carnegie Mellon, it seemed time. However, we understand that projections have scenic properties as well, so feel free to read those pages in conjunction with your scenery unit. At the very least, this will be fruit for discussion!

We welcome students who have little or no theatrical background, but we also hope the book helps those with some theatrical experience to better understand how theatre happens, who makes it, and what they do. You will probably attend theatrical performances while enrolled in this course. Take what you can from these experiences and test what you find in the theatre against what you learn in class. Ask questions, discuss what you see and hear with your professor and your classmates, and please stay open to new points of view. Playwright Paula Vogel suggests that we should "pursue not only joy and pleasure but become curious at states of discomfiture and unease." The acquired taste, she suggests, "is as valuable a tool in the making of selves as the native gift." Stretch yourselves! That is what college is for.

Acknowledgments

We would like to thank our colleagues and friends who have supported us throughout the process of completing this edition—especially Solomon Jordan, whose fine eye and sense for organization made this a better book. Gratitude, as well, to Bridget Sundin, Cristin Essin, Bill Deest, and Wendall Harrington, who all provided valuable information. Thanks for assistance with photographs to Charlie Erickson, Michael Baron, Allie Tabberer, Sean Meyers, Beth Homan, Kyle Haden, Drew Droege, Ellen Lauren, Mary Wayne-Thomas, Anita Ostrovsky, Adrienne Campbell-Holt, Andy White, Richard Hein, Kelly Ullom, Scott Featherly, Bill Ray, Bryan Carpender, Trevor Anderson, Amanda Lederer, Rob Eastman-Mullins, John Friedenberg, James Dodding, Matt Gutschick, Alex Myhre, Joe Anderson, David Phillips, Jenny Graham, Peter Sarafin, Shelby Steege, Bruce Lee, Beth Schachter, Scott Suchman, and Jeff Stander.

Finally, we offer our gratitude to the excellent people at Rowman & Littlefield, without whom this book would not have been possible—particularly Stephen Ryan, our exemplary editor. He, Andrea Kendrick (also R&L), and all the people who have offered articles and ideas have made the book stronger. The faults in the volume remain our own.

Part I

ART

This first part of the book serves as an introduction to the arts. Chapter 1 seeks to stimulate conversation about the nature of art and gives you an overview of the variety of fine art. Chapter 2 specifically introduces you to theatre as a fine art. Chapter 3 concludes the section with a conversation about critics, types of drama, and genre, preparing you to attend plays and to encounter the remaining chapters with an understanding of the breadth of dramatic form.

CHAPTER 1

The Nature of Art

Art enables us to find ourselves and lose ourselves at the same time.

—Thomas Merton, *No Man Is an Island*

From the earliest days of human history, we gathered around fires at the end of a long day's work and shared stories. We told family stories, stories of travel, and tales of battles or exciting hunts. We learned of our ancestry and history, reenacting important events and ritualizing them so as not to forget. We shared sadness and victory. We created myths and gods to explain the unexplainable, to quiet fears, and to excite the imagination.

The act of sharing these stories brought us together, bonded and organized us, and helped us create great cultures and civilizations. Some records indicate that we've been doing this since as early as thirty thousand years ago. Other records show that from 2500 to 550 BCE the Egyptians would reenact the ancient story of the god Osiris's death and rebirth each year. Records of the Shang dynasty in China point to ritualized storytelling, music, and dance since nearly 1800 BCE.

Some six centuries BCE, a group of men gathered on a hillside near Athens, Greece, to sing praises to their god. Following their ancient customs, they began improvising hymns of praise, when one of them stepped out of the group and announced that he had actually *become* the god. The god was Dionysus, the Greek god of fertility and wine. The man who made the startling announcement was Thespis from Icaria, who thus became, according to tradition, the world's first actor.

The Thespian legend has survived over twenty-five centuries. We have little idea what really happened, although we do know that some Athenians—including the philosopher Plato—hated the idea of impersonation, considering it merely a refined form of lying. Theatre nevertheless prospered, and the Greek drama flourished, reaching heights rarely equaled. When the Greeks and their civilization faded from the scene, they were replaced by the Romans, who were superb lawmakers, road builders, and administrators of empire but rarely artists of significance. After a thousand years, the Romans lost their influence as barbarians ransacked Rome, and western Europe

The Theatre at Epidaurus in Greece. ©*ThinkStock*

entered the so-called Dark Ages around 500 BCE. Meanwhile, theatre flourished in India and China.

Around 1500 CE ("common era"), a similar golden age, known as the Renaissance, began in the West as Europe began to coalesce into separate nations. England, France, Italy, Spain, and—later—Germany spread their colonies around the world. Each of them developed a distinct style of theatre. In the English-speaking tradition, which we share with Britain, Shakespeare and the Elizabethan theatre rose to brilliance around 1600.

In the eighteenth century, when English colonies in North America became established enough to pursue entertainment, actors appeared from England, at first using makeshift theatres. Not everyone in the New World welcomed the players. The Puritans outlawed theatre as frivolity, the devil's workshop, a veritable school for scandal. But they couldn't stop it, and the theatre spread from the Atlantic Coast west to Pittsburgh and Ohio, down the Mississippi to New Orleans, across the great American desert to Salt Lake City, then to the gold fields of California near San Francisco and Sacramento, and finally up and down the West Coast.

Early in the twentieth century, some people with a new technology found the quality of light in southern California especially effective for photography and began a film community in Hollywood. Almost immediately the doomsayers predicted the demise of live theatre (a cry that has now been heard for over two thousand years). They believed theatre could never compete with performances recorded on film. Soon thereafter, other people figured out how to send both pictures and sound into their audience's homes, and again the crystal-gazers predicted the end of the theatre.

William Shakespeare (1564–1616). ©*ThinkStock*

Access to entertainment has exploded in the last decade, with streaming services, web series, and more constantly evolving to let us watch what we want when we want to watch it. Video games (and even ways to watch other people play video games) have grown increasingly sophisticated and popular. Still, theatre has yet to disappear, and theatre artists, along with the rest of the culture, have learned how to use new technological advances and how to adapt to each new phase of social and cultural evolution. Something about theatre still seems necessary to human existence.

In fact, perhaps *because* so much of our lives is spent on screens and in virtual spaces, the live experience is something we crave. Some modern critics have called the theatre "a handmade artifact in an age of mass production." Live theatre is locally produced and often bears the hallmarks of its local community, while film is mass produced and mass distributed and may offer little resemblance to the community in which it plays. Perhaps we're lonely for real human contact, and theatre allows us to join one another in a shared experience that calls on us to recognize the actors, not as mere objects for our entertainment, but as human beings like ourselves. Whatever the reasons, millions of Americans still busily produce this "handmade artifact" called live theatre.

Not only does the theatre still flourish, so too do the other fine arts, despite the fact that art can seem intimidating, especially to newcomers. You might find yourself feeling bewildered by, stunned by, or even hostile toward avant-garde forms of art. That is understandable, at least at first. No one wants to feel stupid or left out. Yet education in the arts—as with any subject—can allow us to enjoy things that at first seem difficult. The audience does not need to have painted to appreciate a painting, any more than it needs to have acted to enjoy fine acting. But most of us benefit from some guidance when faced with the unknown, and modern students should not expect the fine arts to be an exception.

Faced with the mind-boggling variety of art, the newcomer might simply give up the search for understanding and turn to other less troublesome and more immediate pursuits. But even a quick study of the arts reveals them as central to life—indeed, as something that attempts to illuminate life and helps make it worth living. Art has been a part of the human experience from the beginning and continues today, not because

Most of us cannot imagine a life without hearing music. However, singing or learning to play a musical instrument can create a relationship to music that takes us deeper into the musical experience. ©ThinkStock

of the decrees of authorities and teachers, but because people find in the arts something of value that they can find nowhere else.

Traditional Fine Arts

There are seven traditional fine arts. In their various forms they have flourished in almost every society since people began to keep records.

1. MUSIC

Music is a tonal language created out of the void of silence, perhaps first suggested by our own rhythmic heartbeats and breathing. As a species we first made drums; some musical devices date back thirty thousand years. More sophisticated instruments began to appear in Egypt as early as 2000 BCE. Music is arguably one of the most powerful of the arts, stirring our emotions and reactions to great degrees. Beethoven, Bruce Springsteen, and Beyoncé all speak clearly to their respective audiences, and those audiences may even overlap.

2. PAINTING

Tens of thousands of years ago, people painted pictures on rock walls and caves in Africa and western Europe showing primitive humans' food supply in surprisingly realistic ways, such as in the Hall of the Bulls in Lascaux and Algeria's Tassili n'Ajjer.

Although the results are aesthetically powerful, the intentions of those unknown cave painters may have been more practical: by painting the animals, the people may have been trying to somehow understand or magically possess them, assuring success in the hunt and thus survival.

These days, we rarely paint what we eat, Andy Warhol's soup cans notwithstanding. A trip through a modern museum will expose the visitor to the more traditional work of the old masters and to the often more challenging work of the moderns, in which the painting becomes the experience, not merely a recording of an experience. Artists have slathered paint on automobile tires, then driven across canvases; others covered nude models with oil paints, then rolled them across the painting surfaces. In 1917, Marcel Duchamp placed a urinal on a gallery wall and named it *Fountain*. Some critics yelled "Fraud!" but others realized that new techniques, ideas, and ways of thinking and seeing are essential to artistic growth. You may not realize it, but along with prodigious technical skill, deep critical thought underpins many great paintings—as it does much great art of all kinds.

3. SCULPTURE

Tucked away in a case in the British Museum in London is a primitive depiction of a woman. The native artist who carved that statue, which is about the size of a softball, attempted to portray the Earth Goddess, the divinity whose will generated the universe. Eventually humanity grew more sophisticated, and the three-dimensional delineations of the gods increased in subtlety. Michelangelo's *Pietà*, housed in the Vatican in Rome, represents a supreme achievement in religious art, whereas Alberto Giacometti's *Tall Walking Figure* (1961) presents us with an equally moving image, however bleak and hopeless, of existential man.

4. ARCHITECTURE

This is the only art that matters, some people say—the only one of the fine arts that requires a license for its practitioners. Structural integrity of buildings can matter enormously, as we discover during earthquakes or hurricanes. When people moved out of caves and began to erect crude shelters, this art was born. A teepee will keep the rain off, and it speaks of a certain relationship between human beings and the landscape in which they live. The Parthenon asserts man's place in the world in another way, singing a hymn to humanity and to a goddess, with unmistakable impact. Architecture, called frozen music by some, is yet another attempt to make the world into our image, to order the irrational universe into an arrangement in which and with which we can live. Few students leave their dorm rooms unchanged; although the walls usually remain in place, the decor is a matter of basic importance. One must decorate the walls of the cave to suit oneself.

The Parthenon, a temple to the goddess Athena on the Acropolis in Athens, Greece. The beautiful proportions of this classical building, even in its damaged state, have won the admiration of artists and architects in all succeeding periods. ©ThinkStock

5. DANCE

Dance is a performing art with much in common with theatre. Sequences of human movement, usually accompanied by music, are combined to create pieces of work (dances) that have symbolic and aesthetic value. It was, and is, frequently seen as an expression of joy, but it can be expressive of any emotional state or intellectual idea. Ballet, modern dance, jazz, tap, and social dance all have roots in both religious and social rituals, as do dances of Eastern cultures. War dances and religious rituals may have originated in an attempt to placate the forces of nature; the techniques employed often resembled theatrical impersonation. By acting out a religious ritual, a hunt, a battle, or any other important event, a group could draw strength before an event, and afterward place it in its collective memory. Recently deceased German choreographer Pina Bausch created work that at face value shared little in common with such dances, but the essential value remains the same. Her work in some way prepared us to better live our lives in a twenty-first-century world.

6. LITERATURE

Literature was the last of the fine arts to develop, from the earliest cuneiform texts to modern novels. You undoubtedly studied various forms of literature before coming to college, but perhaps you take for granted the way we take in language and how it operates symbolically. The little squiggles of ink you're reading right now are an

Dance takes many forms, from ballet to modern to hip-hop. *Courtesy of Wake Forest University Theatre. Photo by Bill Ray*

This production of Shakespeare's *A Midsummer Night's Dream* at Hartford Stage is a good example of the rich and constantly changing art form we are talking about. Here, a four-hundred-year-old play is supported by full use of modern technology, circus elements, a terrific sense of the theatre's architecture, and elements of dance, all to underscore Shakespeare's themes. *T. Charles Erikson*

agreed-upon set of symbols to facilitate the flow of ideas from author to reader. These squiggles convey information, but they can also affect us emotionally.

Theatrical scripts look like literature; playwrights put words on paper just as novelists do. However, we should distinguish between the script and the play, in order to avoid confusion in the future. A play is usually a story enacted by actors on a stage for an audience. A script, strictly speaking, is the written document—the dialogue and descriptions of the event. A play is thus an event; a script is a document. A script is the skeleton or bones, and a play possesses the flesh, spirit, and life put upon that skeleton. Most people use the terms interchangeably, however. You may hear someone speak of reading a play; in the traditional sense of "reading," this is an impossibility. In semiotic terms (reading the "signs" put there by theatre designers, directors, and actors), it is something you will learn to do.

7. THEATRE

Theatre, or dramatic art, is the acting out of events as an art form. The theatre's complex origins, mixed with those of song, dance, and religion, probably grew out of primitive rituals developed to appease the gods. Later these enactments came to have an aesthetic aspect. Today's theatre is a rich and constantly changing art form that may include elements of all the others: painting, sculpture, music, literature, dance, and even elements of architecture.

The fine arts thus represent a long and honorable tradition—an essential part of human endeavor as long as history can record. Even the most repressive societies, such as Sparta in the classic period or Nazi Germany in the twentieth century, could not eliminate the humanistic values of the arts. Both societies tried to pervert the arts to their own purposes. Sparta eliminated almost all arts but retained architecture of necessity and music for military marches. Hitler's Germany was little better; all art was under the Third Reich's thumb and could only glorify the madness of fascism. Thankfully the arts usually exalt humanistic rather than fascistic values.

America's Involvement in the Arts

Many other countries fund the arts at higher rates than the United States does. However, a recent National Endowment for the Arts survey shows that participation in the arts in the United States is on the increase. Twenty-seven percent of Americans enjoy painting, drawing, or some form of the graphic arts; 24 percent write stories or poems; 15 percent participate in some form of folk or ethnic dance; 8 percent sculpt or work with clay; and 6 percent work with a local theatre group. Twenty-two percent of adults, or thirty-nine million people, sing in a choir or some other choral group. All this happens in spite of decreased leisure time for many Americans as they take on extra jobs and work in order to afford an ever-rising cost of living.

Further analysis of the data indicates that whites participate more than African Americans or Hispanics in ceramics, photography, needlework, and playing a musical instrument. African Americans show greater participation in creative writing, ethnic dance, and choral singing. Hispanics, who as a demographic group have the least leisure time, lead all groups in painting, graphic arts, sculpture, and working with theatre groups.

Perhaps even more surprising to most Americans are the statistics comparing American interest in the arts to interest in sports. Forty-six percent of those surveyed by the American Council of the Arts indicated they wished to have more plays and musicals performed where they lived, but only 30 percent wanted more sports events. When one considers both sports and the dramatic arts as parts of the overall entertainment industry, some of the financial ramifications fall into place.

A 2010 survey from Americans for the Arts (their most recent report, and one generated at a less-than ideal economic time) examined the importance of the arts in the United States from an economic perspective. According to that survey, U.S. arts and culture organizations generate $135.2 billion in yearly economic activity—$61.1 million by nonprofit arts and culture organizations, in addition to $74.1 million in event-related expenditures by their audiences. This economic activity supports 4.13 million full-time jobs and generates $86.68 billion in household income, And if you thought the arts were a drain on government or tax resources, the study shows that the arts also give back to the government in taxes each year, with $22.3 billion in revenue going to local, state, and federal taxes each year. When you consider that the National

Endowment for the Arts requested only about $148 million in federal funds in 2015, the arts in this country seem like a bargain if not a profit-making machine.

Performance Research, a marketing analysis company, has proven that corporate marketing and sponsorship of arts events have more potential return benefits than sponsorship of athletic events. According to their data, over half (56 percent) of those with an interest in the arts say they would "almost always" or "frequently" buy a product sponsoring arts or cultural events over one that does not. Compare that with only one-third of NFL fans and one-fifth of Olympic Games fans. Maybe more importantly, nearly 50 percent of those surveyed indicated that they had a higher trust in companies that sponsor arts events compared to those that do not.

Toward a Definition of Art

Readers who have survived the preceding flood of numbers may still wonder about this whole business of art in America, or anywhere else for that matter. What, one may ask, is this thing called art, and why do people seem to seek it out so passionately? What's in it for you?

Definitions are slippery, at best. Observant students will have realized that strict boundaries rarely hold up; exceptions and blurred definitions exist in almost every field of human endeavor. Physicists cannot totally define such basic phenomena as light or gravity. Biologists debate distinctions between the animal and plant kingdoms; some bacteria will not fit into either category. Even the boundaries between life and death are not sharp and have stimulated several notorious court cases.

So we approach defining art with understandable caution. Artists themselves rarely concern themselves with semantics; art is simply what they do. But to illuminate the problems of definition and thereby come to increased understanding remains the appropriate task of critics, scholars, aestheticians, and students in appreciation courses.

A student needs humility to look up a three-letter word—"art"—in a dictionary, but such an assignment can prove enlightening. You will find that most definitions center on the word "skill," but such a general term renders both words fairly meaningless. If any skill is "art," then your ability to quickly tie your shoelaces might fit the definition. We're in search of something a bit different.

Other definitions of art often include such phrases as "the quality, production, or expression . . . of what is beautiful, appealing, or of more than ordinary significance." However, a person may find a natural phenomenon such as the Grand Teton or a starry night sky beautiful, appealing, and of more than ordinary significance. And much modern music and visual art may not be especially harmonious or "pleasing" in the usual sense.

In 1814–1815, Francisco Goya painted the horrors of war with troubling realism. (See his treatment of French troops crushing a rebellion by the citizens of Madrid: *The Third of May 1808*, http://artchive.com/artchive/g/goya/may_3rd.jpg.html.) In contrast, Pablo Picasso's masterpiece *Guernica* presents the horrors of war in a nonrepresentational form, condemning the senseless destruction of a Spanish village. Picasso began work on this painting six days after the bombing of the city of Guernica on

April 26, 1937, finishing it in about two months. (See http://www.museoreinasofia .es/coleccion/obra/guernica.) *Guernica* is considered one of the greatest paintings of the twentieth century. But neither Goya nor Picasso seems involved with the creation of the beautiful in its usual sense, so either we must deconstruct the word "beautiful" (an interesting exercise in itself) or we must seek elsewhere for the essence of art.

People's artistic output results in something concrete: an object (such as a painting, a sculpture, a poem, a novel, a building) or a performance (such as a play, an opera, a dance, or a musical concert). People are restless; they do things to fill their time—dig ditches, take classes, fix cars, plant trees, write books, eat, make babies, sell shoes, vote, fall in love, fall out of love, travel the planet, and play on computers. Which results of all this activity constitute art?

Another term applied to the staggering variety of human endeavor is "creativity." Creativity, a hallmark of humanity, is the combining of elements previously separate, "creating" or resulting in something new. This something may or may not be artistic. A research chemist devising a new analytical technique is most certainly creative. When Henry Ford devised the assembly-line method of manufacture for producing automobiles, he created something that changed the United States in profound ways. His act was certainly creative, but was it artistic?

Pinning all this down can be frustrating. Students should consider the observation made by the great Norwegian playwright Henrik Ibsen (1828–1905) when he suggested that "a student has essentially the same task as the poet [or playwright]: to make clear to himself, and thereby to others, the temporal and eternal questions which are astir in the age and in the community to which he belongs." So, at least from Ibsen's perspective, poets, students, and perhaps other artists are responsible for at least asking good questions about our world.

Another approach to defining art is to try to define the place of quality in our definition. Here again the ice gets thin; people show marked, even violent, differences in their opinions about artistic merit. We might ask why quality so often interferes in assigning the designation of "art" to a piece of work. If an engineer makes a bad bridge, is he still an engineer? Of course. So perhaps it would be best not to assume that "art" must be "good" (whatever the criteria) in order to be "art."

Some people find themselves alienated from art when some domineering authority (a teacher, perhaps) tells them that they should enjoy some piece of art because it's good for them. Appeals to authority rarely bear fruit in a democracy, nor should they. However, if a work of art has won wide admiration for a long time, there might well be something to it; classics are usually classics for a reason, not just because of a conspiracy of professors. Keep in mind, too, that a person may not comprehend all of a complex artwork at once; Picasso's *Guernica* requires multiple viewings for most people before its richness reveals itself. One might say the same of Shakespeare's *King Lear* or of Michelangelo's masterwork *David*.

Appeal based on the subject matter of an artwork can be just as problematic as appeals to authority. Most often, this involves religious art. Art of the highest rank may well have religious roots; indeed, most of the art of the Italian Renaissance grew out of just such origins. Islamic architecture offers sublime sacred space for its inhabitants. But is it better art because it originated in religion? Religious art may be effective as a

Michelangelo's *David* depicts the biblical hero as he returns to confront Goliath. Michelangelo apparently sculpted this masterpiece from a piece of marble rejected by several other artists. ©*ThinkStock*

teaching device, but its artistic merit remains a matter quite distinct. If the corny old country-western tune, "Drop-Kick Me, Jesus, through the Goalposts of Life" advances the cause of Christianity, may heaven help us all. Let's continue to look for more satisfying definitions by turning to questions of what art does and how to understand it.

The Bases of Criticism in the Arts

Examining exactly what it is that people seem to enjoy about the arts offers a possible avenue into understanding and even defining them. Immediately one notes the subjectivity of appreciation of the arts; tastes vary widely. Nevertheless, all people seem to seek some type of transcendent experience. As the French critic Antonin Artaud (1896–1949) put it, "Admittedly or not, conscious or unconscious, the poetic state, a transcendent experience of life, is what the public is fundamentally seeking through love, crime, drugs, war, or insurrection." We seek something larger than the experience of daily routine, something more intense, something transcendent.

A search for the transcendent nature of art might lead you to the work of a critic named Stephen Pepper. In his book *The Basis of Criticism in the Arts*, Pepper examines the nature of the artistic transaction and the means of evaluating artworks. He discusses four typical functions of art:

1. *Art gives pleasure.* Nothing would seem more obvious than that pleasure is good and pain is bad, but Calvinist and Kantian ideas of the wickedness of pleasure still flourish today. Nevertheless, art should be enjoyable in deep and satisfying ways—bearing in mind that judgments of pleasure are subjective. In the theatre, perhaps comedy most overtly induces pleasure in its viewers. Most people love to laugh, and we need feel no shame in wanting pleasure; little enough of it exists for any of us. However, pleasure need not be equated with what is easy or familiar. To use a food analogy, you may find Easy Mac delicious, but there are many other tasty things to eat in the world. Some, admittedly, are acquired tastes, but if you're willing to be a little adventurous, you'll find meals far more satisfying, nutritious, and delicious than microwave macaroni.

2. *Art stimulates intensity of reaction.* This aspect of art correlates aesthetic value with the vividness, extent, and richness of the response to it. Intensity and the depth of experience thus induced in the recipient become the standards of quality. Power becomes a factor; Beethoven or Wagner usually has more brawn than Mozart. Springsteen generally has more heft than your basic boy band.

In the theatre, melodrama usually stimulates the most intense reactions in its audience. The thrill of an automobile chase scene has become a staple of crime films, just as chases on horses have become clichés in westerns. Pearl White, an early film heroine, used to literally hang from cliffs—hence the expression, "a cliff-hanger." Whatever the genre, the most exciting thing that can possibly happen appeals more in this case than the most harmonious or the most truthful.

3. *Art appeals by its coherence, by the internal relatedness or integration of materials.* This idea relates to the harmony of relationships demonstrated by some artworks. If Bach and Mozart do not possess great power, they both offer stunning works of

Sarah Ruhl's play *Dead Man's Cell Phone* blends aspects of contemporary culture, appealing to the mimetic function of art, as well as providing pleasure through more abstract poetic devices. *Courtesy of Kate Bashore*

integrated material. In the visual arts, the mobile offers a striking parallel: Each piece literally counterbalances every other piece in a mutually dependent configuration of elements leading to an overall impression. Bach fugues appeal to many listeners because of their complex internal structure and the implication that the manner of execution may be as satisfying as the content.

In the theatre some musicals might present obvious examples for comparison. *Les Misérables*, for example, is a big show, not only because of the sheer number of cast members and the length of the performance (more than three hours), but because of the size of the ideas addressed. Based on the hugely successful novel by Victor Hugo, *Les Miz* questions the very nature of morality and the reasons for living in this world. But physical size has no relevance here. Edward Albee's four-person, single-set *Who's Afraid of Virginia Woolf?* or Paula Vogel's five-person *How I Learned to Drive* simply have more substance than *Hairspray* or the enormous *42nd Street*. That said, it's perfectly possible to do a fine, coherent, well-integrated production of *Hairspray*, just as one could easily mangle *Les Miz* with illogical production choices. Substance and beautiful structure in a script do not guarantee a coherent production.

4. *Art presents the normal, the mimetic.* This aspect of art deals with the essential, recognizable nature of things. Thus in the representative arts, such as sculpture, paint-

A production of the rock opera *The Who's Tommy* at Muhlenberg College, Allentown, Pennsylvania. *Courtesy of Beth Schachter*

ing, or the theatre, one may find the artist imitating not the individual but the norm or value that the individual represents.

In the theatre, the large category of scripts called dramas would seem most allied to this aspect of art criticism. Not the blood-and-thunder of melodrama or the towering morality of tragedy or the complexity of larger shows but the more recognizable people of modern plays by August Wilson, Bruce Norris, or Beth Henley, or those of Ibsen in their day, illustrate this quality. Yet what one sees as "normal" varies from person to person, and each significant playwright works from a fresh vision of the world. Within the category of drama, playwrights' exploration of the "normal" may seem skewed or exaggerated, even as they illuminate the everyday. All art is selective, after all, and each playwright explores the human experience from a unique vantage point. The *mimetic*—that which imitates life—is therefore as broad a concept as human experience.

Each of us tends to gravitate to one of these four aspects of artistic appreciation, modifying our vision with the other three. Variations and shadings of variations thus cloud the issue of defining art, but we can begin to see how art works and why people need it, even though a comprehensive definition may still elude us.

In 1923 a theorist by the name of Otto Baensch (1878–1936) published an essay titled "Art and Emotion." In it he set out to prove

> that art, like science, is a mental activity wherein we bring certain contents of the world into the realm of objectively valid cognition; and that, furthermore, it is the particular office of art to do this with the world's emotional

content. According to this view, therefore, the function of art is not to give the percipient any kind of pleasure, however noble, but to acquaint him with something he has not known before. Art, just like science, aims primarily to be "understood."

The key phrase "the world's emotional content" seems worthy of investigation, and the late theorist Susanne K. Langer (1895–1985), in her highly admired *Feeling and Form,* built on Baensch's essay and arrived at this succinct definition: "Art is the creation of forms symbolic or expressive of human feeling." Langer thus defined art as an activity, although the forms or objects created are also called art. Thus it follows that human beings (artists) create (by combining previously uncombined elements) forms (objects or events) symbolic or expressive of human feelings (emotions or sentience). Langer spent the rest of her book expanding upon this disarmingly simple definition. Anyone concerned about such matters will do well to consult her works.

But we're not out of the woods yet. Langer's term "symbolic" demands yet another definition, and this one will prove just as slippery as the pursuit of artistic essentials. Langer devotes a large section of her work to the meaning and nature of semblance, or how one thing can seem to resemble or symbolize another. She suggests that art is more than an "arrangement" of things. Something emerges from an arrangement of tones or colors or elements that did not exist before. Here we see that art is both the process (the emergence itself) and the object (what emerges). And we know that what emerges is new because it provokes emotion in the viewer or listener or reader that the original materials never did. The symbols or forms of the new resonate with each new perceiver's subjective feelings. Art is thus forever new.

We have not removed the mystery from the creation of art, but perhaps we can see the mystery more sharply. Consider instrumental music, the most abstract of the arts. It does not (unless unusually mimetic) imitate anything; it does not represent (literally, "represent" or "present again") anything; it simply *is* something, from Beethoven to Danger Mouse.

Langer defined music as a tonal analogue of emotive life. An analogy is a perceived similarity between two things on which a comparison may be based, such as the analogy between a human heart and a pump. Music then, according to Langer, is analogous to human emotive life. Does this mean, going back to Baensch's comments, that listeners would become acquainted with something they had not known before? Yes, indeed, another bit of knowledge would accrue to a listener's persona, but it would not be knowledge he or she could necessarily put into words. The resulting knowledge is experiential, not verbal; one knows more because one has lived more, experienced more. It won't happen with any single piece of music, perhaps, but art at its best will not leave you untouched; you will become a different person, more aware, more human, with more of your potential realized. Indeed, most critics would agree that great art is art that most clearly depicts human potential, the possibilities of living.

When we consider the emotive content of examples of the other fine arts, the function of art begins to emerge more clearly. In architecture the corporate monolith of the Sears Tower in Chicago establishes a far different mood than the Taj Mahal in Agra, India. The U.S. Capitol in Washington, D.C., symbolizes one point of view; a Chili's restaurant symbolizes something else. In the visual arts similar distinctions abound.

You might apply the Langer concept of art as created forms symbolic of or analogous to human feelings to your own experiences. Or stroll through an art gallery; you will always find some artworks more attractive than others. Analysis of why you prefer one painting to another may well reveal something essential about you. As well, it should emerge that art is not so much *about* something as that it *is* something. The mystery of semblance will remain, enriching human existence.

The Functions of Art

Art has commanded much of the world's energy and concern, and many of the finest minds and talents produced by humanity have found art worthy of concern. To determine the purposes and justifications of art, we seek the functions of this sphere of human endeavor, and again we turn to the masters of the past—the artists and the thinkers and the critics—for assistance.

Among the more useful discussions of such matters is the work of Johann Wolfgang von Goethe (1749–1832), the German poet, playwright, theoretician, novelist, and scientist—truly a Renaissance man. Goethe proposed that art had three possible functions: entertainment, edification, and exaltation of the human spirit. Human beings, as is discussed in the following sections, must have these three activities, which are essential to human life. These essentials may occur in non-artistic sources, to be sure, but they constitute the richness of the arts. Art thus emerges as more than merely a "cultural enrichment"; it serves basic needs of humanity and has thus exerted a constant influence on centuries of human existence.

ENTERTAINMENT

Entertainment reveals itself as a human essential when one contemplates a life without it. Just as dreams supply a psychic safety valve for us all, we require diversion for relief from the mundane matters of our lives such as making money or earning grades—or acquiring the basic needs for survival.

Diversion takes many forms; one need not look to the arts to find it. But entertainment, as a word and as a concept, stems from the Latin verb *tenere*, meaning "to hold," and a complete definition would suggest holding the attention agreeably. The variety of what human beings consider agreeable diversion ranges across almost all human endeavor. Some prefer opera; some might choose a bullfight. Video games may seem a waste of time to some people, while others cannot imagine life without World of Warcraft.

The enormous sports industry in this country represents one of the most obvious sources of entertainment we have; thousands of athletes attract millions of spectators who spend billions of dollars on organized sports. Watching sporting events gives pleasure to many people; so does participation for others. Many participants in non-professional or avocational sports enjoy jogging, weight lifting, rock climbing, playing volleyball, and the like, with no intention of ever becoming professional. Improvements in physical strength, health, self-esteem, and the sense of belonging found in team sports are just some of the positive values of sports.

Johann Wolfgang von Goethe (1749–1832). Goethe's outstanding literary achievement was the drama *Faust*. He also contributed greatly as a drama critic and theorist. ©*ThinkStock*

Even those who only watch sports try to increase their level of expertise, their "watching skills," and thus increase their pleasure. For most Americans, for example, watching a cricket match is a study in frustration; few of us have any idea of what's going on. But then, not many Englishmen can get very excited about a suicide squeeze in a baseball game. Perspective, knowledge, and context define what is relevant and important. A queen sacrifice leading to a knight fork can be a thing of beauty, but not if you don't know how to play chess.

You can easily name many other human activities performed strictly for their entertainment value. For some these activities might seem totally worthless, but for others they will offer diversion, escape from the daily grind. This diversion, which can help diffuse the stresses of daily life, is a large part of the appeal of the arts to their audiences. Even so blatantly political and didactic a playwright as Bertolt Brecht (1898–1956) stated flatly in his widely reprinted "A Short Organum for the Theatre," "From the first it has been the theatre's business to entertain people, as it also has of all the other arts. . . . Nothing needs less justification than pleasure."

Many people find beauty chief among the pleasures derived from the artistic experience. The artistic event is essentially an act of communication, most obviously in representational or narrative art forms, but equally so in nonrepresentational or abstract forms. What an artwork communicates may or may not be discursive or factual, but it will inevitably be emotional. Langer's theories, explained previously, support this thesis, as do many other aesthetic theories. Knowing all the theories may not be necessary, but increasing your watching and listening skills is just as rewarding for watching a play as it is for a football game.

EDIFICATION

Edification or enlightenment as an artistic function may seem less obvious at first than entertainment. Most people do not seek out art consciously to learn something; rather they desire an experience. The theatre is first a house of emotion; intellectual matters follow in due course.

A scene from the Wake Forest University production of Frank Galati's adaptation of Steinbeck's *Grapes of Wrath*. Courtesy of Wake Forest University Theatre. Photo by Bill Ray

On the other hand, human survival itself demands continuous acquisition of knowledge. The newborn baby knows nothing of the hostile environment into which it arrives, but the child begins learning survival and social techniques immediately and continues to do so throughout its existence. Learning can be intensely pleasurable: we find new experiences and a wider view of our lives satisfying and gratifying, despite our educational system's occasional corrosion of those pleasures.

Consider, for example, two of the more successful and acclaimed novels of the twentieth century, John Steinbeck's *The Grapes of Wrath* and Alex Haley's *Roots*. Steinbeck's magnificent work describes the 1930s displacement of Oklahoma farmers from the Dust Bowl to California. Three generations of the Joad family fight ever-increasing adversity to achieve their goals, personifying the entire migration. Perceptive readers of the novel will learn a great deal about many things: the Dust Bowl, the Great Depression, human greed, human vulnerability, survival, the labor union movement, and so on. The same readers could learn about such matters by reading historical works and articles, government reports, union meeting records, and census figures. They might even find the factual accounts of the migrants emotionally moving. *The Grapes of Wrath*, however, is another matter; Steinbeck personalized the migrants' plight by creating the Joad family and in so doing intensified the emotional impact of the narrative. Steinbeck's readers learn what it might be like to experience such adversity, and they learn it not as an abstract statistical concept but as a human emotional experience. Such can be the edifying value of art.

Similarly, Alex Haley's *Roots*, based on historical fact and painstakingly researched, allowed millions of readers—and later, viewers of the miniseries—to gain insights into the heritage of African Americans. Histories of black America are many, but Haley's treatment, like Steinbeck's, personified an experience, increasing the impact upon his readers. The knowledge that comes from exposure to new ideas and experiences can substantially increase understanding between people. Emotional edification through an artistic experience may contribute to our quality of life by improving our ability to empathize—helping us understand what another lifestyle or life circumstance might be like. After the success of *Roots*, both as a novel and as a television miniseries, genealogical research in America mushroomed as people researched their own roots.

Although transmission of information can be an important artistic function, the essence of artwork lies, as Baensch suggested, in its emotional content. Yet emotional content may also relate to Langer's idea of symbolism or expression. Beautiful expression may be seen as harmonious unity, giving recipients pleasure and thereby holding their attention agreeably. Beauty in this sense relates most directly to Goethe's suggestion of entertainment as an artistic function.

Goethe's categories thus blur almost immediately; edification is often entertaining, and entertainment often widens the awareness of the entertained. A specific form of entertainment may prove riveting to one person and a complete bore to another. Stamp collecting might lead one person to wider awareness about printing, economy, political and social history, engraving, and so on and provide much pleasure through the process of collecting—and it might bore other people senseless.

A person introduced to one form or type of art may dislike it and later avoid other forms. Unusual or avant-garde forms of any art intimidate many people. We may fear we just won't understand, and we therefore refuse, reasonably enough, to expose ourselves to ridicule. But the person who risks nothing learns nothing. The learning that comes from artistic experiences may not be cerebral or verbal or even factual. One can, through the arts, experience another human being's unique point of view—even one that at first seems incomprehensible. By so doing we can learn something about another human being, about humanity in general, and even about ourselves.

EXALTATION

Goethe's third function of art, exaltation, may seem more commonly related to religion than to art, but the gulf between the two human endeavors is not as wide as one might expect. Art and religion grew from common origins as people used the arts, as in the Lascaux paintings, to understand and thus control an often confusing environment. Primitive (preliterate) people did not always distinguish between art, religion, and science, as they used all three interchangeably, perhaps to try to control their surroundings.

Religion properly concerns itself with humanity's relations with its gods. Art deals more directly with humanity's relations with itself, the interactions between human beings. The two meet when art reveals the potential for magnificence in the human spirit, as when it is faced with adversity. Consider Michelangelo's statue of David, the biblical hero. For many the exaltation derived from this artwork lies in the almost overpowering beauty of the idealized (albeit purposefully distorted) human form wrested by the artist from the marble. But the statue has a metaphorical level as well. It stands in Florence, Italy, a city that had to fight off hostile forces to survive during the Dark Ages. And in the largest sense, *David* presents a statement about the eternal human struggle. The work glorifies a humanity that must fight, fall, and fight again to achieve any worthwhile goal. Humans will keep fighting; *David* dramatically symbolizes that wider and higher view of humankind.

Another example of art's capacity for spiritual exaltation is the script *Oedipus Rex*, written about 427 BCE by Sophocles, a citizen of Athens in what is now Greece. In this famous tragedy, Oedipus, king of the city-state of Thebes, discovers he has committed a hideous although unintentional series of crimes. He falls from his monarchy to the status of an exiled beggar. He blinds himself in punishment for his sins as he accepts his guilt. Paradoxically he achieves a spiritual victory in the face of what seems a total defeat; it is this victory in defeat that reveals the greatness of his spirit. The victory by Oedipus is moral, not traditional. This sort of drama can lead the observer to an awareness of what a human being can be, of what a human can do. We will hope not to experience the same awful situations as Oedipus, but we may hope that if we do, we can bear our catastrophes without whimpering—like men and women, not blindly suffering like beasts.

Tragedy is often considered the highest form of dramatic literature. In it we often see humanity with all the pettiness, bestiality, and smallness blasted out of the protagonists, revealing them far beyond the trifles of everyday life. We gain, from looking on, a wider vision of human potential, a glimpse of what a human being can bear, in a state that we will never encounter. This revelation is ultimately optimistic, and a well-performed and well-received *Oedipus Rex* offers living proof of art's capacity for the exaltation of the human spirit.

More recently, the success of films like *12 Years a Slave* and *The Shawshank Redemption* suggests that we still thirst for entertainment that also edifies and exalts. We may leave the theatre with information about race and power, but we also leave with a deeper appreciation of the capacity of ordinary human beings for courage, resilience, and change.

If the nature of human life requires entertainment and edification, so too does it require some form of exaltation. Just as human beings must have confidence and self-respect to face their existence, so too must they have a wide view of humanity as it struggles toward its future, beset by the trivial and the mundane.

Conclusions

Art is the artist's response to life, offered in the hope of focusing the recipient's view of existence. Hemingway called writing "a hunt for a truth worth expressing." The resultant expression can offer considerable insight and awareness to its audience, depending upon the artist's talent and the perceptiveness of the audience. Much human endeavor, artistic or not, fails, of course, but the best does not; the best elevates us all.

No one can safely ignore so pivotal and central a part of our humanity. Every thinking and feeling person eventually must come to grips with the artistic transaction and what it can offer while realizing that the wide diversity of artistic opinions offers a personal challenge of huge dimensions. Perhaps Leo Tolstoy (1828–1910), Russian novelist and social critic, said it as well as anyone in his essay "What Is Art?" He concluded:

> The task of art is enormous. Through the influence of real art, aided by science, guided by religion, that peaceful co-operation of man now maintained by external means—by our law-courts, police, charitable institutions, factory inspection, and so forth—should be obtained by man's free and joyous activity. Art should cause violence to be set aside. . . . And it is only art that can accomplish this.

Often, artists question the function and form of art itself. Some of the most memorable artworks and significant artists have pushed the boundaries of the purpose and definition of art. These artists are often remembered because they offered a different perspective on the human condition. Sometimes this new perspective is welcomed or, as in the case of Vincent van Gogh, rejected during the artist's lifetime, only to blossom later.

Artists imitate nature. However, interpretations of nature differ, depending upon the individual and the time period. Art can clearly chronicle (through the unique lens of the artist) the time in which it was created, but it can also offer something deeper and timeless to the generations that follow.

Key Terms

aesthetics That branch of philosophy dealing with beauty, emotion, and feeling as opposed to logic and intellect.

fine arts Traditionally, architecture, literature, painting, sculpture, music, dance, and theatre. Students should especially note the distinction between literature and theatre.

form A literary type or kind, as in the form of drama or the form of the novel. Drama as a general form may be said to contain the subforms of tragedy, comedy, farce, and so on. The term is also used to describe the arrangement or structure of materials within an artwork.

Thespis A legendary Greek poet and actor of the sixth century BCE, traditionally considered the first actor and the founder of drama. He won first prize at the earliest recorded drama festival in Athens in 534 BCE.

Discussion Questions

1. What is art?
2. Using the definitions from the chapter as a jumping-off point, discuss the differences and similarities among the arts (visual, music, theatre).
3. Stephen Pepper suggests that art has several functions. Which of these functions do you believe to be the most important and why?
4. Why do we human beings need art? Why do we seem to crave the symbolic and metaphorical?
5. How do Goethe's distinctions among entertainment, edification, and exaltation help define the difference between mass art and the more individualized attention of a live performance?
6. Have you had an experience of art (music, poetry, visual art, theatre, dance) that left you feeling changed? Share those experiences in class and understand what transpired in you to create that change.

Suggested Readings

Aagaard-Mogensen, Lars, ed. *Culture and Art: An Anthology.* Atlantic Highlands, NJ: Humanities Press, 1976. A popular anthology of essays on the nature and definitions of art and creativity.

Dickie, George. *Introduction to Aesthetics: An Analytic Approach.* New York: Oxford University Press, 1997. A relatively new overview of aesthetics.

Fowles, John. *The Aristos.* New York: Vintage, 2001. Originally published 1970. Written by a modern British novelist (author of *The Magus, Daniel Martin, The Collector,* and *The French Lieutenant's Woman,* among others), this volume uses an innovative format to present a life vision that has found considerable favor among university students in all fields.

Koestler, Arthur. *The Act of Creation.* New York: Penguin, 1990. Originally published 1964. A substantial and thorough treatment of creativity manifested in the total spectrum of human endeavor, as perceived by one of the outstanding thinkers of our time. This work includes a detailed theory of comedy.

Langer, Susanne K. *Feeling and Form: A Theory of Art Developed from Philosophy in a New Key.* New York: Scribner, 1953. One of the more widely accepted and articulate theories of art and its function in modern society. Very useful.

May, Rollo. *The Courage to Create.* New York: Norton, 1994. Originally published 1975. An inspirational exploration of the creative process.

Pirsig, Robert M. *Zen and the Art of Motorcycle Maintenance: An Inquiry into Values.* New York: Harper Perennial, 2008. Originally published 1974. A most remarkable and popular book. The subtitle suggests its relevance to aesthetics in modern society.

CHAPTER 2

The Theatre as a Fine Art

You need three things in the theatre—the play, the actors, and the audience—and each must give something.

—Kenneth Haigh (b. 1931)

American playwright David Mamet once said, "When you come into the theater, you have to be willing to say, 'We're all here to undergo a communion, to find out what the hell is going on in this world.' If you're not willing to say that, what you get is entertainment instead of art, and poor entertainment at that." Other writers and practitioners focus on theatre's ability to remind us of everyday truths, still others on the element of surprise. One of the world's most celebrated playwrights, Tom Stoppard, has said that when we go to the theatre there should always be "some kind of ambush involved in the experience. You're being ambushed by an unexpected word, or by an elephant falling out of the cupboard, whatever it is."

Different people find different values in the theatre. The exact nature of theatre as a fine art defies easy definition, and theatre—which has connections in all the fine arts— may be the most complicated of all. If, as we discuss in chapter 1, art is the creation of forms symbolic or expressive of human emotion, applying this definition to the seven traditional fine arts may illuminate the distinctions between their essential natures.

As Susanne Langer suggests, *music* presents a tonal analogue of emotive life. Ludwig van Beethoven, John Lennon, and Michael Jackson, each working in completely different times, places, and forms, created totally distinct music, yet each caught part of the emotive life of their times, and their fans found them admirable.

You might consider *painting* and *sculpture* as visual analogues of emotive life, painting using two dimensions and sculpture using three. Picasso and Goya both opposed war (artists are often pacifists), but the visual statements of their opposition took far different forms, both highly regarded.

Architecture seems to relate most closely to sculpture in its three-dimensional qualities, but unlike sculpture, its creators intend people to inhabit the artworks. Like sculpture, architecture uses form, color, and texture to symbolize and express human emotion.

The *literary fine arts*, prose and poetry, are verbal analogues of emotive life. Not everything written intends to offer such an analogue, of course; college catalogs do not function as art forms, nor do business letters, government documents, or textbooks. Commonly, novels, poetry, short stories, essays, and similar forms constitute the art of literature.

Dance is an art form using the human body in motion, usually without any use of language and usually (but not always) accompanied by music. The expressive nature of movement is the essence of dance; we should therefore evaluate the music only by its appropriateness as accompaniment to the movement.

But what sort of emotive analogue is theatre? Surely not verbal, or we would not have to distinguish between literature and theatre as fine arts. True, some scholars and critics examine scripts as works of literature, but playwrights rarely so intend them. So what exactly is the art form in the theatre? The acting? The designs? The directing? All of the above? In a search for a workable definition, we try to illuminate this complex art.

Toward a Definition of Theatre

Even among those who work in the theatre, the art form resists clear definition as to its nature and function. Traditionally, theatre occurs when actors appear on a stage and enact a story for an audience. Even so simple a definition leads to arguments. Is "story" really necessary? If the audience and actors exist in separate spaces, as happens in live radio or television drama, is that theatre? If the performance and the audience exist in both different times and spaces, as in recorded theatre performances, should we consider that theatre? Perhaps until some more sophisticated distinctions emerge, we should consider the electronic and cinematic dramatic media as separate art forms, theatrical rather than theatre.

This chapter considers only live theatre, that form of dramatic art distinguished by one important element: *feedback*. By feedback we mean the circular response possible by having an audience exist in the same place at the same time as the actors, in a shared social environment. The immediacy of the live theatre allows an actor to become aware of the audience's response and to react to that response. Conversely, no matter how strong on-camera performances may be, the medium freezes what the actors are doing, and they cannot respond to their audiences. Even if a situation comedy is recorded in front of a live audience, as many of them are, we see only a recording of the performance. Actors may well react to the audience in the room with them, but we, watching them at home, are not part of that encounter. The actors are gone. They may simply have finished that recording, but they may also have retired, died, or gotten out of the business. Watching films of actors now gone—Philip Seymour Hoffman, Marilyn Monroe, Sidney Poitier, James Dean, and others—illustrates the point.

The skilled stage actor makes the most of the feedback loop with the audience. For instance, actors playing in a comedy onstage will "hold for laughs"—that is, they will wait to deliver a line until the audience has almost quit laughing at a successful comic line. Most stand-up comedians learn this sort of rhythm very early in their careers, or

Lookingglass Theatre's wildly imaginative production of *Lookingglass Alice*, directed by David Catlin. Caterpillar is (from top to bottom) Anthony Fleming III, Molly Brennan, and Kevin Douglas, with Lindsey Noel Whiting as Alice. *Courtesy of Rich Hein. Photo by Liz Lauren*

their careers do not continue. Since no two audiences will laugh exactly the same way at exactly the same time, no matter how consistent the performance, the performer must remain attuned to the audience and alter the timing of the act accordingly. When actors do this skillfully, the audience notices nothing mechanical about such techniques. We may sometimes notice, watching a comic film on television, that the rhythm seems a bit off. Filmmakers often follow an expected laugh with a few seconds of material that does not depend on dialogue or the sound track. A large film crowd in a movie theatre will fill in the space with laughter, but smaller groups of people rarely laugh as much or as often. Thus the timing may seem off to the home viewer. This is, perhaps, the most obvious way that audience response is noticeable from the outside, but much subtler forms of connection occur during every good night in the theatre. Hopefully you will have the chance to experience (and notice) this connection with the actors when you attend a play this semester.

Theatre's Unique Relationship to the Other Fine Arts

To a casual onlooker, the theatre seems to be a conglomeration of arts rather than a distinct art itself. We have already mentioned the potential study of scripts as literature, quite apart from their theatrical function. However, playwrights create their scripts hoping to see them produced rather than read. They write dialogue and arrange a series of actions for performance by live actors on a stage before a live audience. The script, like the scenario for a film, thus represents a statement of intention. Playwrights produce a plan, an outline, for achieving the finished artwork, but they do not create the completed work itself. This statement does not negate or belittle the quality of dramatists' writing; rather, it makes plain that playwrights seek goals sharply different from those of the novelist or the poet.

In the same way, scenic artists do a lot of painting in the theatre; backdrops, murals, curtains, and other two-dimensional scenery often call for detailed and meticulous painting. Even though this painting requires many of the same techniques used by easel painters, we should not evaluate the results in the same way. Theatrical painting results in objects to be used as part of a production; the easel painter's output stands alone.

Sculptural techniques are theatrically useful for arranging actors in the performance space, in some forms of scene design, and in some makeup constructions. But one must not confuse the techniques of an art with the art itself; sculpture and theatre, though they may share techniques, remain separate.

Music and dance, being performing arts themselves, can create even more confusion in this regard. Often composers create music and choreographers create dances specifically for a theatrical performance, and a casual observer might evaluate them quite apart from the total performance. But only the contribution of the music or dance to the total production should determine their success or failure. A magnificent piece of music might prove totally inappropriate to a particular production. Beethoven's Fifth Symphony, rightfully considered a masterpiece, would be a wretched choice as background music for a Neil Simon comedy. "Cabaret" was a climactic musical number in both the stage play and the film, but no one would want to include it in *Macbeth* or *The Lion King*. Adding to the confusion, several musical art-

Elizabeth Homan's production of *Rent*. *Sean Meyers Photography*

ists—Louis Armstrong among them—recorded "Cabaret" and established its distinct popularity as a hit record. The song thus became a separate entity to succeed or fail on its own, quite apart from its function in the original stage production.

In the past few decades Broadway producers have staged some "nonbook" musicals—musicals without any story line to hold them together, such as *Jerome Robbins' Broadway*. These shows are nonnarrative revues—more like concerts than plays. In the Robbins show, for example, the entire production consisted of musical numbers taken from previous shows Robbins had presented on Broadway; nothing new appeared. The audience thus experienced music once removed from its original intention.

Another common relationship exists between film and theatre. The popularity of a film or Broadway show can spur endless loops of re-creations. For example, many Broadway musicals have been made into films: *Into the Woods, Dreamgirls, Rent,* and *Les Misérables* to name just a few. Many popular films have also become Broadway productions: *Xanadu, The Lion King, Legally Blonde, Beauty and the Beast,* and Mel Brooks films like *The Producers* and *Young Frankenstein*. Similarly, *Monty Python and the Holy Grail* became the musical *Spamalot*. John Waters's cult film *Hairspray* became a hit Broadway musical and then was filmed again with new songs and a new cast. After an interview on *The Daily Show* at the release of the second film, Waters said, "I made a joke on the Jon Stewart show that now I wanted to do *Hairspray* on ice. And the next day I had real ice producers calling and were serious and wanted to do it."

A final consideration of the theatre in relation to the other arts would include architecture. Like architects, scenic designers are interested in creating environments for people to inhabit. Scenic designers also find themselves studying architecture and construction techniques so that they can place accurate representations onstage. As will emerge later, the actual design of any theatre, created by architects, has ramifications for almost everything that takes place in it. Some of those severely affect the economics of the production; other elements affect everything from acoustics to scenic and lighting design to the kinds of plays best for that space.

One must be careful from the beginning, then, not to confuse the wide spectrum of artistic activities within a theatre. Certainly theatre is a multidisciplinary endeavor. Yet, one must evaluate these activities in their theatrical context, not as an accumulation of techniques gathered from the other arts.

The Complexities of Theatre Art

A theatrical production is a living thing; when it is over, it dies. Any performing art has the advantages of life and the disadvantages of death. A painting may last for centuries, as might a work of literature or a piece of sculpture, but a play lasts only a few hours, then exists only in the memory of the audience members and the artists who made it.

Film and video actors may do several takes, but eventually their performance is "in the can"—finished and safely recorded. Stage actors face the challenges over and over, usually eight times a week in the Broadway theatre. But even though they do the same show over and over, they cannot actually repeat it. Human personalities change from day to day, and actors have good days and bad days, like athletes or students. These changes can be very healthy. Good actors continue to make discoveries even after productions open, and because acting works as a kind of chain reaction, what one actor does inevitably affects at least some of the others. These discoveries help keep performances feeling "fresh." Audiences also differ remarkably, and each audience modifies a production by its responses. Actors often speak of good audiences and bad audiences. Some audiences simply have greater powers of perception than others. Some audiences give nothing; others stimulate the performers to their best work. Just as athletes talk about the crowd "getting into" the game, so audiences get into the production; they can actually make or break a performance. Actors may rehearse to a relatively empty auditorium, but they would not care to perform to one; the audience completes the artistic transaction.

Another complicating factor in the performing arts is the box office—the financial need for an audience. A production's appeal, especially in the commercial theatre, determines its life or death. Commercial producers commonly spend enormous sums of money, enough that they take few unnecessary chances with risky productions.

In 1981 investors put up $2.4 million for a production of a musical version of *Frankenstein*. After a few weeks of preview performances the show closed after opening night and investors lost all the money they had put up. Who was to blame? Everyone and no one, really.

Being a communal art, the theatre combines the work of a wide variety of people and thus entails human interaction: communication, compromise, and the sharing of a common vision. We discuss the following contributors to the theatrical experience in future chapters:

- Playwrights, who conceive and prepare the script to be performed
- Directors, who select the actors, rehearse them, and approve all elements of the production
- Actors, who perform the play
- Designers, who conceive and supervise the preparation and use of scenery, lighting, costumes, makeup, hair, properties, and sound
- Carpenters, stitchers, drapers, electricians, video artists, sound editors, and others who help make the designs reality
- Stage managers, who assist in rehearsals and run the performance after the show has opened
- Assistants, who help the director, producers, stage managers, or designers
- Crew chiefs and crew members, who execute scene shifts and supervise the properties, hair, and makeup, as well as maintain equipment and execute lighting and sound cues
- Dramaturgs, who research aspects of the show and help with analysis
- Critics, who describe and assess the production for the public

Many more people usually contribute to productions in various ways. We touch on many of them in passing as the book progresses, but in the meantime, it's worth noting that a whole cadre of people shape your experience of a production. Producers must raise the money for the production and supervise all financial matters. Publicists advertise the production to the public. Box-office personnel sell you tickets, and front-of-the-house personnel and ushers see to it that you are safe, seated, and comfortable. Building personnel maintain and guard the theatre and the production elements. In addition, there are specialists who may supply unique requirements for a specific production: animal trainers, puppeteers, stunt performers, pyrotechnicians, acrobats, musicians, and so on. Although the audience may see only the actors, box-office personnel, and ushers, everyone listed here can affect the success or failure of a production to a greater or lesser degree.

The Theatrical Spectrum

Much human activity looks like theatre but is, in fact, not theatre. Even if we restrict our definition of theatre to actors enacting a story on a stage in front of an audience, we will find some nontheatrical endeavors that qualify. In fact, a whole field of study was established in the late twentieth century, called performance studies, to account for how these kinds of events incorporate the theatrical.

Consider, for example, the ritual of the Roman Catholic High Mass, in which costumed performers (the priest and the altar boys) appear in an area before a congregation/audience and perform a highly conventionalized narrative of the death and resurrection of Christ. The Mass seeks religious, not aesthetic, goals, but if spiritual exaltation constitutes a proper function of both art and theatre, many common elements can link the theatre and religious ritual. All the theatrical elements come into play, and congregations find some church services more moving, more effective, more exalting—and thus more artistic—than others.

Sporting events may seem remote from theatre at first glance, but if you consider Improv Olympics or Comedy Sportz, the analogy is easy to make. In fact, even scripted drama has connections to sports, since most plays depict the enactment and resolution of a conflict. The analogy can work in reverse as well: a baseball game presents costumed performers resolving a conflict in a specific playing area before an audience gathered to watch. The performers/players have practiced for the event, but until the conflict begins with the other team, no baseball game exists and no one knows the outcome in advance. No one seriously proposes baseball as theatre except in the widest possible sense, but the relationship between theatre and sports as parts of the entertainment industry indicates some comparable appeals to their audiences.

Likewise, theatre often frames or enhances sporting events—and the bigger they are, the more the theatrical comes into play. Consider, for instance, the opening ceremonies of the Olympic Games, which are lavish theatrical productions, often with dancers, musicians, and designers, directed and choreographed by people drawn from theatre and film.

Even rioting and public demonstrations have some theatrical overtones. As in sports, the event is real, not staged (in most cases), and the outcome is usually in doubt. Participants enter a space to engage in or resolve a conflict, often surrounded by onlookers. The line between performer and onlooker can blur, and people can pass from one category to the other as observers find themselves swept into the melee. The goal is not artistic, so street action does not qualify as art or theatre to most people, but we cannot deny some of the structural and ritualistic commonalities. Critics and scholars have recently shown increased interest in performance studies, the study of all manner of performances rather than the specifically aesthetic.

While these examples have theatrical elements, their *intention* is not often consciously artistic. Theatre is. Theatre, then, exists in any consciously artistic attempt to delineate human existence for an audience in a performance presented by living actors to a living audience. Theatre is traditionally verbal, narrative, and conflict centered, although it may not depend upon any of these qualities. New York writer/director Richard Foreman creates plays that have no obvious story line or conflict but nevertheless provide exhilarating theatrical experiences for adventurous audience members.

People create theatre for a wide variety of motives and in a wide variety of circumstances. Each context is unique, and while we wish we had the space and scope to look at theatre from all over the world, the theatre scene in the United States provides a good microcosm of theatrical endeavor. The following pages outline many of these. However, please bear in mind that a combination of for-profit, not-for-profit, professional, and nonprofessional theatre exists in many places in the world, not just in the United States. Additionally, while we focus on New York in these early pages, it is not the only place that great theatre can be seen in the United States—far from it. Instead, we use it as shorthand for the categories that exist in other metropolitan areas—designating a continuum from large for-profit commercial/professional theatre, to smaller experimental professional (but often not-for-profit) companies, all the way to not-for-profit community theatres staffed by volunteers.

BROADWAY THEATRE

Although a decentralization process has been under way for some time, many people still equate professional theatre in the United States with the Broadway stage in New York City. Broadway in the theatrical sense is that part of midtown Manhattan bounded by Forty-first Street on the south, Fifty-third Street on the north, Sixth Avenue on the east, and Eighth Avenue on the west. Forty professional theatres exist in this space, eighteen of them owned by the Shubert Organization and eleven more by James M. Nederlander.

Professional theatre was first performed in New York by visiting companies from England in the mid-eighteenth century, but the theatrical center of the country was Philadelphia until about 1825. New York theatre then rose to the forefront and has remained there ever since.

The Broadway theatre is the most expensive theatre in America—the most expensive to produce and the most expensive to attend. Production costs have risen steadily; at present a Broadway producer works with about two dozen labor unions in order to stage a show, including:

- The Dramatists Guild of America (playwrights)
- The International Alliance of Theatrical Stage Employees, or IATSE, in New York City's Theatrical Protective Union Local 1 (stagehands and crew members)
- The League of American Theaters and Producers, aka the Broadway League (producers and owners)
- Actors' Equity Association (actors, chorus performers, stage managers), the American Guild of Variety Artists, and the American Guild of Musical Artists
- Treasurers and Ticket Sellers Union Local 751
- Theatrical Wardrobe Attendants Union Local 764
- Doorman's Union Local 183
- Association of Theatrical Press Agents and Managers
- Theatre Transfer Local 817, a branch of the Teamsters Union in companies hired to move scenery and other materials
- American Federation of Musicians Local 802
- Theatre and Amusement Service Employees Union (porters, cleaners, and lavatory attendants)
- International Union of Operating Engineers (building employees)
- Society of Stage Directors and Choreographers

It appears that everyone concerned with a Broadway production has a union except for the audience. The generally inflationary trend of the American economy has led to increasing costs for all concerned on Broadway; theatre rents have increased, and costs for production materials have escalated, all of which result in escalating ticket prices. We discuss the work of union members more in chapter 7, but many things contribute to the expense of live theatre in Manhattan, one of the most expensive and populous cities in the world. Astronomically expensive rents and real estate, cost of living, and material and transportation costs make the basic cost of doing business in New York high for everyone. Add in the hiring of the best actors, directors, designers, stage managers, musicians, and choreographers in the world, and you can begin to see why tickets cost so much.

As of August 2016, Broadway.com listed thirty-one Broadway shows currently running (twenty-one musicals and ten plays). Ticket prices are widely variable, even if we ignore the unusual variation in prices for shows like *Hamilton* (see the sidebar). For instance, if you want to see the glowingly reviewed *Oslo* in 2017, you can purchase a seat for $104.72 and sit near the back of the theatre, or buy a "premium" seat for $270.00, after fees. Discount tickets can be picked up for most shows at the TKTS booth (www.tdf.org/nyc/7/TKTS-ticket-booths) in Times Square if you're willing to wait in long lines.

The *Hamilton* Phenomenon

Told through the language and rhythms of hip-hop and R&B, the smash musical biography of Alexander Hamilton by Lin-Manuel Miranda is on track to become one of the biggest commercial and critical hits in Broadway history. In 2009 Miranda sang a number from the show at a night of poetry and music at the White House, and a long development process ensued. Six years later, a full-fledged *Hamilton* opened Off-Broadway at the Public Theatre to glowing reviews, then transferred to the Richard Rodgers Theatre on Broadway in July 2015.

Commercial success: With no movie stars on the marquee and no special effects, *Hamilton* nevertheless sells out the 1,321-seat Rodgers Theatre eight times a week. In just a few months it easily recouped the $12.5 million it cost to mount, and though it is expensive to do—$295,000 a week for rent, house staff, musicians, stage hands, and more—it nevertheless was profiting over $600,000 per week *before* ticket prices were raised in June 2016. Scalpers had been making about $150,000 per show by reselling tickets at more than four times their normal prices. This meant that people who had nothing to do with making the show were pulling in a projected $60 million per year. *Hamilton* producers decided to add cheap lottery seats and raise the prices on the most expensive seats. Now tickets range in price, at the theatre, from $10 lottery seats to a top price (brace yourselves) of $1,580 a seat. All this means that producers and investors could make hundreds of millions of dollars from ticket sales, profiting as well from merchandising (T-shirts, CDs, books, etc.). These investors split $13 million annually, plus 3 percent of adjusted gross income. Tours (in Chicago, San Francisco, London, and probably more) will rake in millions more. And unlike many financial arrangements, *Hamilton* shares the wealth with actors from the development process and with the director, designers, choreographer, songwriter, and more.

Artistic success: In 2016, *Hamilton* was nominated for sixteen Tony Awards (a record), winning eleven. It also won a Grammy and the Pulitzer Prize. Critics were effusive in their praise:

> What's great about *Hamilton* is *Hamilton* itself. Its combination of 21st-century music and 18th-century history is amusing, entertaining and dazzlingly ingenious, but the show is also surprisingly moving; audiences leave feeling wrecked and exhilarated. The musical really is everything: a drama, a comedy, a character study, a spectacle, a lesson, a romance, a war story, a historiographical critique.—*Time Out*

The show matters to our society, and to the theatre, in part because it is speaking to you, a new generation of theatregoers, in both what it talks about and how it tells the story. Written by a liberal arts grad (Miranda graduated with a theatre degree from Wesleyan University), it is smart, diverse, and fast-moving. The characters, the lyrics, and the story are complex, and there is so much to squeeze into a night at the theatre that perhaps only hip-hop can make it possible. "The sheer volume of words facilitates the flow of information and complexity," says *Time Out*. "It expands the scope of the story Miranda can tell. Hip-hop doesn't just make *Hamilton* better—it makes *Hamilton* possible."

Led by a cast of mostly black and Latino actors, *Hamilton* foregrounds the experience of minorities and along the way helps support Broadway's growing commitment to stories about people of color—something it has not always done well at all. This story about immigrants, made by people who are the children of immigrants, has become part of the national conversation and has inspired a new generation of theatregoers.

Good articles on the show are plentiful. Here are a few you might want to read:

- http://www.nytimes.com/2016/06/12/theater/hamilton-inc-the-path-to-a-billion-dollar-show.html?_r=0
- http://www.nytimes.com/interactive/2015/08/06/theater/20150806-hamilton-broadway.html
- https://www.timeout.com/newyork/theater/why-hamilton-is-the-broadway-musical-to-see-now

Investors for Broadway productions face unique circumstances. Unlike most business investments, an unsuccessful Broadway venture loses all the money put up; it is an all-or-nothing sort of business. With large sums at stake, most producers subordinate aesthetics to fiscal prudence, preferring old and familiar procedures. As gamblers say, scared money never wins.

But if Broadway producers run substantial risks, they can also win enormous rewards. The numbers from fifty years ago seem positively quaint, but they set the stage for what is happening today. In 1966, the musical *Cabaret* cost $500,000 to stage, but it cleared a profit of $1.74 million. Today, *Wicked*, which initially cost $14 million to mount, has since 2003 grossed approximately $4 billion worldwide. *The Phantom of the Opera* and *The Lion King*, which have been running even longer, claim to have grossed $6 billion each. If *Hamilton* continues its current pace, it is on track to bring investors a great deal more.

That said, at least four out of five Broadway productions fail to return their investments, and costs continue to escalate. Shows still open, however, and investors still appear. Some years ago, Hal Prince was one of Broadway's more successful producers. As of 1972 he had produced nineteen shows, of which eight were flops. Those disasters lost him about $1.5 million, but his hits (*Fiddler on the Roof*, *Follies*, *Cabaret*, *Damn Yankees*, *West Side Story*, and so on) yielded him profits of ten times that much. With a success rate of just over 50 percent, Prince's investors had received a 230 percent profit. The longest-running show in American history, *The Fantasticks*, which opened in 1960, amassed some amazing statistics. The original investors each put in $55, for which they each earned more than $750,000—a profit of 13,500 percent. Truly, there is no business like show business.

Only London's legendary West End, with its fifty theatres, can compete with Broadway. London used to be a joy for theatregoers to visit, with cheap tickets and an incredible range of productions from which to choose. Ticket prices have increased substantially; *Book of Mormon* tickets will run you £66–£256 (or $88–$330), while a straight play like *King Lear* runs £45–£71 (or $58–$92). Good seats are often available for considerably less, though—and even at full price are still below the Broadway average.

Who is going to see Broadway shows? Demographics seem to be changing, and the numbers are still out on what the impact of *Hamilton*, *Book of Mormon*, and *The Color Purple* are having. However, in 2014, 13.1 million people saw Broadway shows, with an average age of forty-four. About 2.75 million of those attendees were non-Caucasian (or about 79 percent Caucasian). Theatregoers still continued to be predominantly female (68 percent), and non–New Yorkers accounted for 65 percent of the tickets sold, making Broadway one of the top U.S. tourist destinations. Theatre audiences are highly educated, and they spend a lot of money. Broadway's estimated economic contribution to NYC in 2014–2015 was $12.57 billion and eighty-nine thousand jobs. (See the Broadway League's website as updated information becomes available.)

THE ROAD

Although the Broadway theatre technically occurs only in midtown Manhattan, Broadway shows appear in other cities as road companies. Shows in preparation for Broadway used to have tryouts near New York in Philadelphia, Boston, and Washington to polish the performances before opening on Broadway. Rising costs of all production elements have almost eliminated this practice; shows now hold a few weeks of previews in New York before officially opening and receiving critical reviews.

If a show has a successful Broadway run, however, the producers will consider a touring version. The market for such shows across America and Canada is substantial; this market is considerably larger than for Broadway itself. As is evident from the profits for such shows as *The Phantom of the Opera*, *Wicked*, and *The Lion King*, touring can exponentially increase a show's profits. It is not cheap, though. In 2012–2013, there were approximately forty-five Broadway touring shows traveling the country. Producers spent $752.7 million to run the tours. With ticket sales and ancillary spending, the economic impact of Broadway tours was approximately $3.2 billion, $2.8 billion of which went to the communities that presented the shows.

Road shows usually tour in one of three varieties of production:

1. First are the national companies, comparable in almost all ways to the Broadway originals and staged by the original producers. These shows appear in "key cities," such as Los Angeles, Washington, Chicago, Boston, Detroit, San Francisco, Philadelphia, Baltimore, Miami, Dallas, Cleveland, St. Louis, Charlotte, and Pittsburgh. Such shows typically require that 75 percent of tickets be sold for the producers to clear a profit.

2. At the second level are the bus-and-truck companies that play engagements of less than a week, usually three days. Such engagements require 50 percent to 60 percent attendance for financial success. The staging approximates but does not duplicate that of the original production.

3. At the third level are the bus-and-truck companies that perform one-night stands, often performing six times a week in six different locations. The company uses simplified settings to facilitate putting them up and taking them down. The producing agency receives a straight fee rather than a percentage.

OFF-BROADWAY THEATRE

The term "Off-Broadway" originated after World War II to describe both productions and theatres outside the Times Square area of Manhattan. These theatres were Equity houses but seated only 100 to 499 patrons. The Off-Broadway theatres had a major impact on American theatre in the 1950s and 1960s by offering low-cost performance opportunities to unknown playwrights and other theatre artists. Some of the outstanding companies to emerge included the Circle in the Square, the New York Shakespeare Festival, the Negro Ensemble Company, and the Manhattan Theatre Club, most of which are still operating, along with the Public Theatre, SoHo Rep, Cherry Lane, the Pearl Theatre Company, and many more.

So who goes to these theatres? In part because the tickets tend to be cheaper, audiences for Off-Broadway shows tend to be younger and more diverse. The theatres tend to be located in neighborhoods where you can find reasonable meals and cheap transportation.

Many shows from Off-Broadway transfer uptown to Broadway, like the hit musicals *Avenue Q, A Chorus Line, Stomp, Hair, Urinetown,* and even *Hamilton,* which premiered at the Public Theatre, to name a few.

OFF-OFF-BROADWAY THEATRE

By about 1960, the Off-Broadway theatres found their production expenses increasing, and an even less commercial theatre began to emerge in New York, eventually called the Off-Off-Broadway theatre. It grew to a collection of approximately two hundred small experimental groups. Equity regulations defined the Off-Off-Broadway theatre as performances with limited runs using unsalaried Equity performers in houses of not more than one hundred seats. (Los Angeles, Chicago, and other large cities have many similar venues.)

At first located around Greenwich Village and lower Manhattan, these productions tended to be more experimental than those in the Off-Broadway theatres. Most of them paid little or no salary to participants. Several theatres and companies rose to eminence, however, as they fostered new playwrights by giving them inexpensive showcases for their work. Among them were the Caffe Chino, the Café La Mama, the Open Theatre, and the Bread and Puppet Theatre. Several productions moved from these humble beginnings to Off-Broadway or even to Broadway. Some companies that have won wide followings and substantial critical acclaim continue to create their work in small, low-budget spaces. They may prefer the intimacy of a small theatre, and they certainly avoid the box-office pressures felt by those involved in multimillion-dollar productions.

Today, Off-Off-Broadway productions may range from the highly experimental to simply produced revivals—and tickets tend to cost less than $20 a seat. In 2016, you could see a production of *Othello* or take your chances with *Canuck Down Under*; *Fxxx'd 'Til Payday*; or *Erik Dies, You're Stupid and We Hate You*, among other imaginative and edgy things. In New York there is surely a theatrical experience to suit every taste. What's more, similar venues may be found in many large cities in the United States and, indeed, all over the developed world.

REGIONAL THEATRES

Perhaps the most striking innovation in the American theatre in the last half-century has been the rise of the regional theatres. These professional theatres, usually working in repertory of some sort, have sprung up all across the United States. The oldest regional theatres are the Hudson Guild Theatre, founded in 1896 in New York, and

The Williamstown Theatre Festival 2015 production of Nobel laureate Eugene O'Neill's final play featured six-time Tony Award-winner Audra McDonald, and lighting and scenic designs by Jennifer Tipton and Ming Cho Lee—two of the most respected theatre designers in the world. Regional theatre is therefore not to be seen as "second best." *T. Charles Erikson*

the Cleveland Playhouse, founded in 1915. Before 1963 only 32 of these theatres operated; the rest have appeared since then. By 1989 there were 233, and in 2014 the Theatre Communications Group counted 1,770 not-for-profit professional theatres, most of them regional theatres. The largest concentration is still on the East and West coasts, but the regional theatre movement has now spread to almost every state, making it a truly national phenomenon.

Regional theatres rely on loyal audiences that they foster over time. By paying close attention to the communities out of which they develop, these theatres become an integral part of the cultural life of a city. Regional theatres also tend to be particularly careful about providing basic services. Such things as wheelchair access and headsets for the hard of hearing, which are sometimes hard to come by in Off-Off-Broadway and Off-Loop (Chicago) theatres, are commonplace in regional theatres. Subscribers—those who buy season tickets—get reduced prices per ticket and special perks, such as free ticket exchanges and replacements, as well as priority offers to non-subscription events.

No one theatre typifies regional theatres, but the Mark Taper Forum in Los Angeles has gained a reputation of merit since its founding by Gordon Davidson in 1967. The Forum operates in three theatres: the Mark Taper Forum, a thrust stage with a seating capacity of 742; the Ahmanson, with flexible seating of between 1,600 and 2,000; and the Kirk Douglas Theatre, a 317-seat venue located in a renovated historic theatre, which opened in October 2004. Regular subscribers at the Taper number over twenty-one thousand, and annual attendance exceeds two hundred fifty thousand. The Mark Taper season, which usually runs twelve months (September to August), includes five or six plays. Gordon Davidson has said the mission of the Mark Taper Forum is

> to create and maintain a theatre that is socially and culturally aware, that continually examines and challenges the assumptions of its culture, and that expands the aesthetic boundaries of theatre as an art form while attempting to find the timeliness of the classics in contemporary terms. We continue to attempt to enlighten as well as entertain our audience. . . . The future of the . . . Forum lies in the pursuit of artistic excellence, aesthetic daring and community service.

Other regional theatres express similar goals, with some individual distinctions. The Actors Theatre of Louisville (Kentucky) has specialized in presenting original scripts, several of which have moved to successful runs on Broadway. Chicago's Steppenwolf Theatre (which helped jump-start the careers of John Malkovich, Joan Allen, Gary Sinise, and others) prides itself on being an actors' company, dedicated to choosing and producing plays that provide particularly challenging roles for actors. Shakespeare and Company in Lenox, Massachusetts, states that they are dedicated to inspiring "a new generation of students and scholars to discover the resonance of Shakespeare's truths in the everyday world." They do more than Shakespeare but are committed to "demonstrating the influence that classical theatre can have within a community." Budgets and expenses for such theatres are far smaller than they would be on Broadway or on the road. For example, the musical version of *Frankenstein*, which cost $2.4 million to produce in New York and ran only one performance, originally cost only about $30,000 at the St. Louis Repertory.

Some critics have remarked that regional theatres' successes have brought problems—those of power and commerce. Directors note that they must walk the line between artistic independence and the need for commercial success. In other words, what started as experimental hothouses have become a significant part of the establishment. While the pioneering stages have become multimillion-dollar operations, some sources of revenue have decreased. Federal funding used to contribute about 10 percent of the theatres' budgets; now the government supplies only half that much. State government contributions have also dwindled, and arts council budgets have decreased. Private foundations have helped take up the slack, but the shortage remains severe. About thirty important theatres closed for good in the 1980s. Yet others, like the Alliance Theatre in Atlanta and Oklahoma City's Lyric Theatre, are maintaining high production standards and playing to substantial audiences.

Perhaps the regional theatres' situation in the late 1980s and 1990s was best summed up by Zelda Fichandler, founder and producing director of the Arena Stage in Washington, D.C., when she said, "We made the revolution. We've pulled the wagon up the hill; our long 'Mother Courage' journey is over. The next generation will be about evolution. The theatre is a living organism that must change. That is

Regional theatre is thriving in places you might not expect, like Oklahoma City, where Michael Baron directs the Lyric Theatre of Oklahoma. High production values and a thriving audience base are likely the result of the crowd-pleasing qualities of large-scale musicals like this production of *Big Fish*. *Courtesy of Keith Rinearson*

both encouraging and sad." Fitchandler died as this book was going to press in the summer of 2016, able to look back on the growth of a theatre scene that would have been unimaginable sixty years ago.

The evolution continues, as regional theatres find ways to make themselves viable. Worldwide economic troubles in the early 2000s hit companies hard, causing some to close and others to economize drastically. Some companies have had to do fewer shows—five or six instead of eight—or reduce the number of expensive shows. Casts of two for such single-set shows as *Topdog/Underdog* or *'Night, Mother* cost far less than full-stage musicals, but theatres can charge the same amount for tickets.

A number of new companies have also emerged, many without the expensive budgets of an operation like the Mark Taper Forum. You can find great theatre in places like Oklahoma City (Lyric Theatre); New Orleans (Southern Rep); Atlanta (Alliance Theatre); Seattle (Seattle Rep); Cleveland (Public Theatre); Iowa City (Riverside Theatre); Milwaukee (Milwaukee Rep); Memphis (Playhouse on the Square); Minneapolis (Guthrie Theater); Chicago (Lookingglass, Steppenwolf, the Goodman); and many others.

Regional theatre is also thriving in the Shakespeare festivals that exist around the nation. Despite their name, such "festivals" produce far more than Shakespeare, and many are permanent theatrical establishments, not festivals in the usual sense of the word. The Oregon Shakespeare Festival (OSF) in Ashland, Oregon, has for years been listed as one of the top regional theatres in the United States. Their 2016 season included eleven plays, including, naturally enough, five Shakespeares (*Timon of Athens, The Winter's Tale, Hamlet, Richard II, Twelfth Night*) as well as *Great Expectations, The River Bride, Vietgone*, and more. OSF employs 325 full-time and 175 part-time company members and has upward of five hundred volunteers. They also have a number of programs focused on new play development—their American Revolutions program; a Shakespeare translation/adaptation project; a musical commissioning program; their hip-hop Nexthetics initiative; and a program to commission adaptations, translations, and new plays. Well-endowed, well-attended, and an important employer and tourist attraction, OSF even posts their audited financial statements and annual reports online for anyone to see. They aren't going anywhere.

Not all regional theatres are doing such booming business, and some of the theatres now listed by Theatre Communications Group will eventually disband. However, many will survive, and others will emerge. In an age of increasing technical gadgetry all around us, the theatre still offers the rare handmade, live (nonvirtual) experience. Regional theatres further offer the kind of community connection that can make this experience particularly personal.

BEYOND TRADITIONAL THEATRE

Though mainstream white, heterosexual America has tended to dominate the theatre in the United States, minorities and women have increasingly made an impact. African Americans and Latino, for example, have developed and continue to expand diverse contributions to the nation's theatre. Women's groups produce a wide variety of works, as do gay and lesbian companies. Native Americans, Yiddish groups, Irish, Japanese, Indian, Chinese Americans, and others continue to find new theatrical expressions of the American experience. Such performances are often overtly political; to some degree, all these groups work toward foregrounding lives and viewpoints that have tended to be overlooked by the commercial theatre.

With the incredible success of Lin-Manuel Miranda's *Hamilton* on Broadway, along with the success of musicals like *Fun Home* and *The Color Purple*, our culture's thirst for new voices and stories is more visible than ever. Meanwhile, smaller productions and companies continue to expand our understanding of human experience.

African American/Black Theatre

A long and complicated history of black actors and performers exists in the United States, beginning with African-inspired performance as well as theatre based more on white European drama. Ira Aldridge and James Hewlitt were early-nineteenth-century black Shakespearean actors, but it was not until the 1960s, when government funding was made available, that black companies truly flourished in this country.

While funding was eventually withdrawn and many of the companies folded, some survived, including the Free Southern Theatre in New Orleans and the Negro Ensemble Company in New York. The National Black Theatre Festival, founded in 1989, occurs biannually in Winston-Salem, North Carolina, and is an important place for black writers and performers to share their work. In the past fifty years, influential writers, such as August Wilson, Suzan-Lori Parks, Ntozake Shange, Amiri Baraka, Anna Deavere Smith, Charles Fuller, Lynn Nottage, George C. Wolfe, and Lorraine Hansberry, along with many talented performers, designers, and directors, have infused African American theatre with purpose and energy.

Lesbian/Gay/Bisexual/Transgender Theatre

LGBT theatre has also added fresh energy to the American theatrical scene. Julliard professor Roger Oliver remarked a few years ago, "It seems almost inconceivable today, with the abundance of openly gay playwrights and gay-themed plays, that less than 50 years ago a drama critic for the *New York Times* felt the need to call for 'social and theatrical convention' to be 'widened so that homosexual life may be as frankly treated in our drama as in contemporary fiction.'" Indeed, many of the twentieth century's best gay playwrights, such as Noel Coward, Tennessee Williams, William Inge, and Edward Albee, did not write many openly gay characters, though careful reading of their work reveals plentiful gay themes. Matt Crowley's *The Boys in the Band* (1968), with 1,001 performances Off-Broadway, helped change a tradition of caricature or closeting.

By the late 1970s, such groups as the San Francisco Gay Men's Theatre Collection and Theatre Rhinoceros were firmly established, and the Gay Theatre Alliance was formed in 1978. The Broadway hit *La Cage aux Folles* (1982) added further stability to the gay (men's) movement, along with other drag-loving playwright/performers like Charles Ludlum and Charles Busch (*Psycho Beach Party*). Martin Sherman's *Bent,*

Black playwrights have contributed richly to the American theatre, giving voice to many different African American experiences and reaching wide audience acclaim. For instance, Lynn Nottage's plays, like this one, *Intimate Apparel*, about a lonely African American seamstress (here played by Aleshia Price), are regularly produced in regional and university theatres. *Courtesy of Wake Forest University Theatre. Photo by Bill Ray*

Well-known LA actor Drew Droege portrays Miranda Priestly in the unauthorized musical parody version of *The Devil Wears Prada*. *Courtesy of Bryan Carpender*

Terrence McNally's *Love! Valour! Compassion!* and Tony Kushner's lauded *Angels in America* plays (among others) added visibility, complexity, and artistic achievement to the movement. Since then, out gay playwrights have become too numerous to mention, even as the complexities of sexual orientation—especially for transgender people—dominate the headlines as this book goes to press.

Festivals of LGBT work have also burgeoned in cities all over the Western world, the longest-running of which may be the international Dublin Gay Theatre Festival, occurring during the first two weeks of May every year since 2004. Performance art has also been important to the development of gay narratives, with activist/performer/author Tim Miller at the forefront of this work.

Lesbian theatre has a slightly different trajectory, focused as many women's companies are on feminist issues as a whole and having been less well-documented than gay (male) theatre. In fact, our culture's early relationship to lesbian characters may be seen through the lens of Lillian Hellman's 1934 *The Children's Hour*, in which a woman who has (and admits) sexual feelings for her female friend ends up committing suicide. Since then, lesbian theatre companies, including the Lavender Cellar in Minneapolis (1973), the Lesbian-Feminist Theatre Collective (Pittsburgh, 1977), and others have emerged, doing highly collaborative work in which plays were often collectively written by three or more women. Groups such as Split Britches, WOW (Women's One World), and the Five Lesbian Brothers (founded by five members of WOW) helped foreground lesbian characters and viewpoints in their innovative New York productions. Lesbian playwrights have also found homes in mainstream theatre, with Paula Vogel, author of *How I Learned to Drive*, *The Baltimore Waltz*, and other plays, as the most visible example. Another milestone was the lesbian-centered musical *Fun Home*, written by Lisa Kron and based on Alison Bechdel's graphic novel, which won five Tony Awards in 2015, including Best Musical.

The theatre is about exploring the human condition, so as we move toward greater understanding of each other as human beings, including our sexual orientation, our complicated personal stories will continue to find expression in the theatre.

Latino and Portuguese Theatre

Is difficult to talk about in a unified way, connected as it is to a variety of Spanish-speaking cultures. Cuba, Spain, Mexico, Puerto Rico, and much of South America may share a common language, but the theatre produced by each group reflects the diversity of those cultures. Nevertheless, Spanish-speaking theatre in this country, which seems to have begun with religious plays performed near Santa Fe in 1598, predates American English-speaking theatre by nearly a hundred years. By the early 1900s, places with large Spanish-speaking populations like Florida, Texas, Arizona, and California were becoming active places for such work, which included variety shows and circus, musical, and more traditional plays. The depression of the 1930s saw the deportation of nearly half a million Spanish-surnamed people to Mexico, resulting in at least one play about the crisis for Mexican Americans. In 1936 the Federal Theatre Project was inaugurated by the Roosevelt administration, and it worked with the Centro Asturiano theatre of Tampa, Florida, staging approximately forty-two productions there. Growing Puerto Rican and Mexican populations in the 1940s–1960s led to the Teatro Hispano of New York, the Teatro Cuatro, and other companies. Today, we may look to the influence of these groups, as well as El Teatro Campesino (Farm Worker's Theatre), founded in 1967 by Luis Valdez, and companies in Arizona, Texas, Colorado, New Mexico, Washington State, and more.

Luis Valdez's play *Zoot Suit*, at Mark Taper Forum (1979), was a landmark production, and indeed Valdez's influence can be seen throughout the 1970s–1990s, even as such influential playwrights as Cherri Moraga and Milcha Sanchez Scott began to be produced. Meanwhile, plays in English and occasionally Spanish by such esteemed playwrights as Puerto Rican–born Jose Rivera (*Marisol*, *Cloud Tectonics*, *Another Word for Beauty*) and Cuban-born Maria Irene Fornés (*Fefu and Her Friends*, *The Conduct of Life*, *Letters from Cuba*) came into the mainstream of American theatre.

Today, some Latino/a playwrights enjoy consistent careers and accolades. For instance, in 2012, Caridad Svich (b. 1963) won an award for lifetime achievement, having written over forty full-length plays staged all over the world. Still, American mainstream theatre has far fewer prominent playwrights from Spanish-speaking backgrounds than we might expect, given that at least 17 percent of the total American population is Hispanic and that some states have over 40 percent Hispanic and Latino populations. We are hopeful that the increasing diversity of the country will be reflected in our theatres in the coming years. Certainly the success of *In the Heights* and *Hamilton* which, at its core, is an immigrant's story, portends positive change.

Feminist Theatre

Any attempt to define feminist theatre will display some of the same complications we find with the aforementioned groups. No single viewpoint or mode of production exists simply because people share certain common experiences, values, or roots. Feminist theatre groups therefore vary from grassroots organizations to more commercial setups, from revolutionary aims to more psychologically driven explorations of women's experience. A few of the better-known groups include the Omaha Magic Theatre, the Spiderwoman Theatre Workshop, and Rhode Island Feminist Theatre. Many feminist collectives reject entirely the hierarchical structure of traditional theatre, including the way that plays are made. Companies may create scripts in workshops, through improvisations that explore specific themes, often emphasizing the power of transformation, as well as incorporating Epic Theatre devices and particular social concerns of women. Because of the way these plays are often made, a list of important feminist playwrights is always limited. It is also worth noting that the concerns of white feminists have sometimes seemed to speak for *all* women, without acknowledging their whiteness as a factor. Indeed, many important female writers of color, already mentioned in this chapter, write feminist plays, and we would be remiss if we did not introduce the concept of intersectionality. The central idea of intersectionality

Different strands of world theatre weave through educational theatre. *Emilie: La Marquise Du Chatelet Defends Her Life Tonight,* **by Lauren Gunderson, explores history, math, and women's history to create a wonderful theatrical experience that is also educational.** *Courtesy of Wake Forest University Theatre. Photo by Bill Ray*

is that class, race, gender, geography, religion, sexuality, and many more factors overlap and combine to make us who we uniquely are. The theatre is just as complicated. And though this discussion of "alternative" theatre sets these groups apart from our mainstream discussion, it is important to remember that the theatre, and indeed all culture, is more fluid than this structure implies. Ideas, performance strategies, and people flow from group to group.

In any case, a short list of women writing feminist plays would certainly include (among many many others) Lynn Nottage, Caryl Churchill, Maria Irene Fornés, Timberlake Wertenbaker, Caridad Svich, and Suzan-Lori Parks.

EDUCATIONAL THEATRE

Educational theatre refers to production programs generated by universities, colleges, secondary schools, and primary schools, often as a part of their curriculum. Ticket prices for such productions are usually nominal; the institution absorbs the bulk of the production costs.

College and University Theatre

Past figures have indicated that some twenty-five hundred colleges and universities in the United States presented about seventy-five hundred productions—thirty thousand performances—for audiences numbering about nine million. For many Americans such performances are the only local live theatre available, especially in smaller communities.

Although colleges and universities stage many productions, they also function as institutions of higher education. Thus they serve a dual purpose of increasing their students' understanding of the theatre as well as making live theatre available to their audiences. Some institutions consider their educational mission primary and center their efforts on classroom training; other institutions focus their efforts on production. Most combine the two, melding the relatively unhurried and theoretical classroom study of theatre with the creation of public performances.

A college education implies that students should obtain both a wide general education and some degree of vocational training; theatre students who seek to study only performance skills usually attend a conservatory rather than a college. At the undergraduate level in a traditional program, perhaps a third of students' coursework is in their major field; the remainder consists of minor fields and general education requirements, although enormous variations exist throughout higher education.

At the graduate level, the degree programs leading to the master of arts (MA) or doctor of philosophy (PhD) seek to prepare students for teaching or scholarly careers, whereas degree programs for the master of fine arts (MFA) or doctor of fine arts (DFA) are preparatory for work in production as an actor, director, playwright, or designer. However, some programs defy these easy distinctions. For instance, some MFA programs now include more theory and history than in the past, and PhD programs sometimes work with an artist/scholar model.

A production of *The Best Christmas Pageant Ever*. Middle and high school theatre helps develop students' abilities as theatre practitioners while also giving them important social and bonding experiences and a creative outlet for self-expression. *Spencer County Middle School, Taylorsville, Kentucky. Courtesy of Shelby Steege*

The production budgets and salaries of all concerned in educational theatre tend to be lower than those for commercial theatre, including the regional theatres. However, teachers usually have greater job security.

Secondary School Theatre

Recent figures from the National Endowment for the Arts indicated that some thirty thousand high school theatre programs in the United States—averaging one production a year for a total of one hundred fifty thousand performances—played to a total of forty-five million audience members. The secondary school theatre is thus the single most active producing agency in America.

Quality varies enormously, as it does in all forms of production. Although more than 90 percent of American high schools engage in some sort of theatre activity, surveys indicate that only about a quarter of them offer "strong programs." However, outstanding high school programs have grown up around the country. Some secondary school programs struggle on in the most appalling conditions; untrained but well-intentioned casts put on plays in cafeterias or gymnasiums. Strong programs require trained leadership from the faculty, funds to support the programs, and commitment from the administration.

As more theatre majors have made their way into the world as educators, the quality of high school theatre has improved a great deal. Among educators, there is a growing appreciation for experiential learning and of different learning styles (kinesthetic, aural, visual, etc.)—and these have obvious links with theatre. As an after-school program, working on plays is also a good way to build community, give students positive outlets for their creative energy, and satisfy their need for personal connection.

COMMUNITY THEATRE

In many American cities, residents who share an interest in the theatre have organized into producing agencies, most of them nonprofessional. Such organizations form and disband, making an accurate count difficult, but estimates range upward from three thousand, not including churches, camps, civic groups, and other agencies that might stage plays.

Some community theatres employ salaried staff and have their own theatre. Others have their own theatre but do not employ a paid staff. Still others work without either a permanent facility or a professional staff, using volunteer labor for all duties, and renting or borrowing performing spaces wherever available.

The production quality of such organizations varies widely, depending upon the experience and expertise of the participants, as in any other theatre. In the early part of the twentieth century, however, American community theatres were a major factor in the development of American drama, and they continue to serve as a vital and dynamic part of the total theatre scene in this nation.

CHILDREN'S THEATRE AND CREATIVE DRAMATICS

Children's theatre producers intend their work for audiences composed of children. Professional companies, educational organizations, community theatres, and other producing agencies may stage such shows. In the past decade, support for these theatres has increased dramatically in places like Omaha, Nebraska (the Rose Theatre), and Seattle, Washington (Seattle Children's Theatre), where these organizations teach classes, provide free or reduced-price tickets for kids and their families, and work hard to build seasons that are both inviting and challenging for children. The goal is not only to nurture them as children but also to encourage their love of theatre by making high-quality art that kids from ages three to sixteen can enjoy and connect to.

Children in Omaha, Nebraska, have a terrific resource in the Rose Theatre, where they can take classes and see high-quality productions. Here, Rochelle Pickett and Brandon Shostak play two of the title characters in *Diary of a Worm, a Spider, and a Fly*, directed by Rob Urbinati. *Courtesy of Matt Gutschick*

Some children's theatres are professional touring companies that take their shows into schools. Companies like Chamber Theatre Productions of Boston and the Missoula (Montana) Children's Theatre have met with great touring success.

Creative Dramatics

Somewhat resembles children's theatre, although it is less often performed for audiences. In creative dramatics, children improvise stories, usually as an educational technique to stimulate their imaginations and allow them self-expression. In creative dramatics, the techniques that an actor uses to train the mind, voice, or body can prove beneficial for primary students. A teacher might, for example, while teaching the alphabet, have students form their bodies into the shapes of various letters. Such a practice can facilitate learning, promote motor functions, and dissipate excess energy, while establishing learning as a pleasurable activity. In most instances these activities are directed by a classroom teacher or sometimes by a person specifically trained in such techniques.

Both children's theatre and creative dramatics are growing in popularity, and both can contribute richly to children's imaginations, audience development, and future theatrical participation.

OTHER THEATRICAL ACTIVITIES

Psychodrama, an improvisatory technique used in treating mental disturbances, became popular in the 1990s. By acting out frustrations or wish-fulfillment under the supervision of a qualified professional, patients gain understanding of their dilemmas and themselves. The goals are therapeutic rather than aesthetic, but the techniques are similar to those used in the theatre.

Many religious organizations produce theatre, dramatizing biblical events or subjects on a religious theme. Perhaps the most lavish are the outdoor productions of Passion plays (the Passion and Resurrection of Christ being the narrative), such as those in Disney, Oklahoma; Wauchula, Florida; or Spearfish, South Dakota. The most famous of all and the one with the longest tradition is that in Oberammergau, Germany, which the residents have presented approximately every ten years since 1634.

Although a relatively minor form today, religious drama dominated western Europe from about 1000 to 1500 CE; the Church kept the theatre alive in Europe after the fall of Rome. As we recall, the very origin of scripted drama took place on the Athenian Acropolis during religious festivals.

Conclusions

Human beings tell stories to connect with each other, to make sense of their world, to inspire, to gain perspective, and to relax. Theatre lets us do that together, forging stronger communities and gaining empathy for people, places, and times we might otherwise find alien. How many of us knew much about Alexander Hamilton before Lin-Manuel Miranda decided to tell his story in a contemporary theatrical vernacular? How much closer to each other do we come when we learn the details of each other's joys and suffering? The theatre will always be here to help bridge our differences and connect us as people.

The theatre remains a vital and integral part of American life, whether audience members seek entertainment, edification, or exaltation and whether they find it in the commercial, the educational, or the avocational theatre. The appeal of the theatre may remain essentially a mystery, but playwright Eugene Ionesco came close to explaining it when he said, "Theatre is not literature, propaganda or philosophy. . . . It is simply what cannot be expressed by any other means . . . a complexity of words, movements, gestures that convey a vision of the world inexpressible in any other way."

Key Terms

Alliance of Resident Theatres/New York (www.art-newyork.org) Formerly the Off-Off-Broadway Alliance, an organization of producers of Off-Off-Broadway shows.

American Alliance for Theatre and Education (www.aate.com) An organization concerned with theatre education for the young, including children's theatre and theatre at the secondary school level.

American Association of Community Theatre (www.aact.org) Founded in 1986 to replace the American Community Theatre Association, which was founded in 1958.

American College Theatre Festival (http://www.kcactf.org/home/index.html) An annual series of festivals during which plays staged on college and university campuses may advance to state, regional, and national festivals. The national festival is hosted by the Kennedy Center for the Performing Arts in Washington, D.C., with the assistance of the Association for Theatre in Higher Education. Awards are given for acting, playwriting, and scenic design.

Association for Theatre in Higher Education (www.athe.org) A national organization open to anyone interested in theatre but primarily concerned with postsecondary theatre training, production, and scholarship.

Broadway A street running diagonally across Manhattan in New York City, crossing Seventh Avenue at Times Square, forming the heart of the theatre district. **Broadway theatre** usually refers to the professional theatre in that area, although few of the theatres are actually on Broadway. *See also* Off-Broadway.

children's theatre Productions presented either by children or by adults for child audiences. *See also* creative dramatics.

community theatre Avocational theatre—that is, theatre performed not by professionals, students, or educators but by community members. Larger community theatres often hire permanent directors and other staff.

creative dramatics Although practitioners vary widely in their usage of this term, most define it as theatre by children that may or may not be presented to the public.

didactic Instructive, intended to teach. Thus, in drama, referring to scripts whose primary purpose is to edify rather than to entertain.

educational theatre Theatre associated with institutions of learning, especially universities, colleges, junior colleges, and high schools.

happening An unstructured, frequently improvised event with some theatrical overtones that emerged during the late 1960s. At the time, happenings raised significant questions about the nature of art.

League of Off-Broadway Theatres and Producers (www.offbroadway.org) An organization of producing agencies.

Little Theatre movement A nationwide movement, primarily in U.S. community theatres between 1910 and 1930, that attempted to put into practice the European ideals of strong directing, noncommercial goals, and new staging techniques. *See also* New Stagecraft.

long run The common practice of running a successful production as long as it shows a profit at the box office.

New Stagecraft A term used to describe the nontraditional staging techniques first advanced in Europe by Edward Gordon Craig and Adolphe Appia. Many of these innovations were first seen in the United States as a part of the Little Theatre movement.

Obie First given in 1956, Obies are awards for excellence in the Off-Broadway theatre. They are presented by the *Village Voice* newspaper.

Off-Broadway Commercial theatre productions away from the central theatre district in New York City (*see* Broadway) with somewhat lower production budgets.

Off-Off-Broadway A term that refers to even less expensive and more experimental productions in New York City. Distinctions are not sharply defined.

producer In the commercial theatre, the person or persons in overall charge of financial matters; sometimes the person or persons funding the production. The term is usually used to distinguish this person's role from that of the director, who has charge of all aesthetic decisions but who is hired by the producer.

regional theatre Professional theatres outside New York City, such as San Francisco's American Conservatory Theater, the Repertory Theatre of St. Louis, and Minneapolis's Guthrie Theater.

repertory theatre A professional theatre with a resident or in-house company of actors that work from a repertoire or group of plays in rotation.

stock A production scheme in which several plays are presented for limited runs of perhaps a week or two, as in summer stock, as opposed to repertory or the long run.

Tony An award named in honor of Antoinette Perry (1888–1946), actress, producer, and director. The Tonys are awarded annually for excellence in the Broadway theatre. They were first given in 1947; the presentations are now televised each spring.

Discussion Questions

1. How is theatre different from and yet similar to the other arts? How might knowledge of other arts help theatre artists make better theatre?

2. In an age of digital communication and mass production, what separates mass media (videos/DVDs, television, CDs) from live performance?

3. How do finances (personal as well as global) figure into the production of live performances as opposed to recorded media?

4. What happens in the relationship between live performances and a live audience? Why attend live theatre instead of just watching a video or going to the movies? What are the advantages/disadvantages of live performances?

5. Discuss the similarities and differences between the various types of theatre explored in this chapter. That is, how are expectations different for a Broadway show, a community theatre production, and a university theatre performance?

6. What statistics listed in this chapter do you find most interesting, and why? Were there any surprises?

Suggested Readings

Banham, Martin, ed. *The Cambridge Guide to World Theatre.* Cambridge, UK: Cambridge University Press, 1988. A one-volume encyclopedia of world theatre, compiled by over a hundred theatre scholars. Highly recommended.

Bordman, Gerald Martin. *The Oxford Companion to the Theatre.* 2nd ed. Oxford: Oxford University Press, 1992. A one-volume encyclopedia of world theatre.

Brockett, Oscar C. *History of the Theatre.* 8th ed. Englewood Cliffs, NJ: Prentice Hall, 1998. The most popular one-volume text in theatre history, this book is well illustrated and comprehensive in its scope and treatment of theatrical heritage.

Carlson, Marvin. *Theories of the Theatre: A Historical and Critical Survey from the Greeks to the Present.* Expanded ed. Ithaca, NY: Cornell University Press, 1993. An important overview of not only dates and movements but also the progression of ideas throughout theatre history.

Fergusson, Francis. *The Idea of a Theatre.* Princeton, NJ: Princeton University Press, 1949. Considered one of the most influential studies of this century. Fergusson uses ten important plays to examine both technical and textual ideas.

Hartnoll, Phyllis. *A Concise History of the Theatre.* 3rd ed. Updated by Enoch Brater. London: Thames and Hudson, 1998. Originally published 1968. Less comprehensive than Brockett's book, this volume is perhaps more appropriate to the newcomer to theatre history. Richly illustrated.

Langley, Stephen. *Theatre Management and Production in America: Commercial, Stock, Resident, College, Community, and Presenting Organizations.* New York: Drama Publishers, 1990. One of the best guides to the financial end of theatrical practice.

Londré, Felicia. *The History of the World Theatre from the English Restoration to the Present.* New York: Continuum, 1991. Another fine general history, more readable than most others of its kind.

Loney, Glenn. *Twentieth-Century Theatre.* 2 vols. New York: Facts on File Publications, 1983. A comprehensive listing of most twentieth-century theatrical innovations.

Macgowan, Kenneth, and William Melnitz. *The Living Stage: A History of the World Theatre.* Englewood Cliffs, NJ: Prentice Hall, 1955. For many years this book was the most popular theatre history text in colleges and universities; it still offers eminently readable prose and accurate scholarship.

Robinson, Alice M., Vera Mowry Roberts, and Milly S. Barranger. *Notable Women in the American Theatre.* Westport, CT: Greenwood, 1989. An indispensable source for anyone interested in key women in the history of American theatre.

Wilmeth, Don B., and Tice L. Miller, eds. *Cambridge Guide to American Theatre.* Cambridge, UK: Cambridge University Press, 1993. A spin-off of *The Cambridge Guide to World Theatre,* complete with a bibliography and biographical index.

CHAPTER 3

The Audience and Critic

To avoid criticism, do nothing, say nothing, be nothing.

—Elbert Hubbard (1856–1915)

Audiences today are generally not as well versed in the traditions of live theatre as they were before electronic forms of entertainment emerged. Some people have never seen live theatre and may therefore be unfamiliar with the traditions of taking an intermission or clapping after a scene, song, or act. They may think it's okay to put their feet up on the seats or to text-message friends during a live performance. They may not realize that they have a part in enhancing the performance—that their attentiveness and responsiveness can actually strengthen the actors' performances and thereby make everyone in the theatre enjoy the evening more.

This is not to say that today's audiences are unsophisticated about performance. They are familiar with television and film but may not understand how theatre is unique or important. Certainly live theatre can't compete with the spectacle of film or the mass audiences of television. So why should audiences attend or support live theatre? Professional theatre tickets are much more expensive than a video rental or legal download. You could probably pay for all your other entertainment for a month with what you would spend for an average ticket to a Broadway production.

Many students are introduced to theatre in college or high school settings by attending a student production on campus. You might even experience theatre on video, mistaking that awful thing you see on screen as live theatre. Remember that even if the production is filmed well, the actual experience of live theatre has been defeated by putting it on video. And student amateur productions, though heartily staged and very often powerful in their own right, rarely equal a well-crafted professional production. Students just learning what live theatre is may mistake these amateur productions as the limits and heights of what theatre can offer. Audiences may have to travel to New York City, London, or a nearby regional theatre (most states have them) in order to experience the excitement and impact that live theatre can offer.

Artists still produce theatre because it can offer one primary thing that no other medium can offer: the power of the interaction of live actors with a live audience.

Television and film are ultimately flickering light on a wall or screen. Having a live person right in front of you who vaults you through a well-crafted production can be breathtaking. You may liken the experience to listening to a recording of your favorite musicians and then seeing them live. In a great performance, the energy of the exchange between performer and audience is as unmistakable as it is difficult to describe.

Just like any other art or entertainment form, professional theatre can also produce weak performances. Sometimes you have to sift through a fair amount of bad theatre to find the good. But when you do find excellence, the experience can be transformative. The course you are taking right now will give you the perspective and knowledge to develop opinions of your own. In the meantime, one way to avoid bad theatre and to find the good is to rely on the writings of a trusted critic.

To those outside the theatre, and often to those within it, the relationship between theatre artists and critics seems utterly hostile. If a critic attacks a performer for "running the gamut of emotion from A to B," the actor may call the critic "a virgin teaching Don Juan how to make love." Yet critics continue to operate in the modern theatre, and they show no signs of dying out. The theatre has always had its critical observers, from Aristotle and Plato in ancient Greece to the reviewers of next week's Broadway premiere. Just as the spectrum of theatrical activity covers a multitude of possibilities, theatrical criticism also varies widely in form and function.

Modern theatre artists continually seek to evaluate themselves and their work, but they receive feedback of great impact from two sources: the professional critics' reviews and the responses of the theatregoers. The critic offers an abstract reply to a produc-

The Real Inspector Hound, by Tom Stoppard, focuses on two pompous theatre critics, Moon and Birdboot, seen here, in a Metro Stage production, Washington, D.C. ©*Michael Bailey*

tion and affects the theatregoers' actions; the theatregoers then respond in the most concrete of terms: either they pay for a ticket or they do not. Any examination of the theatre should thus include the critical conditions of the time.

The Professional Critic

There are five categories of professional critics:

1. Newspaper
2. Magazine
3. Television/radio
4. Online/social media
5. "Analyst"

Most theatregoers equate the professional critic with the reviews they find in print, online, and in various broadcast forms. In larger metropolitan areas, these critics can wield considerable power over the success or failure of commercial productions. In New York City, the critics have an enormous effect on Broadway and Off-Broadway theatre, particularly the critics who write for the *New York Times*.

Newspaper critics usually attend the opening night of a production and write their reviews immediately afterward for publication the next day. Broadway casts traditionally wait into the wee hours of the morning to read such reviews, which in large part determine whether a show will continue to run or not. If the reviewers disapprove of the show, a production may not even have a second performance. If the reviews seem favorable, the producers and publicists quote them in subsequent publicity. Most shows get mixed reviews—part positive, part negative—in which case carefully selected extracts of the reviews appear in the publicity.

Critics whose reviews appear in magazines or in Sunday newspapers can take more time to prepare their essays. Because such critics can work more carefully, they tend to offer more thoughtful and polished insights. An editor often allots more space for them so that they can offer more detailed reactions.

Some metropolitan television stations reserve a few minutes for theatrical reviews on late-night news programs and repeat them the next day. Television reviewers often work under the same deadline pressure as newspaper reviewers to get their material in front of the public while it's still fresh. Under these circumstances, they can offer little more than first impressions.

Online sources can vary in speed and length, from the tweet sent out during the show to a long blog about the production weeks later or anything in between. Theatre critic Nick Reichert notes, "Social media has definitely changed the game for theatre criticism. Though it's not as ubiquitous as social media's impact on TV shows and movies (with new episodes and new movies trending on Facebook and Twitter nationally) it definitely has started to make or break a show's chance of succeeding, especially in the Broadway realm." There is also overlap in media, as professional newspaper and magazine critics all have social media presences. Conversely, superfans can have big followings—though there are limits to their influence. Reichert notes that "though social media has democratized our notion of criticism, there is a drastic difference in the impact theatre reporters and critics have, [compared to] bloggers who are theatre super fans."

A fifth category of critic, rarely encountered by the usual theatregoer, is comprised of the analysts, those critics who examine scripts in detail, often in book-length treatments. Examples might include Felicia Londré's *Tom Stoppard* or Jan Needles and Peter Thompson's *Brecht*, in which the authors examine a collection of works by the playwright. Cecil Smith and Glen Litton took another approach in *Musical Comedy in America*, in which they analyze a genre of production. Jan Kott's excellent *The Eating of the Gods: An Interpretation of Greek Tragedy*, a volume some six years in preparation, offers yet another method. Such analyst-critics may take up the work of a single playwright, a particular period of dramatic history, a dramatic genre, or even drama in general.

The Functions of Criticism

As we have just mentioned, analysts are typically academics who offer historical and/or theoretical context, as well as explore themes, patterns, and the impact of certain works. To a great extent, the rest of this section focuses on critics who do shorter-form work, especially those we know as "reviewers." A review should:

- Function as a news item
- Describe and/or present an impression of the production
- Assess the production's value
- Acknowledge the reviewer's preferences

The functions of the critic and of criticism emerge from the types of critics and the forms they employ. At the most elementary level, a review should function as a news item, reporting that a specific company in a particular theatre is staging a specified script. The reviewer usually includes information about the production's remaining performances and how to get tickets.

Second, the critic presents the reader with his or her impression of the production. The critic may describe the production, its style, the audience response, and the work's overall nature. A careful critic will not confuse this function with the next, however.

An assessment of the production's value may appear in reviews. Here critics consider the production against their total theatregoing experience and their concepts of what the theatre at its best can be. Good critics also encounter each production on its own terms. If, for instance, a critic goes to *Medea* and spends the evening wishing the play were funnier, the reviewer is not doing his or her job. Rather, a reviewer should encounter the play as freshly as possible and examine the particular production choices made, then assess their impact.

Critics make themselves most responsible and leave themselves most vulnerable by admitting their preferences, but in this way they can make their greatest contributions to the theatre. The great critics of the past rose to eminence in this way. Gotthold Lessing (1729–1781), for example, served as a critic for a German company. The productions he reviewed have long since sunk into obscurity, but the theories he advanced still have great value to the modern theatrical student. Similarly, Aristotle's analyses of the theatre of his day form a body of critical thinking that no modern critic or theatre artist can safely ignore. Other important critics of the past include George Bernard Shaw (1856–1950), who became an important playwright after his stint as critic; Jacques Copeau (1879–1949), who was a critic before becoming one of the early twentieth century's most influential directors; Brooks Atkinson (1894–1984), who won an enviable reputation for his fairness and perception; and Walter Kerr (b. 1913), a critic for the *New York Times* and winner of a Pulitzer Prize in 1978.

Theatrical criticism is justified for two reasons. First, critical response offers the only substantial reply to the theatre artist. Productions certainly succeed or fail at the box office in terms of ticket sales, but perceptive critics can help illuminate theatre artists' choices through their evaluation or analysis. Of those who participate in a theatrical production, including the audience, only the critic does not have a vested interest in the show's success. A critic who has the necessary qualifications can make a substantial and valuable contribution.

A critic usually shares his audience with the theatre artists; theatregoers read theatre critics; non-theatregoers do not. A critic can serve the higher purposes of theatre by illuminating a work for its actual or potential audience. This second justification for criticism in no way demeans the audience or brands them as too stupid to understand what they see. It rather suggests that expert assistance may increase understanding and therefore appreciation. Anyone who has ever sought out explanation for a difficult piece of writing, film, or painting, for example, can appreciate the critical function.

For example, were it not for two critics, we might not know the work of theatre icon Henrik Ibsen, who stirred up great controversy with his late-nineteenth-century works. Today, his plays, including *A Doll's House*, *Hedda Gabler*, and others, seem tame, but many of his contemporaries considered Ibsen a pornographer. Two English theatre critics (George Bernard Shaw and William Archer), themselves playwrights, placed Ibsen's work in a new light and paved the way for his plays' future success.

Requisites for Excellence in Criticism

There are five requisites for excellence in criticism:

1. Love of the theatre
2. Fairness
3. Theatrical knowledge and experience
4. Writing skills
5. Concentration

Some critics win widespread respect, both among their colleagues and among theatre artists. Circumstances vary, but the qualities of excellence in criticism usually include the following.

1. LOVE OF THE THEATRE

That a theatrical critic might not enjoy attending the theatre might seem incredible, but evidence shows such an unhappy state of affairs can indeed exist. A newspaper editor may, for example, assign the theatrical beat to a reporter with various other responsibilities, and that reporter may not prove ready, willing, or able to review productions capably. Excellence in any endeavor demands enthusiasm for one's work, and critics who have lost their sense of theatrical values will have little to offer. Those who have never had it to begin with should seek other assignments.

2. FAIRNESS

Anyone expressing opinions or value judgments on any subject reveals his or her prejudices and preferences. Critics cannot eliminate their human frailty, but they can minimize its interference in their work. A critic who attends on consecutive evenings a Greek tragedy, a musical comedy, a Shakespearean comedy, an Absurdist drama, a Neil Simon comedy, and a drama by Chekhov may find it difficult to apply the same objective standards to all of them. Critics face this problem continually, and the best of them find individual means of solving it.

We should note that bloggers who write about theatre are under little pressure to preserve this aspect of criticism, nor are they necessarily qualified in any other way to offer an informed—let alone well-written—opinion. However, there's a decent chance that bloggers who know something about theatre are out there, and they may reliably lead you to some great performances.

3. THEATRICAL KNOWLEDGE AND EXPERIENCE

Ideally, theatre critics should have considerable awareness of the heritage and evolution of the theatre, as well as substantial insights into contemporary developments. The highly regarded Walter Kerr, at one time drama critic for the *New York Times*, for example, began as a film critic for two newspapers while in high school. He later directed some fifty plays as a drama professor and wrote or collaborated on several Broadway plays and one musical. Having served as drama critic for the magazine *Commonweal* for two years and for the *New York Herald Tribune* for fifteen, he then joined the *Times*.

However, mere exposure to theatre will not stimulate critical excellence, any more than seeing hundreds of baseball games will create an effective sportswriter. Experience and study of the essential nature of what one writes about will contribute to growth in any profession. It is not unusual to find reviewers in relatively large cities in the United

States who have never had a theatre class, let alone participated in theatre at any level. In addition, the Internet has spurred a financial downturn for newspapers over the past decade, resulting in severe cuts in arts reporting. Unfortunately, many audience members therefore end up deciding to attend a play (or not) based on the advice of someone totally inexperienced.

4. WRITING SKILLS

Theatre critics reach their audience primarily through the written word. They should therefore be able to articulate their observations and opinions precisely. Their writing circumstances may vary from the solitude of their home office to the backseat of a speeding New York taxi as they try to make a deadline, but their work will influence a number of theatregoers. Such responsibility demands accuracy and precision.

5. CONCENTRATION

Like the actor, the critic must ignore matters irrelevant to the production and concentrate on the matter at hand. Audience members may let their minds wander or may stew about something in their personal lives, but critics should not allow themselves this luxury because their responses go to the public. Outstanding critics must have the mental discipline necessary for intense, concentrated perception, analysis, and response.

Critical Preferences

- Pleasure
- Impact
- Form

People's preferences vary widely in most matters: automobiles, music, clothing, food, politics, sex, and religion, to name a few. We should then readily accept that people have sharply distinct expectations of the theatre. Audience members attend the theatre for a variety of reasons, and they tend to evaluate their experiences positively if the production meets their expectations. Specific artworks have distinct dominant qualities that tend to attract the audiences who will most appreciate them. Individual audience members may thus find their appreciation based on some of the values outlined, citing Stephen Pepper, in chapter 1: pleasure, impact (or intensity), and form.

APPRECIATION OF PLEASURE

Nothing seems more difficult to define or less necessary to justify than pleasure. Recalling Goethe's insistence on entertainment as an essential function of art, we can

Steve Martin's hilarious play *The Underpants* **at the University of Wisconsin-LaCrosse.** *Courtesy of Joe Anderson*

realize that whatever seems good to one theatregoer is, in that person's opinion, good. But the very word "good" represents only an indefinite commendation, a subjective response. If a production captures the agreeable attention of a viewer for a few hours, it has served a viable function for that viewer. Another person may require more than mere diversion, but even diversion alone need not be mindless—unless the audience is equally mindless, an unusual case.

APPRECIATION OF IMPACT

Some audience members equate value in the theatre or in other art forms with the intensity of their response. Comedic plays can sometimes be quite intense. For instance, Michael Frayn's *Noises Off*, like most farce, is action packed and highly charged. However, audience members who want big impact often find themselves attracted to more serious drama, perhaps the classical tragedies, usually seeking a greater personal involvement in the artistic experience than is offered by milder art forms. The film *No Country for Old Men*, as well as plays like Lin-Manuel Miranda's *Hamilton*, appeal at least in part because of their emotional impact.

APPRECIATION OF FORM

Yet another type of artistic appreciation grows from the perception of the integration of artistic elements or the internal relatedness of the artwork. In the theatre, both the script and the production offer opportunities for evaluating form. Does the script seem focused or unfocused? Does everything seem to operate coherently? In looking at form, one might ask if the themes extend outward to the characters, the language, and the structure of the play. So, in a play that values societal rules, we may encounter a disciplined form with few subplots, uncluttered language, character behavior that is generally restrained, and a logical plot progression. Conversely, in a play about rebellion (e.g., the Broadway hit based on a nineteenth-century Wedekind play, *Spring Awakening*), we might find more extravagant language, complicated relationships, a chaotic impression given by highly emotional character behavior, and so forth. The production choices then play their part.

Looking at the 2006 Broadway production of *Spring Awakening*, for instance, there were both surprising (rebellious) choices, and choices that explain what's being rebelled against. For instance, the actors wore rather restrictive costumes that in many cases gave the impression of being unable to contain the characters' life force and energy. (Naturally, this was an illusion, since the actors needed to run, jump, and dance in these clothes. We'll tell you more about the designer's job in later chapters.) In any case, such costume choices were consistent with the themes of the play and the struggles of the characters and were, therefore, rather "fitting" choices. Form is, therefore, not a matter of good or bad but of coherence. So, as one looks at the more recent *Spring Awakening*, originated by Deaf West in Los Angeles, and featuring deaf performers, another series of choices was made that highlighted the intense (and private) emotional life of the teenagers in the play. You might fruitfully compare these productions to discuss the form of a production, as opposed to the form of a play script.

Most of us find within ourselves a propensity toward one or more of these forms of appreciation (pleasure, impact, or form), and we tend to seek these qualities in our artistic experiences. Some artists follow a similar inclination in their work. But enduring artworks tend to amalgamate all three aspects and thus offer a rich potential to all who experience them. The three aspects are not mutually exclusive; they rather offer three relatively identifiable responses.

Moonchildren, by Michael Weller, is a good example of a representational play. Though set in the mid-1960s, most college students would find the characters recognizable, and the setting is usually treated realistically. *Courtesy of Wake Forest University Theatre. Photo by Bill Ray*

Thoughtful theatregoers do well to examine their own preferences, lest they find themselves out of sync with a production. This possibility represents a very real danger for professional critics, who may inadvertently divert an artwork from its intended audience or completely misinterpret it, condemning it for not achieving purposes to which it never aspired. We therefore reassert the need for critics (and students) to do their best to encounter each production on its own terms.

Types of Drama

Twenty-five centuries of playwriting have seen a bewildering number of attempts at dramatic styles, genres, and "isms." Scholars and critics have attempted to categorize these multiple types and describe the stylistic alternatives that have emerged. Audience members will find they have a higher potential for appreciation if they are aware of the main types of drama.

REPRESENTATIONAL THEATRE

One of the oldest and widest divisions of drama types lies between the *representational* and the *presentational* types of scripts. Historically, presentational theatre dominated the world's stages until the late nineteenth century, when modern realism (the representational theatre) emerged and rose to the popularity that it still enjoys.

In representational theatre all elements of the production seek to give the illusion of reality. The events on the stage seem to be real, just as they do in most of television and film. It does not matter that the events are not what they seem; the audience willingly, if temporarily, suspends its disbelief, an act essential to the dramatic arts.

To suspend disbelief is a lot different from believing that what you see is really happening. If audience members believed that the actor playing Othello in Shakespeare's tragedy was actually strangling the actress playing his wife, Desdemona, they would have to get up and stop him, since not doing so would make them complicit in murder. But they do not believe they are watching a real murder; instead, they enter into the contract with the actors that establishes a work of theatre.

Two important factors have to be in place. First the audience must achieve *empathy* with one or more of the central characters—a rapport or affinity with that character and his or her apparent goals. But at the same time the audience must retain *aesthetic distance*, a detachment from the action taking place on the stage. Audience members must willingly suspend disbelief to become involved in a performance, but they must also remain aware that they are watching an artwork, not a real event. This dual involvement requires a delicate balance, an artistic contract between performers and audience.

The members of the audience may—indeed often do—become so engrossed in the stage action that they forget they are in a theatre. You may have had that sort of experience. But when jolted out of that involvement, the onlookers rarely have any doubt that they are in a theatre, watching actors, either live or on film.

If a person grew to maturity without ever hearing of the theatre, if he or she were innocent of the very idea of impersonation, watching a live stage performance would strike them as a very strange experience. In an early American script, *The Contrast* by Royall Tyler (1757–1826), a New Yorker takes a simple-minded rustic to a theatre. Having never seen a play, he believes that when the show started "they lifted up a great green cloth and let us look right into the next neighbor's house" and wonders if many New Yorkers build their houses that way. Similarly, a somewhat untrustworthy story relates that in the nineteenth century a second-rate Shakespearean company presented *Romeo and Juliet* in a Colorado mining camp to an audience of miners. All went well until Romeo began to commit suicide, at which point the miners stopped the show, woke up Juliet, dragged a startled Friar Lawrence from backstage to remarry them— and they all partied uproariously for the next three days.

Actors in the representational theatre usually seem to ignore the audience; they act as if there were a "fourth wall" between them and the onlookers. Even with this convention in place, the actors can, nevertheless, remain aware of the audience and its reactions.

PRESENTATIONAL THEATRE

Presentational theatre makes no attempt at ignoring the audience. In fact, the cast may deal directly with the audience in a face-to-face confrontation. Most musical comedy

This Illinois Wesleyan University production of *The Drowsy Chaperone*, with its painted airplane and focus toward the audience, is a terrific example of presentational theatre. *Courtesy of Pete Guither*

is presentational: The singers come to the front of the stage, look directly at the audience, and perform without any pretense of a "fourth wall." You might also think about the soliloquies in Shakespeare, monologues, one-person shows, and any play with a narrator as being similarly presentational. During the course of the semester, you are likely to encounter a number of plays that acknowledge the audience or that make no effort to replicate everyday life as you know it. Actors play ducks, frogs, and swans in the children's show *Honk!* and the audience simply accepts the convention as part of the storytelling. Much theatre asks you to use your imagination in this way, speaking to truths about human existence in a different way than in the representational theatre.

Representationalism versus presentationalism, therefore, does not suggest a right and a wrong way to do theatre. They are two distinct approaches to a theatrical event, determined by the form of the script and the intentions of the director or producer. Many plays, including most contemporary musicals, combine elements of both.

Genres

The main genres of theatre include tragedy, melodrama, comedy, satire, and farce, though scripts often resist categorization, presenting a world in each play that is unique in and of itself. Nevertheless, we can see patterns in individual playwrights and in groups of plays and playwrights—hence the usefulness of having such classifications.

Modern experimental theatre does not fit easily into the traditional classifications, nor need it, but regular theatregoers will find that much drama does indeed fall into one of the types just mentioned. Playwrights often mix the various forms to excite greater interest in their audiences. The tragedy of Hamlet becomes all the darker when juxtaposed with the low comedy of the gravediggers; similarly, many of Shakespeare's comedies have very serious elements. *Measure for Measure*, for example, deals with sexual blackmail and *The Winter's Tale*, with the loss of love through pride.

Such variations may prove troublesome, but playwrights rarely sit down and say, "Today I will write a melodrama." It is, nevertheless, helpful to understand the forms as they originated.

TRAGEDY AND MELODRAMA

As suggested in chapter 2, tragedy seeks to exalt the human spirit. The tragedian often seeks this response by revealing a central character in the most serious of dilemmas, beset by forces that eventually defeat him or her. Melodrama similarly places its central characters in awful circumstances, the prototypical example being the heroine tied to the railroad tracks while the hero races to the rescue. Most melodrama achieves a satisfactory end in that the hero arrives just in time, defeats the villain conclusively, and marries the heroine. But no one arrives to save Oedipus or Hamlet; they meet their sufferings head-on and seem to lose.

To determine the essential distinction between tragedy and melodrama is to dig into the very essence of drama. Both tragedy and melodrama put the protagonist in peril, but melodrama excites the audience with amazing events and satisfies them with the eventual success of the "good guys." One need look no further than TV thrillers, cop shows, westerns, war stories, and so on. A "happy" ending is perhaps the clearest difference but not the only one.

Tragedy engrosses an audience in the tightening circle of adversity surrounding the protagonist, so while suspense is a part of tragedy, its satisfaction stems from the depiction of a human being transcending the fate that brought seeming destruction. Melodrama often proves the more suspenseful of the two forms, whereas tragedy offers more profound insights.

Right triumphs in melodrama; the playwright cleverly shapes the plot and portrays the world as it ought to be. In tragedy the protagonist, although destroyed socially, even killed, triumphs in defeat; the playwright reveals his or her comprehension of humanity and portrays the world as it is. Put simply, melodrama suggests that human beings can triumph over adversity; tragedy proposes that they can transcend it.

Another aspect of the distinction between tragedy and melodrama lies in the nature of the protagonists and their capacity to perceive. Several dramatic theorists have observed what they call the tragic pattern of *purpose, passion*, and *perception* in tragedy. In this pattern, the protagonist first discovers a goal to pursue (Hamlet must avenge his father's murder; Oedipus must lift the curse from his kingdom), then sets out to achieve that goal. Because the matter is of some significance to the protagonist, he or she becomes passionately involved in the action.

So far there seems little difference between the two forms, but at the play's resolution, when the protagonist either succeeds or fails, they differ sharply. In tragedy, the central character understands deeply the nature of his or her condition and the nature of existence. As Hamlet dies, he knows he has avenged his father's murder and restored order to Denmark. As Oedipus gropes his way out of Thebes, blinded by himself, banished by his own edict, he knows what excessive pride can lead to. Thus, as some theorists propose, the protagonist's degree of perception distinguishes tragedy from melodrama.

Thus far we have considered tragedy and melodrama in their purest forms. Playwrights rarely cooperate with such neat pigeonholing of their work. Whereas tragedy as a distinct form began in the fifth century BCE in Athens, melodrama as a distinct literary genre arose at the turn of the nineteenth century, although melodramatic elements have existed from the beginning. Students may avoid some confusion if they regard tragedy and melodrama not as distinct categories but as the two ends of a continuum, with specific scripts tending toward one end of the spectrum or the other.

Thus, for example, we need not expend great energy in trying to categorize Arthur Miller's well-known script *Death of a Salesman*. Rather we tend to agree with the critic Brooks Atkinson (1894–1984), who suggested that this script "reached the foothills of tragedy." One might view similarly *M. Butterfly, Angels in America, Amadeus*, and a host of other modern, serious scripts. They are more substantial than melodrama but do not neatly fit the designation of tragedy. Modern melodrama—films such as *The Martian* or *Mission Impossible* or any of the numerous *CSIs* on TV—cause far less difficulty in categorization.

In the fourth century BCE, Aristotle, the Greek critic and philosopher, proposed that theatrical productions consist of six elements:

1. Plot, the arrangement of events in a script
2. Character, the representation of the personalities in action
3. Thought, the ideas contained within the script
4. Diction, the expressive use of language
5. Music, the accompaniment to productions
6. Spectacle, the visual elements of production

This scheme of analysis, which still has considerable value, reveals still further the differences between tragedy and melodrama if one examines each element in a prototypical script. Melodrama tends to concern itself more with plot and spectacle than does tragedy and less with thought and character. One might propose humans as creatures of hope and therefore more attracted to melodrama, with its ordered good and evil and the hope of escaping adversity, than to the more complex tragic concept of transcending one's fate. Certainly melodrama has had greater commercial success in the history of the theatre, but tragedy has had greater impact. Literary critics especially have found the enduring qualities of tragedy far more worthy of their attention than the temporary values of theatrical melodrama. Audiences tend to appreciate excitement more than profundity; Shakespeare spoke of "the judicious few."

Although no precise list of essential characteristics seems possible, we can describe the general tendencies of the forms. Tragedy typically:

1. Concerns a serious subject, which the playwright treats seriously
2. Presents a protagonist of high stature, often of royal birth, or a person representing a class of people (at least, the protagonist represents more than a mere individual)

3. Avoids the element of chance or coincidence, focusing upon what *must* happen as opposed to merely what *could* happen

4. Evokes in the audience emotions of pity and fear, which Aristotle called catharsis—pity for the protagonist's suffering and fear that a similar calamity might befall him or her

5. Brings the protagonist—and by extension the audience—to a heightened perception of the human condition as personified by the central character

In contrast, melodrama usually:

1. Treats a serious subject

2. Presents characters more loosely, often as stereotypes (i.e., good guys and bad guys), allowing the audience a more immediate empathetic response

3. Employs the element of chance to generate excitement in the audience, even at the risk of improbability

4. Evokes sentimentality rather than catharsis

5. Brings the protagonist to eventual victory, possibly with no real enlightenment or perception

Other terms have emerged over the centuries to differentiate serious drama from tragedy. Italian Renaissance scholars, for example, coined the term "tragicomedy" to

Scapin, **a highly physical comedy, directed by Shirley Huston-Findley at College of Wooster.** *Courtesy of Sidney Martin*

describe scripts they considered a mixture of tragedy and comedy. Anton Chekhov's *The Three Sisters* and Samuel Beckett's *Waiting for Godot* are considered great works of tragicomedy. These plays present worlds in which melancholy and irony mingle with physical comedy and wit, but they also reflect a serious worldview. The French used another term, *drame*, to characterize contemporary plays of serious intent.

COMEDY, SATIRE, AND FARCE

Just as critics have considered melodrama somehow inferior to tragedy, they have considered comic forms of less substance than serious drama. It seems that if playwrights want serious consideration they must write serious dramas. Yet the comic forms may also explore serious issues, and they often hold greater audience appeal.

Seeming to seek merely to amuse, comedy does not evade the substantial; rather it approaches our existence from a viewpoint different from tragedy and the other serious forms. Theoreticians have suggested that life is a tragedy to those who feel and a comedy to those who think. Or, as actor Kevin Kline has said, "As a tragic hero, I can appear noble, but as a jester, I can tell the truth."

Comedy frees us, temporarily and harmlessly, from the strictures of society. We may not, by nature, be chaste, obedient, subservient creatures, but we come to expect that of one another through the conventions of the society in which we live. Release must happen, through dreams, through sublimation, and through comedy.

Satire, perhaps the most overtly purposeful comic form, uses irony, sarcasm, and ridicule to expose, denounce, and deride human vice and folly. Often savage in its attack, satire hardly avoids matters of consequence and in fact often addresses them directly. Examples include the works of Aristophanes in Greece in the fifth century BCE, Molière in seventeenth-century France, Mark Twain in nineteenth-century America, and present-day comic strips. Such television shows as *The Daily Show* and *Saturday Night Live* qualify richly, as does the work of many contemporary stand-up comics. Such comedy seeks to correct society and its ills by ridiculing its undesirable aspects; there's more to it than just being silly. Aristotle's concept of thought in drama is very much in evidence.

At the opposite end of the comic scale lies farce, a comic form seeking only to amuse, with little, if any, conscious function beyond evoking laughter. This is the comedy of slapstick, pratfalls, pie fights, chase scenes, seltzer bottles, and the like. Included are many Charlie Chaplin films, the Three Stooges, the Marx Brothers, most Ben Stiller movies, and the frequently revived work of playwright Georges Feydeau (1862–1921). To some critics, farce represents the least substantial of all comic forms—indeed, of all dramatic forms—divorced entirely from thought or idea. But other critics find merit in farce. Who hasn't had days when everything seemed chaotic, unpredictable, and a bit overwhelming? Yet, seen in the rearview mirror, such days can seem hilarious. This is the worldview of a *farceur*. Audiences often find farce delightful, and theatre artists know that successful farce calls for skill and precision of the highest order. See a good production of *Noises Off*, and you will see what we mean.

Between satire and farce, then, we find comedy, although the term refers to all comic forms. In this sense comedy corresponds to the great bulk of serious drama lying between tragedy and melodrama. Comedy definitely employs thought but does not call attention to the fact. Many of the more successful situation comedies on television, such as *The Big Bang Theory* and *The Office*, have definite points of view but do not always hammer them home. Theatre companies have also formed, in this country and others, that are devoted entirely to producing comedy. The Theatre of Comedy Company, formed in 1983 in London, is one notable example. Since its founding it has had a string of West End successes, including brilliant productions of *Hay Fever* and *Six Degrees of Separation.*

The essence of comedy seems to be the collision of two planes of thought in a suddenly revealed new combination. The punch line of a joke triggers the listener's grasp of this new relationship. We can apply this theory to any joke we know. Invariably, a story will start developing along one line of expectation, then suddenly thrust itself into a totally new one. Cartoon television shows such as *South Park* or *Family Guy* frequently reveal a similar collision of thought planes, and the viewer's sudden realization of the new relationship triggers laughter. A viewer, however, who doesn't understand the collision, doesn't see the new relationship—doesn't "get it"—will be frustrated and will not laugh or smile.

Comedy is usually quite topical and timely; what might have been hysterically funny to our parents leaves us cold, and our children will find our humor quaint at best, mindless at worst. When viewing classical comedy, an audience needs help desperately. Aristophanes's brilliant political satires of the Athenian administrator Cleon require a considerable knowledge of Athenian history, and his outrageous, often obscene puns simply do not translate from ancient Greek into English. Similarly, Shakespeare's jokes depend on a specific usage of language and a set of circumstances long past. When Hamlet advises Ophelia to "Get thee to a nunnery, go," few modern audience members will realize that the Elizabethans equated nunneries with houses of prostitution. Yet much of Shakespeare's comedy still appeals strongly to modern readers and audiences, attesting to his relative avoidance of the trivial.

Viewed from another angle, the terms "tragedy," "*drame*," "melodrama," "satire," "comedy," and "farce" indicate six distinct methods of considering a specific human action or even existence in general, ranging from the spiritual optimism of tragedy to the raucous irreverence of farce. Thus a playwright can choose to treat a single dramatic theme or situation in any of these ways. Consider adultery, long a popular subject for drama. Playwrights treated this theme tragically in *Othello*, comically in *The Country Wife*, satirically in *What the Butler Saw*, as *drame* in *A Streetcar Named Desire* or *The Crucible*, as farce in *Noises Off* or *A Flea in Her Ear*, and as melodrama in everyday television soap operas. If tragedy and satire are the forms that depict humanity most thoughtfully, farce and melodrama suggest a world in which good can triumph over evil. *Drame* and comedy, combining the most popular of both extremes, have both critical worth and popular appeal and have thus succeeded most consistently over the long history of the theatre.

Playwrights rarely consciously select one of these six genres when they begin to create a script. In the modern drama, they often combine all the dramatic forms in varying degrees, selecting the elements that seem most appropriate for their specific intentions. Shakespeare, for example, mixed the comic and serious in most of his tragedies, intensifying each by juxtaposing one with the other. Just as painters use highlight and shadow to depict a three-dimensional form, playwrights commonly perceive life as a mixture of the serious and the comic, the substantial and the trivial, and often meld both approaches in depicting human existence on the stage.

Theatrical Styles and Trends

Style is individual to each play. However, it is helpful to identify stylistic trends within groups of plays and playwrights. Whether playwrights consciously or unconsciously choose the genre or style in which they work, such divisions can help contemporary theatre students understand that the *way* something is done (its style) conveys meaning, demonstrates social values, communicates mood and atmosphere, and more. The following are some of the major trends you should know about.

1. Realism
2. Symbolism
3. Expressionism
4. Epic theatre
5. Absurdism
6. Postmodernism

Clybourne Park*, Bruce Norris's sharp, witty spin-off of Lorraine Hansberry's *A Raisin in the Sun*, demonstrates how satire and realism can coexist. Wake Forest University, directed by Sharon Andrews. *Courtesy of Wake Forest University Theatre. Photo by Bill Ray

1. REALISM

As a conscious movement, realism is first discernible around 1853 in France. It has been the dominant theatrical "ism" in some form or another since the 1880s. Realism owed much to the development of positivism, which emphasized the application of the scientific model to human behavior. Behavior, in a realist's view, was determined by the forces of heredity and environment. Realists, therefore, focused on objectively *depicting or representing* the tangible physical world, believing that the ultimate reality was discoverable only through the five senses. Henrik Ibsen's early works were some of the most influential realist plays, and such writers as August Wilson and Arthur Miller were important twentieth-century proponents of the genre. Bruce Norris's work, particularly his 2010 Pulitzer Prize–winning *Clybourne Park*, is another good example. Psychologically coherent characters, recognizable (illusionistic) environments, logical cause-and-effect plots, and a strong emotional component have for years made realism one of the most popular forms of modern drama.

However, shortly following the advent of realism, philosophers and writers began to doubt that objectivity, the central premise of the genre, was possible or even desirable. Other components of the genre also came into question, and many new forms emerged to give voice to other perspectives.

2. SYMBOLISM

Symbolism has been with the theatre forever. All theatre, to a certain extent, is living metaphor. All of a production's words, actions, and even plot lines are made meaningful through interpretation, conscious or subconscious. However, as a conscious movement, symbolism was short lived, appearing in France in the 1880s and lasting only until about 1900. Symbolist plays are allegories in which the immediate dramatic action must be reinterpreted on another (hopefully higher) philosophical plane. Its ultimate aim was to convey intuitions about a higher truth that the playwright felt could not be adequately expressed in words. Maurice Maeterlinck, William B. Yeats, and Henrik Ibsen wrote many of the important symbolist plays.

3. EXPRESSIONISM

A short-lived but influential movement, expressionism emerged out of post–World War I Germany. These intensely subjective plays, which externalize the writer's inner feelings, are clearly antirealistic and are frequently seen as a young person's revolt against passivity and conformity. Expressionist plays almost always have a Christlike figure at their center. Everything in the play is filtered through him or her, revealing an intensely personal vision of reality. Though often frightening and nightmarish, these plays also hold a belief in mankind's ability to undergo a spiritual rebirth. Georg Kaiser, Elmer Rice, Sophie Treadwell, August Strindberg, and Henrik Ibsen all wrote important expressionist plays.

***Machinal,* by Sophie Treadwell, is a prime example of an expressionist play.
*Courtesy of Wake Forest University Theatre. Photo by Bill Ray***

4. EPIC THEATRE

Made famous by noted theorist and playwright Bertolt Brecht (1898–1956), epic plays seek to enlighten as they entertain. Epic theatre influenced much of the political theatre written during the second half of the twentieth century, and Brecht is regarded by some as the most influential playwright since World War II. The central aim of these plays was to redefine the relationship between spectator, theatre, and society. Brecht believed that realistic, dramatic theatre lulled audiences into passivity; he wanted to spur them to action. Therefore, he sought to "alienate" or distance audience members from the onstage action, allowing them to judge the actions of the characters rather than empathizing with them as they would in the "dramatic" theatre. Epic plays try to arouse spectators' capacity for action by (a) helping the audience to maintain critical distance and (b) refusing to resolve conflict in a traditional dramatic (Aristotelian) structure.

Brecht championed the use of episodic structure, in which each scene stands for itself, and also refused to adhere to linear cause-and-effect plot development. Brecht's staging ideas have been particularly influential, and techniques that he and others developed can be found throughout popular culture. One example is his use of titles that precede the action of each scene. These titles inform the audience of what is about to happen, thereby attempting to keep their attention on *how* things happen rather than allowing suspense to sweep them away. The film *Babe*, as well as dozens of plays, have made use of this device, though sometimes without the kind of overt political purpose

Waiting for Godot,* Beckett's dark and funny absurdist play has enjoyed many revivals, including such pairings as Steve Martin and Robin Williams and Ian McKellan and Patrick Stewart. In this production at Wake Forest University, directed by Brook Davis and designed by Rob Eastman-Mullins, Zac Pierce-Messick and Phil Kayser take on the roles of Vladimir and Estragon. *Courtesy of Wake Forest University Theatre. Photo by Bill Ray

Brecht intended. A television show your parents may have watched, called *Frasier*, tended to use these titles as a way to set up the punch line of each scene. Nevertheless, epic plays tend to be overtly theatrical, focused on social questions, and directed at making the audience think more than feel.

5. ABSURDISM

After the atrocities of World War II, a number of writers strongly influenced by existential philosophy began to explore ways to express the absurdity of human existence. Not bound by any manifesto or a defined set of objectives, these writers were, instead, grouped together in 1961 by critic Martin Esslin, who saw a pattern of dramatic strategies emerging. Absurdist plays:

- Describe a nonrealistic world without cause-and-effect logic
- Reject the use of Aristotelian plot structure in favor of a circular structure, or one in which the end of the play demonstrates an intensification of the initial problem or situation
- Explore the breakdown of communication and the limits of language. Dialogue is therefore often disconnected and full of repetition, jargon, and baby talk

- Contain characters who lack a clearly defined psychological past and whose behavior often seems irrational or indecipherable
- Are often quite funny and extremely dark. Humor and pain coexist in almost all of these plays

Included among the absurdists are such important figures as Eugene Ionesco, Samuel Beckett, Jean Genet, and Harold Pinter, among others.

6. POSTMODERNISM

Postmodernism is not so much an "ism" as it is a trend away from defining works in the kind of bounded, unified ways previously described. Postmodernists, like other nonrealistic theatre practitioners, also dismiss cause-and-effect determinism. Self-consciously splicing together styles, genres, moods, and cultural levels (high/low), postmodern artists are indifferent to questions of originality and relish the use of irony. The heroic individual with a unified, coherent psychology has no place in this worldview, nor does the notion of high culture as opposed to popular culture. For instance, stage director Robert Wilson calls his works "operas" but makes no attempt to adhere to the traditions of this most conservative of theatrical forms. His operas, such as *Einstein on the Beach*, instead use dancers as the featured performers and work on a poetic rather than narrative level. More easily accessible postmodernists include Sam Shepard, whose *True West* reveals two brothers who, during the course of the play, blur and transfer identities.

Postmodern theatre is perhaps most visible in the New York avant-garde, and it is not without its critics. Writer Todd Gitlin has remarked, "Alongside the blasé brand of postmodernism . . . there is another kind—one in which pluralist exuberance and critical intelligence reinforce each other." *Hamilton* is an excellent example of such pluralist exuberance, mixing old and new with abandon to say something new in a new way.

Stage directors such as Peter Sellars and Robert Wilson, as well as such multimedia artists as Laurie Anderson, helped open the door for transcending the traditional barriers between visual art, theatre, and music. Directors Richard Foreman and Elizabeth LeCompte and playwright/performers John Leguizamo, Spalding Gray, and Anna Deavere Smith also contributed meaningfully to the birth of postmodern theatre in the United States. In fact, the kind of blurred boundaries that these—and many other—theatre makers of the 1970s–1990s created has made possible things like *Hamilton*, *Avenue Q*, *Book of Mormon*, and much more.

The Theatregoer as Critic

Prepare to write your play responses by doing the following:

1. Find out something about the production before you go.
2. Go with an open mind.

3. Go with a friend.
4. Stay focused.
5. Offer feedback.
6. Don't get discouraged.

Just as you take a chance when you go to a movie, you take a chance when you attend the theatre. You may be entertained or bored; you may leave transformed or annoyed. You may encounter a portrayal of humanity's darkest aspects or a feather-light piece of fluff. The theatre may test society's values and customs; such testing is an appropriate function of art in general and theatre in particular. You may find a production completely disagreeable, but you can considerably increase the odds in favor of avoiding such unpleasant experiences through some fairly simple techniques.

1. FIND OUT SOMETHING ABOUT THE PRODUCTION BEFORE YOU GO

Unless you plan to see a production of a new script, you can usually find out some-thing of its general nature fairly easily. The producing agency will often be happy to describe a production to you; just ask whomever answers the phone in the box office. Above all, the most effective means of theatrical publicity and the most effective means of learning about a production is word of mouth. Nothing brings customers into a theatre like satisfied audience members, and nothing keeps them away like disgruntled patrons. Your friends, especially because they know your tastes, can help you consider-ably in making your theatrical choices.

You can look online for information, of course. Publicity releases try to entice you into the theatre, but they also describe to some extent the sort of event you may antici-pate. Published reviews sometimes include descriptions, and hopefully our discussion of genre earlier will help you decode what you read even further.

With all that in mind, it can also be fun to see a play when you know absolutely nothing about it. If you are especially adventurous, you may find it more enjoyable to see the play and then learn all you can about it.

2. GO WITH AN OPEN MIND

To whatever degree you choose to educate yourself before a production, with an open mind, and try to meet the production at least halfway. Don't be that person who condemns everything, hoping to be thought of as the smartest, most insightful person in the room. Such attitudes contribute nothing to any aspect of human endeavor, any more than does the attitude that everything is wonderful. Both views are counterpro-ductive and unrealistic. Rather, recognize that there is often something to enjoy in a production if you will give it a chance.

3. GO WITH A FRIEND

Most people prefer to attend a production with someone rather than alone. Theatre is nothing if it isn't a sharing experience; to share it with friends seems to increase the enjoyment. Just make sure to invite someone who is likely to enjoy the play rather than someone who thinks it's cool to hate everything.

4. STAY FOCUSED

Stay focused on the performance. On behalf of theatre workers and audience members everywhere, let us take this opportunity to suggest that, while you're in a theatre during a performance, you simply let go of life outside of the play. Listen and respond to the performance with generosity, and even when you see a production you don't enjoy, keep it to yourself for the time being. You never know if you're sitting in front of one of the actors' grandparents, who are proudly enjoying the show. In fact, it is rare that a production is so bad that someone doesn't enjoy it, just as it is rarely so good that someone doesn't hate it. Give the rest of the audience a chance. You might even look for something that you can enjoy—the design elements, the performance of a particular actor, or the singing in a musical. Please don't distract others by flipping open your cell phone, checking e-mail, or digging around in your purse. If you can't find anything redeemable in the show, leave—just wait until intermission. You can let the cast and company know you didn't like their work in more effective ways than disrupting the performance. Theatrical productions are complex interactions, usually requiring intense concentration by audience and performers alike. If you cannot or will not enter into that contract, have the courtesy to let the cast and the rest of the audience try.

5. OFFER FEEDBACK

Consider giving the producing agency some feedback. Write them and let them know what you thought about the work. They may disagree, and they may not take your advice, but they will not ignore it. In selecting and preparing production schedules, producing agencies try to predict the future and read the minds of their audiences. This difficult task becomes much easier if audiences make their opinions known. Critics offer one sort of response, but the public can offer a very substantial one as well. You will, as an audience, get the entertainment you deserve.

6. DON'T GET DISCOURAGED

Don't feel discouraged if you encounter a streak of disagreeable theatre. Baseball teams have losing streaks, individuals have slumps, and students have bad semesters, but they

In *Eurydice*, playwright Sarah Ruhl tells us that the title character descends into the underworld in an "elevator" that rains on the inside. All kinds of gorgeous (if difficult) scenic opportunities live in that simple stage direction. Here's one, at Catawba College, in a production directed by Elizabeth Homan. *Sean Meyers Photography*

usually keep at their tasks and eventually do better. Hang in there. Great theatre may be right around the next corner.

Theatre needs audiences for its survival, and it tends to get the audiences it deserves. Perhaps not all audiences need theatre; the functions of art and the theatre exist in many and various human activities. But for twenty-five centuries, since Thespis stepped out of that Athenian chorus and began to enact Dionysus, the theatre has offered a uniquely direct form of aesthetic enjoyment to millions of human beings. As long as people seek vital interaction with other people, the theatre will continue to delight and stimulate its patrons. Perhaps you will never again enter a theatre, and you may live a happy, prosperous, and productive life without it. But if the actions and interactions of humanity still intrigue you, the theatre will have much to offer.

Reviewing a Production

The golden rule of good criticism is: deal with the work of art *on its own terms*. The following are several groups of questions to jump-start writing responses to theatrical productions. Your professor might ask you to address one or more of the following elements in writing your response. Our questions should be a good jumping-off point for thinking about a production's directing, acting, and design elements, as well as the structure and content of the play.

THE DIRECTION

1. What was the overall direction/goal of the production? (Take a stab at it. Don't let yourself off easy with lazy responses like "There was no point to this.")
2. How would you describe the style of the production? How would you describe the overall mood or tone?
3. Movement: Was the blocking/movement clear? Give examples. Did the blocking have motivation or a purpose? Did it tell the story clearly? Give examples.
4. Was the stage space well used? Give examples.
5. Acting: Were the actors well cast? Were characters and relationships well developed?
6. Pace: Did the pace or rhythm seem appropriate to the material? Give examples.
7. Having considered these elements, how would you characterize the direction of the play?

THE ACTING

Separate the character from the actor. It is possible to dislike a character but admire the actor's performance. When discussing a character, use the character's name; when discussing an actor playing a character, use the actor's name.

1. Were the actors convincing in their roles? Why or why not?
2. Did the characters seem to have a purpose or goal to achieve? Explain.
3. Did the actors/characters interact well—listening and responding to one another fully?
4. Did the actors' behavior (physical, vocal, emotional) fit their characters? Give specific examples.
5. Could they be heard/understood? Did their use of language fit the character?
6. Choose an actor and examine the progression of his or her character. Did the character change over the course of the play? If so, how did you observe that change? What did the actor do—physically, vocally, emotionally—that made this change observable?
7. Having considered all these elements, how would you describe the acting in the play?

THE DESIGNS

1. Did the costumes, sets, lights, and sound work well together? Did they support the action of the play?
2. Did the style chosen suit the production? How so? Give examples.
3. What contribution did the scenery make to the production? Did it help frame the action and act as a machine for the action? Did it help you understand time period, socioeconomic status, and location? What was the overall effect of the scenery?
4. What contribution did the costumes make to the production? Did they help establish relationships between characters? Were there differences between costumes for one faction or class and another? Were they appropriate for the individual characters? Were they cohesive as a group?
5. What was the overall effect of the lighting? Could you see the faces? Did it create appropriate moods? Did light changes (cues) help the show's rhythm and pace? Did the lights help you know where to look? What was the overall effect of the lighting design?
6. Did the sound design support the production? Did it help create mood? Did it help set the time period or location? Did it help with transitions? Did it support appropriate changes in rhythm and pace? How were volume levels? Were they too loud or too soft? What was the overall effect of the sound design?

STRUCTURE AND CONTENT

1. What was the plot of the play? Was there a clear build? Who was the protagonist, and what was his or her central journey? Who was the antagonist? A battle between those two characters surely suggests something about the themes of the play. Consider that conflict.
2. What was the play thematically about? Were the ideas put forth in a coherent way? Did the playwright take sides? How were the themes manifested in words, actions, characters, and symbols?
3. Were the characters in the play clearly defined? Were they realistic or symbolic? Which characters were in conflict? Was there a character you can closely identify with? Who and why?
4. Was the play serious or comic? Realistic or fantastic? Presentational or representational? Did it mix elements (serious with comic, realistic with fantastic)?

GUIDELINES

Whatever your professor asks you to write about, you will want to follow some basic guidelines:

1. Make sure to critique the production on its own terms. Yes, we know we've said this already, but it bears repeating.

2. Avoid words like "good" and "bad" and such phrases as "I just thought . . . " or "I just don't like . . ." Do not allow your response to deteriorate into a paper about your likes and dislikes. It's fine if you don't like the production; it's fine if you love it. However, your job is to make sense of the production choices and/or to point out how the production choices failed to make sense of the play. This does not mean that the production should fit the picture in your head; it means that the production needs to hang together and communicate something.

3. Be specific. Once you have established a point of view about the production, cite specific moments to support your ideas and explain your reactions. Include both positive and negative reactions. Make sure you're being as clear and fair as you can be.

4. Do not give a plot summary.

5. Consult your program for spellings of actor/character, director, and designer names.

6. When responding to university productions, we also suggest starting from a point of graciousness and humility. Remember that the actors in these plays (and the directors and designers in student productions) are not necessarily professionals.

7. Please also assume that the people who constructed the show know something and that they have made their choices deliberately. Such remarks as "This was just stupid and confusing" generally do more to expose your lack of investigational skills or imagination than anything else. If something confuses you or sticks out, ask first, "Why might they have made this choice?" It's likely that there's a good answer. It's also perfectly possible that there isn't one, but it's worth examining first, if only to avoid looking foolish when there is.

Final suggestions for a good paper: Write clearly and descriptively. Support your views with examples drawn from production choices (not only lines of dialogue). Finally, we suggest that you write these responses as soon as possible after you see a play. Our memories are rarely as good as we think they are, and far more descriptive detail will be possible if the production is fresh in your mind. Good luck, and enjoy!

Conclusions

In a period of so many forms and varieties of entertainment, an audience member may become overwhelmed with choices. Unfortunately, the most common response is to stick with the familiar and comfortable instead of taking chances. The backlash in the entertainment world then is to produce only what some people call corporate art—art that is homogenized and sanitized for a consumer economy. Corporate art does not take risks or cover new ground. Through a productive and communicative relationship between audiences and critics, such blandness and deadly theatre can be avoided. Critics at their best push theatre companies to excel and create bridges for new audiences to attend live theatre for a variety of new experiences. We encourage you to tap into your most adventurous side when it comes to theatre.

Key Terms

Atkinson, Brooks (1894–1984) Widely considered the dean of American drama critics. He spent much of his career with the *New York Times*. He received a Pulitzer Prize for his reporting on the Soviet Union and a Tony Award in 1962 for distinguished achievement in the theatre.

drame Although rarely used today, this French term was formerly used to describe a play that was neither tragedy nor comedy but a mixture of the two, usually tending more toward the serious.

epic theatre A didactic form of theatre that arose in Germany under Erwin Piscator (1893–1966) and was later associated with Bertolt Brecht (1898–1956). It was characterized by the use of nontraditional techniques (films, treadmills, cartoons, segmented scenery, etc.) and often called for political and social reform.

existentialism Modern philosophy associated in drama with the Theatre of the Absurd. It varies widely among its many proponents, chief among whom were Albert Camus (1913–1960) and Jean-Paul Sartre (1905–1980).

expressionism A literary movement that developed before and after World War I in Germany, spreading thence to other nations. Expressionism seeks to portray inner emotions of human beings and thus is opposed to realism and naturalism.

farce A comedic form seeking primarily to amuse. Comedy in the narrowest sense seeks a more thoughtful amusement, whereas farce seeks the release found in laughter.

Kerr, Walter (1913–1996) One of the more highly regarded drama critics, for a long time associated with the *New York Times*. He is the author or coauthor of several books about the theatre.

Lessing, Gotthold Ephraim (1729–1781) A German playwright and dramatic critic who sought with some success to free German literature from the neoclassic strictures under which it suffered at the time. His best-known treatise is *The Hamburg Dramaturgy*.

melodrama Originally a term applied to drama with songs but now used to describe scripts that seek to excite audiences emotionally by sensation; spectacle; and, frequently, improbable events.

naturalism A literary and artistic movement that emerged in the second half of the nineteenth century, growing out of the increasing scientism of the time. Although sharing realism's concern with external forms, naturalistic approaches tend to be even less selective.

Nietzsche, Friedrich Wilhelm (1844–1900) German philosopher who wrote valuable and insightful treatises on the nature of art and tragedy.

presentational A term sometimes used to describe theatrical productions that do not attempt to give the illusion of realism or naturalism. *See also* representational.

protagonist In Greek drama, the leading character, now usually the "hero" or "heroine," or that character for whom the audience has the most sympathy.

realism A theatrical movement that arose in the latter half of the nineteenth century and sought to depict nature and life with great fidelity. Scientism and positivism contributed considerably to the movement. *See also* naturalism.

representational A style of production seeking to create the illusion of reality of action and actual environments onstage. Usually associated with realism. *See also* presentational.

Theatre of the Absurd A term originated by Martin Esslin in an essay by the same name, referring to dramas based on existentialism, such as those by Sartre, Camus, Ionesco, Genet, Adamov, Beckett, and Pinter.

tragedy A serious type of drama, the form of which has varied widely in different eras, usually ending with a protagonist destroyed socially or physically though having won a spiritual victory in defeat.

vaudeville An immensely popular form of entertainment from about 1865 to the 1930s, consisting of a series of acts—singers, dancers, comedians, acrobats, trained animals, and dramatic sketches. The advent of motion pictures and radio eradicated this valuable training ground for performers, although the television variety show offered comparable appeal to audiences.

Discussion Questions

1. What does it take to be a good critic? What do you think would be the most fun—and the most challenging—aspects of writing good criticism?
2. Look at the three critical preferences—pleasure, impact, form—and discuss what each offers us as theatregoers. How does our desire for these three things extend to our other entertainment options? That is, what do we love and expect from sporting events, music concerts, video games, and more? What do we expect from the theatre that is similar and different?
3. What are the differences between representational and presentational theatre? Identify key elements from plays you are reading this semester that seem to be one or the other.
4. What are the differences between melodrama, tragedy, and drama? Identify some contemporary plays and films you have seen and read that fit into (or straddle) these genres.
5. Discuss the different kinds of comedy. Again, choose plays, films, TV programs, and/or web series that fit these distinct forms. Talk about how they are different and similar and what makes them funny.

Suggested Readings

Brook, Peter. *The Empty Space: A Book about the Theatre.* New York: Touchstone, 1996. Originally published 1968. A discussion of the theatre by one of the most important directors of the last half of the twentieth century. Invaluable to the theatre student.

Corrigan, Robert, ed. *Comedy: Meaning and Form.* 2nd ed. New York: Harper & Row, 1981. Originally published 1965. A good collection on the nature, makeup, and form of comedy.

———, ed. *Tragedy: Vision and Form.* 2nd ed. New York: Harper & Row, 1981. Originally published 1965. A good collection on the nature, makeup, and form of tragedy.

Dolan, Jill. *The Feminist Spectator as Critic.* Ann Arbor: University of Michigan Press, 1988. An excellent and accessible exploration of feminism and the theatre.

Dukore, Bernard. *Dramatic Theory and Criticism: Greeks to Growtowski.* New York: Holt, Rinehart & Winston, 1974. A massive sourcebook of edited writings from the past and present on dramatic theory and criticism, with lucid introductions by Dukore.

Reinelt, Janelle G., and Joseph R. Roach. *Critical Theory and Performance.* Ann Arbor: University of Michigan Press, 1992. A significant collection of contemporary theory and criticism.

Schechner, Richard. *Public Domain.* New York: Avon Books, 1969. A series of essays and articles in which the author seeks to justify and explain modern theatre. Especially recommended is perhaps his best-known article, "Six Axioms for Environmental Theatre," in which he correlates public events and traditional theatre.

Schmitt, Natalie Crohn. *Actors and Onlookers.* Evanston, IL: Northwestern University Press, 1990. An insightful look at contemporary theatre and theory.

Selden, Samuel. *Man in His Theatre.* Chapel Hill: University of North Carolina Press, 1951. Selden writes especially clearly about the origins of the theatre and its relevance to society by placing theatre in context with human action.

Shank, Theodore. *The Art of Dramatic Art.* Belmont, CA: Dickenson, 1969. A most provocative book in which the author sets out to define the parameters of the theatre. A work that tends to stimulate considerable fruitful discussion.

Part II

THE PLAY

This section is focused on the work of playwrights, directors, and actors, who develop the play, both as a written text and as a play in performance.

CHAPTER 4

The Playwright

Writing for the theatre is both isolation and collaboration.

—Lin-Manuel Miranda (b. 1980)

Take some wood and canvas and nails and things. Build yourself a theatre, a stage, light it, learn about it. When you've done that you will probably know how to write a play.

—Eugene O'Neill (1888–1953)

In a draw poker game with no wild cards, the odds against being dealt a full house in the first five cards are about 700 to 1. A full house (three of a kind and a pair, such as three aces and two eights) usually wins the pot but not always.

Playwrights face similar odds. Americans write tens of thousands of full-length scripts a year, only a few hundred of which receive serious consideration for production. Of the scripts produced, only one in ten achieves any sort of success. Compound this problem with the fact that good plays can take anywhere from several months to several years to write, and you can see the difficulties playwrights face. As writer-director Moss Hart once observed, "Playwriting, like begging in India, is an honorable but humbling profession."

If the odds against success are enormous, so are the potential rewards. A few American playwrights have earned sizable incomes from their scripts. As mentioned earlier in this book, Lin-Manuel Miranda stands to make $6.5 million a year for his *Hamilton* script, as well as for licensing of *In the Heights* to both theatres and for film rights. We might also mention Andrew Lloyd Webber and Stephen Sondheim and their many successes in the musical theatre, but this discussion concerns mainly "straight" plays. That said, Neil Simon, David Mamet, Christopher Durang, and a few others have made very good livings from their writing—though all three benefited from extra-theatrical income. It is telling that the United States has more professional poker players than professional playwrights; the odds for financial success at poker are better. Playwrights in other countries face similar odds and—as in the United States—

Playwright Suzan-Lori Parks (b. 1963) was the first black woman to win the Pulitzer Prize—for her play *Topdog/Underdog* **(2002).** *Courtesy of Stephanie Diani*

find it more lucrative to write for TV and film. Name a well-written TV show or film, and it's likely the writers have tried their hand at playwriting, as well.

Without the playwright we have no theatre. That "writing" may happen when one person sits alone in a room with a laptop or paper and pen, or it might occur through nontraditional processes like "devising," which we cover later. Either way, a repeatable form must somehow take shape—and this is the work of the playwright. We may have difficulty imagining playwrights, such as Sophocles or Shakespeare, sitting down to blank papyrus or paper, but every playwright begins with the blank page, whereas the other theatre artists usually work in response to the playwright's creation. For this reason, most people have traditionally considered the playwright the primary theatrical artist.

Note the spelling of the word "playwright." We do not spell it "playwrite," although one correctly calls what a playwright does "playwriting." The word "wright" refers to a worker or a maker of things, such as a shipwright or wheelwright. "Wright" is a form of the verb "work"; "wrought" iron refers to iron that a craftsman has worked into a desired form.

The Narrative Form

Playwrights make up the situations that actors enact onstage. We might get closer to what playwrights do if we consider the word "plot" in a double sense: the traditional definition of what happens on the stage and the less usual sense of the playwright's scheme or plan for the play. In traditional drama, the playwright establishes a situation, disrupts that status quo by placing various forces in conflict, and then resolves that conflict.

In so doing, the playwright finds most stories follow a pattern, although the same pattern may unfold in thousands of different ways. Some successful short-story writers

Shakespeare remains one of the most produced and most admired playwrights in the world. If you don't understand why, you probably haven't seen great Shakespeare yet. Here, in the 2008 DC Shakespeare Theatre production, Kyle Haden as Laertes and Jeffrey Carlson as Hamlet duel in the final scene. *Scott Suchman*

claim they follow the same pattern in every story, a pattern in which "an attractive protagonist (hero or heroine) overcomes great adversity to achieve a worthwhile goal." Almost every word of this formula implies some substantial meaning. "An attractive protagonist" indicates that the audience should empathize or sympathize with the hero or heroine and that a play or story usually deals with only one such protagonist. Many stories have multiple heroes, but the majority present only one. Sometimes you'll be presented with an "antihero," a person for whom you feel ambivalence or who has great flaws, like Tony Soprano in *The Sopranos* or Macbeth in *Macbeth.* Something attractive almost always emerges, however, to help you empathize with this character. "Overcomes great adversity" suggests that the struggle should be of some size, of some consequence, not just a trivial problem. Yet some comedies succeed through exaggeration of the trivial; drama has no rules that always apply. Finally, "to achieve a worthwhile goal" indicates that in most plays the hero succeeds, and further supports the need for a substantial achievement by the protagonist. If you apply this disarmingly simple formula to whatever dramatic media you experience for a few months, you will find that everything from *Hamlet* to *South Park* fits this narrative pattern.

Traditionally, over centuries of playwriting as well as other forms of storytelling, a sequence has emerged with the following structural components.

1. EXPOSITION

The play begins, and somehow the audience needs to learn when and where the events of the play take place. What is the status quo (also called "stasis") at the start of the play? In Shakespeare's *Hamlet* we find ourselves in the castle Elsinore in Denmark, just after the death and funeral of the elder Hamlet. We learn this, and other salient facts of the situation, or "given circumstances," in the first scene. Playwrights weave exposition through the early scenes of most plays.

2. INCITING INCIDENT

An event upsets the status quo and launches the conflict. It is not always the first event, but it is the one that sets the forces of opposition against one another. By the third scene of *Hamlet*, the young prince has learned from his father's ghost that the father was murdered and that Prince Hamlet's stepfather (and uncle) Claudius was the murderer. The lines of battle emerge clearly, although Hamlet's disdain for his stepfather has already been established by this point in the play.

3. RISING ACTION, OR A SERIES OF COMPLICATIONS

During the rising action, the important events in the plot may be seen as "complications" that lead to the resolution of the conflict. Again, a complication in this sense is an *event*, not a fact. For instance, Hamlet's supposed madness is not a complication in the structural sense. However, his attempts to discover Claudius's guilt, the moment when he nearly murders Claudius but decides not to because Claudius seems to be praying, his accidental murder of Polonius—these are part of the rising action. They are complications, important structural moments in the main plot revolving around Hamlet as the protagonist and Claudius as the antagonist.

4. CRISIS OR CATASTROPHE (VARIOUSLY DEFINED)

The crisis may be seen as the last complication before the climax. It is an event that immediately precipitates the resolution of the conflict. In *Hamlet*, the prince's return to Elsinore ("This is I, Hamlet the Dane," act 5, scene 1, lines 257–58) ensures that the showdown will come soon. You might even choose a somewhat later event—perhaps Hamlet's discovery that his mother, Gertrude, has been poisoned—as the crisis leading to Hamlet's murder of Claudius.

5. CLIMAX

A major event resolves the conflict in a story. Hamlet kills Claudius; the conflict is resolved, and the play is almost over.

6. DENOUEMENT

A French term meaning unraveling, denouement occurs after the climax to illuminate the climax and may tie up loose ends. Some critics call the denouement "falling action," because of the lessening of tensions and excitement reached at the climax. At the end of *Hamlet*, Fortinbras returns to take charge; life will go on at Elsinore.

Some scripts do not follow this pattern so clearly, but if conflict seems to be missing, we do well to look for the source of tension in the enacted events. We should seek to discover what's at stake, who might lose what, and who might gain and see if a pattern does not begin to emerge.

The Playwright's Alternatives and Restrictions

Playwrights:

1. Devise a blueprint for an event
2. Have a profound knowledge of the theatre in production
3. Know the differences between playwriting and literary writing

Playwrights write words that audiences usually don't see. The playwright thus devises a *blueprint for an event*, for a series of actions and transactions, showing rather than describing a set of events that reveal human relationships.

Anton Chekhov (1860–1904), perhaps the best known of all Russian dramatists, wrote plays most closely associated with the Moscow Art Theatre. They are, however, still widely produced today. *The Cherry Orchard, The Three Sisters, The Seagull,* and *Uncle Vanya* are still considered masterpieces. *Library of Congress, LC-USZC2-5544*

Writing for the stage presupposes that the writer has a profound knowledge of the theatre in production. With some notable exceptions, many of the great playwrights first worked in some capacity as production personnel, often as actors. Shakespeare supposedly broke into the theatre by holding horses outside the theatre for patrons; later he became an actor and a playwright. Literary and theatrical values may resemble one another but often differ sharply. Only a few writers succeed on both fronts.

Requisites for Excellence in Playwriting

To succeed, playwrights should:

1. Match their creative urge with hard work and perseverance
2. Develop deep powers of perception
3. Develop their ability to use language
4. Understand human psychology and sociology
5. Learn to critique their own work
6. Develop a practical understanding of theatre
7. Get a good education and develop a sense of "craft"
8. Learn their markets

1. MATCH CREATIVE URGE WITH HARD WORK AND PERSERVERANCE

To begin with, any writer must have the creative urge, the drive to invent something new. This requirement in itself eliminates many people who merely "want to be writers," something distinct from wanting to write. Playwrights are perhaps the most solitary of theatre artists, spending most of their time alone, trying to get their ideas and words into acceptable form. Clear writing results from hard work. Perseverance thus becomes a primary requirement for writers—the dogged persistence and stamina to see them through the conception, creation, revision, and rewriting of their work.

2. DEVELOP DEEP POWERS OF PERCEPTION

Another essential quality is perception, the ability to see the world around them with a profound penetration and understanding, usually leading them to a somewhat sympathetic view of the human circumstance.

3. DEVELOP AN ABILITY TO USE LANGUAGE

Since writers use words as their primary means of communication, most of them study and develop their ability to use language their entire lives.

4. UNDERSTAND HUMAN PSYCHOLOGY AND SOCIOLOGY

Human psychology and sociology are also usual areas of study, since playwrights must often function as social scientists. Not only must they understand human behavior, but they must also understand the varieties of interpersonal human relationships as well as the nature of groups (such as, but not limited to, audiences). Though the task seems well beyond human ability, playwrights must seek a total understanding of humanity.

5. LEARN TO CRITIQUE OWN WORK

Writers also function as critics of their own work. No writer can be both writer and critic at the same time, so they usually go through several revisions of their manuscripts, altering, changing, deleting, adding. As Ernest Hemingway put it, "The most essential gift for a good writer is a built-in, shock-proof shit detector. This is the writer's radar and all great writers have had it."

6. DEVELOP A PRACTICAL UNDERSTANDING OF THEATRE

If one is to write scripts for production, a considerable theatrical background seems highly desirable. A few exceptions notwithstanding, writing for so specialized a field as the theatre demands intimate awareness of the unique qualities of live performance. Mere exposure to the theatre rarely suffices; playwrights must usually participate in the theatrical interaction before they can hope to create it successfully.

7. GET A GOOD EDUCATION AND DEVELOP A SENSE OF CRAFT

Formal education, such as that obtained at a university, can contribute to the playwright's overview of humanity, but several highly successful playwrights have had little formal education—including the erudite August Wilson. Most have drawn on their own perceptual acuity and solitary study. The majority of playwrights constantly read scripts and attend the theatre to gain an appreciation of other playwrights' techniques and unique visions of humanity. Whatever the source, a solid education and natural curiosity can deepen and widen a playwright's view of the world. The playwright gains something else, usually called "craft," from the very act of writing, a sort of "paying one's dues," or the accumulation of experience and insight into one's art. All artists seem to serve comparable apprenticeships; for example, musicians spend time learning scales. Eventually the artist emerges with a better sense of what he or she can do and how to do it, just as one learns to drive a car. A personal style also emerges, born out of personal experiences and preferences, as well as external reinforcement.

8. LEARN THE MARKET

Finally, playwrights have to study their markets, examining all the possible producing agencies and theatrical movements of their time. Beginning playwrights must especially concern themselves with the various playwriting contests around the world; they offer a beginner some opportunities for production.

Producing the Script

Whatever form their stories might take, playwrights depend upon others to bring their work to life. Playwrights almost never create a script just as literature; they write in hopes they'll see it staged. A director or producer must select the script and decide to produce it. The actors selected by the director must learn the lines and actions; develop characterization; and, to the best of their ability, present the script to the audience. The actors (as well as everyone else connected with the production) can illuminate, distort, or expand on what the playwright has written.

A great script can receive a miserable production, just as a great piece of music can suffer in the hands of a poor musician. Theatre history offers examples of many cases of poorly received premieres followed by great success. *The Seagull*, by Russian playwright Anton Chekhov, is a classic example. *The Seagull* opened on October 17, 1896, at the Alexandrinsky Theatre in Saint Petersburg, performed by an uninterested and insufficiently rehearsed cast. The actors' flamboyant styles clashed with the quiet naturalism of the script. In addition, the audience that gathered had come to see broad comedy. They could not relate to this new form of theatre, which they suspected made

Anton Chekhov's *The Cherry Orchard* at Catawba College. *Sean Meyers Photography*

fools of them. The play failed. Chekhov stormed out of the theatre when the second act ended, and he swore never again to write for the theatre.

Soon after, a new company formed in Moscow, the Moscow Art Theatre, and they understood Chekhov's play. A representative persuaded the playwright to try another production, and on December 17, 1898, the Art Theatre, Chekhov, and director Konstantin Stanislavsky became the leaders of the Russian theatre. Chekhov continued to write wonderful plays, which theatre companies still perform throughout the world.

A similar case in the United States involved Samuel Beckett's *Waiting for Godot*, which provoked considerable hostility in its first American audiences. Not until much later did a full understanding emerge, and *Waiting for Godot* has become a metaphor for modern life, as audiences and critics have come to recognize Beckett's profound, sad, and funny view of the human condition.

The Contemporary Situation for the Playwright

Very few playwrights today earn a living just by writing for the live theatre; most need supplemental income. Television and film writing pay better than does the theatre; many playwrights today move back and forth between stage, screen, and television to earn a living. The time and effort involved in writing a stage play seldom wins commensurate financial rewards.

Playwright José Rivera. *Courtesy of José Rivera*

José Rivera on Writing for Film and Theatre

The theatre, for a lot of living playwrights who aren't world famous, always contains a lot of risk—and you're as likely to get your heart broken in the theatre as anything else. Paradoxically, part of the thrill of theatre is that risk that it will break your heart and crush your spirits. It's like a game of Russian roulette sometimes, for playwrights. So commercial or critical success is sweeter because the writer has already paid a significant price.

Writers like me who also work in film tend to be rare because film's material rewards usually overwhelm the rush you would get in the theatre. As writers age they want to substitute rush for stability. I stay in the theatre because I love the world of it more than I love the world of film. Artistically it's just not as rewarding to write film because you don't ultimately own the film you're writing. As a screenwriter you're in the weird position of being the writer of a film but not its author. That authorship is usually claimed by the director. When screenwriters become directors, they regain their authorship—at which point the artistic rewards in film match those of the theatre and the writer may never come back to writing plays.

(from a personal communication with Gendrich)

In spite of all the barriers, more and more playwrights appear, both professional and amateur. Some artists, however, still prefer writing for the stage over the screen. For some insight into this, see the sidebar from José Rivera, the acclaimed writer of both plays (e.g., *Marisol, References to Salvador Dali Make Me Hot*) and films (e.g., *The Motorcycle Diaries*).

Colleges and universities meet increasing demands for playwriting courses and offer more and more production and workshop assignments for their students. Aspirants assume they will always find room at the top, and they continue to turn out scripts by the thousands.

Few playwrights achieve excellence, since the excellent, by definition, rarely occurs. For the fortunate and persevering few who do receive early reinforcement for their work, submitting scripts to literary agents for possible professional production seems to be the major hurdle. If a writer can convince an agent of a work's commercial potential, the agent then circulates the script to possible producers. Commercial factors may supersede aesthetic considerations at this point; the huge sums of money required for professional production tend to make investors and producers cautious. On the Broadway stage, for example, only about 10 percent of the plays that open earn back their original investment. Still, hope springs eternal in the human breast, and successful playwrights can reap both artistic and financial rewards. Income not only from stage productions but also from television series, motion picture rights, the publication of scripts, and royalties from amateur productions all contribute to the income from a successful script.

So the playwright, after having created a script as described in the next section of this chapter, moves from aesthetic considerations to commercial matters. New playwrights almost never receive production in large regional theatres or on Broadway. They do better to find online listings of play competitions and their submission guidelines. Or, if they prefer a more analog approach, they can obtain copies of *Writer's Market*, an annual publication carried in most large bookstores and libraries, listing many of the outlets for new scripts.

Often playwrights submit their plays to playwriting competitions for publication, production, and/or monetary awards. Some competitions also fund residencies for the playwright to work with directors, dramaturgs, and actors in the initial production of their script.

The two leading script publishers, Samuel French, Inc., and Dramatists Play Service, Inc., both have readers to examine new scripts, but they prefer to deal with proven commodities. Quite a few college and university theatre departments solicit new scripts for possible production, as do an increasing number of community theatres. For college students, the most obvious outlet would be the American College Theatre Festival, which offers regional and national competitions for student writers.

An aspiring playwright should also contact the professional organization for playwrights—the Dramatists Guild of America, a corporate member of the Authors League of America. Throughout the guild's long history, it has organized and fought for the rights of American authors, scoring significant successes in such matters as copyright law, sales of film rights, income averaging for tax purposes, and negotiations with producers. Every summer, the guild releases a directory of producers and outlets for original scripts, an invaluable guide to young playwrights.

Surveying playwriting texts also assists the newcomer to this field; one cannot know too much about one's craft. See the suggested readings for recommended volumes.

José Rivera's 1993 Obie Award–winning magical realist play *Marisol*, also seen on the cover of this book. *Courtesy of Wake Forest University Theatre. Photo by Bill Ray*

In spite of all good efforts, most aspiring writers of any sort just don't make it; playwrights are no exception. Those who receive continual rejection do not tend to remain in the arts. Starving painters in their wretched garrets may be romantic figures, but they do not continue to starve in most cases; they will either die or seek income elsewhere. The purist may consider financial concerns a corruption of aesthetics, but such considerations are inescapable. Thousands of people consider themselves artists while working in other jobs to make a living. New York and Los Angeles teem with cab drivers, waiters, secretaries, and tour guides who are actors, painters, dancers, or writers. Some artists have received little or no recognition during their active careers, then had their work recognized later. Kafka, van Gogh, Rembrandt, Melville, and the like come to mind—but theatre is a living art, so posthumous recognition is nearly impossible.

Creative Procedures for the Playwright

The steps to production include the following:

1. Conception
2. Execution
3. Revision
4. Production

Playwrights, unlike other theatrical artists, mainly work alone. They do not, in the early stages of creation, usually have significant interaction with other artists, and they thus enjoy a greater freedom in approaching their work. Until they submit a draft of their script to a potential producer, they can work in whatever ways they prefer. Most playwrights, however, have found some systematic procedures to be most productive, and the following steps typify writers' working methods.

1. CONCEPTION

The playwright must have both the general creative urge and the specific stimulation to work on a particular script or story. For many playwrights, creating scripts evolves naturally from their participation in the theatre; they may move from acting to directing to playwriting, each step marking an increase in overall effect upon the production. If one examines the lives of the great playwrights, this pattern occurs frequently, if not inevitably. Usually, however, very little of merit appears before the playwright has reached artistic, social, and theatrical maturity. To quote Macklemore, "The greats weren't great because at birth they could paint. The greats were great cause they paint a lot."

As for the genesis of a particular script, ideas can come from practically anywhere. Playwrights are always open to the next script idea; such stimulation may come from a person or an imaginary character, an incident, a circumstance, an idea, a message, even a specific location. Anything may spur the playwright into the act of creation. Reading a metropolitan newspaper from front to back—every word, including advertisements and mastheads—can provoke several (or several hundred) ideas for plays.

Writers—indeed, all artists—speak with terror of "drying up," of failing for one reason or another to find the necessary creative stimulation, and they find various means of overcoming this problem. Amateurs often just quit writing forever, but professionals discover how to get back on track. Some announce their new projects to friends and editors, forcing themselves to follow through. Some find physical exercise clears their mind, while others use their downtime to take care of other chores: correspondence, query letters to editors, paying the bills, and so on. Usually they write something, anything, even describing the weather, until the words begin to come again.

2. EXECUTION

Scripts do not come flashing full-fledged into the minds of artists. An idea arrives, but the writer must nurture it, think it out, do research, and experiment with it before the script can actually begin to come forth. However a playwright begins, the first version is almost always just a draft.

There is no one way of working; plays, like other creative works, develop in a huge variety of ways. Some playwrights begin with a rough sequence of events, called a scenario. Simple at first, this blueprint for the play grows more and more detailed and comprehensive as the work continues. Writing a scenario parallels outlining a speech or a term paper. The writer may plan and structure the event as a whole before dealing with the details along the way. When the playwright has completed the scenario as fully as possible (Ibsen usually did three increasingly more detailed scenarios), he or she then executes a first draft of the complete work. Does any human endeavor go according to plan? The playwright will usually find it necessary to refine the scenario or go back to earlier stages of the plan to solve unforeseen problems.

Other playwrights don't use outlines at all but discover structure as an outgrowth of writing dialogue and/or action. Whatever the method, the process continues until the writer has a completed first draft.

3. REVISION

Most playwrights—indeed, most writers—would agree that their works are not written but rewritten. Revising a script seldom seems as exciting or creative as conceiving the scenario and completing the first draft, but revision frequently determines the script's eventual success or failure. At this point the playwright may seek out a reading of the script—that is, having actors read the roles aloud. A more complex technique is the staged reading, when actors move about on a stage, using minimal properties and furniture but holding the scripts in their hands while they act the roles.

Such first attempts to bring a script to life almost invariably suggest further revisions: Scenes need cutting, adding, or changing; characters may require elimination or expansion; the story demands a different sequence of events; and so on. As the playwright hears the script rather than reads it, it seems more like a production, less like a literary work. Eventually, however, the playwright completes the draft he or she expects to submit to producers for consideration.

4. PRODUCTION

Most people assume that a script has reached its final form as production nears, but in the commercial theatre, rewriting may continue even during the first few productions. The cast may not perform exactly the same script two nights in a row until the opening; the playwright may rewrite sections of the script after one evening's performance, have the cast rehearse the next morning or afternoon, and see them play it that evening. This can be a stressful process, but eventually a final script emerges.

Often, if the show is successful, the playwright publishes the script in its final version. Film or television spin-offs may follow, but those are different media, and the playwright will frequently need to revise the original script.

VARIATIONS

Although the four stages of conception, execution, revision, and production describe the creative sequence for a good many playwrights, the actuality can vary considerably.

Joe Turner's Come and Gone by August Wilson (1945–2005) at Lincoln Center Theatre. Before his death, Wilson wrote a series of ten plays called "The Pittsburgh Cycle," exploring black characters' experiences in each decade of the twentieth century. *Joe Turner* was purportedly Wilson's favorite, but *Fences* and *The Piano Lesson* are also well known and widely produced. *T. Charles Erikson*

Bursts of creative inspiration and energy occur frequently in the arts, and artists of all sorts employ any means helpful to them and the process. Being an art, theatre does not have to obey any set of scientific laws or regulations.

In a few cases, scripts have come to playwrights very suddenly. Eugene O'Neill claimed he woke up one morning with a new play "fully in mind," even to the title, and in less than a month, he had finished the enduring *Ah, Wilderness!* If we can believe theatrical legend, Arthur Miller's *Death of a Salesman*, Edward Albee's *Zoo Story*, George Farquhar's *The Recruiting Officer*, John Osborne's *Look Back in Anger*, and several of Noel Coward's scripts had similar origins.

Still other playwrights approach the process through highly collaborative "workshops." These workshops may be dedicated to improving a working draft of a play, or they may be used to devise an entirely new work. In the workshop process, a writer may offer a story line, rough draft, concept, or topic to a production company, which then works together over a period of weeks and even months to create dialogue and events. With a basic philosophy that many heads are better than one, the playwright here may function as an editor as much as originator of the dramatic work. However, a workshop may simply be a jumping-off point for creation or a way to solve problems in a new play, basically supporting an otherwise fairly traditional playwriting process.

Caryl Churchill wrote her play *Cloud Nine* with the Joint Stock Theatre Group using a workshop process. Churchill simply suggested the issue of sexual politics to company founder Max Stafford-Clark. After weeks of improvisation, experimentation, and research with company members, Churchill then left the group and wrote the play based on their work, returning later to rehearse the final script with the company. Churchill says of this process, "Though no character is based on anyone in the company, the play draws deeply on our experiences, and would not have been written without the workshop."

Though collaboratively written plays appeared before Churchill's, the work of the Joint Stock Theatre Group and others has attracted much attention since *Cloud Nine*. In fact, since then, this kind of collaborative work has come to be known as "devised" theatre. One might start with a theme, as Churchill did and as performance collectives like the Japanese group Dumb Type did, or with a troubling problem, an image, or—as performance artist, teacher, and deviser Tim Miller likes to do—a "fierce moment." From there, many techniques can be employed to elicit not only the spoken language of the piece but also the physical and theatrical language of it. The Tectonic Theatre Project, founded by Moises Kaufman in 1991, has developed what they call Moment Work, a process using all theatrical elements to make original pieces. In fact, it has been the foundation of all of Tectonic's pieces (*The Laramie Project, Gross Indecency: The Three Trials of Oscar Wilde, I Am My Own Wife*, and *33 Variations*). A highly structured training process is used for both Moment Work and for Viewpoints, a process popularized by theatre director Ann Bogart. Expanding on the work of choreographer Mary Overlie, Viewpoints relies heavily on the physical exploration of actors.

Devised work has become popular in colleges and universities, giving rise to numerous original plays and one-off performances. And it has also helped create Off-Broadway successes like the Obie Award–winning play *The Woodsman*.

2016's *The Woodsman*. Puppetry, devising techniques, a compelling story, haunting images, and a unified ensemble of performers made this relatively inexpensive production a successful, critically acclaimed hit for the Strangemen Company. *Matthew Murphy*

Not many audience members care how a playwright creates or how long it takes; they care only about the quality of the finished work. However, craft, hard work, courage, and inspiration are all needed for a successful creative process in any of the arts.

Evaluating the Playwright's Contribution

Because a play in production combines the artistic efforts of many people, separating one element, the script, from the total effect requires considerable theatrical experience; a lifetime of theatregoing is not too much.

Each element of a production modifies and affects every other element, leading to an interdependency of effort and making it most difficult to evaluate anything less than the show's total effect. If a scene or speech plays especially well in a production, for example, to what degree does one credit the playwright for writing an effective speech, the actor for delivering it well, or the director for having shaped the actor's performance? Ideally, all have contributed, and all can share the credit. But could a playwright create a splendid speech only to see it delivered miserably by a terrible actor? It happens every night around the world. And sometimes a brilliant actor makes a playwright look better than he or she deserves.

Devising work like this 2014 production of *Vox*, created by students at Wake Forest University and actor/director/playwright Tim Miller, draws deeply on the personal narratives of the writer/performers. *Courtesy of Wake Forest University Theatre. Photo by Bill Ray*

Because the playwright's work exists in a separate form—the script—it might seem easier to divorce that element from the rest of the production. But few playgoers read the script of a show they are planning to see. Nor does reading the script from a printed page always help, especially to theatrical newcomers. Some scripts "read better than they play"—that is, they impress the reader with qualities that never appear on the stage. So, too, some scripts play better than they read. Eugene O'Neill's plays, for instance, are notoriously "bad reads," playing better onstage than they seem on the page.

Those who read scripts must, then, envision a production in their minds; they must cast, set, direct, light, design, and costume the play in their imaginations. Even experienced professionals may encounter considerable difficulty in reading scripts and predicting success or failure. Remember, the success ratio on Broadway is one in ten productions.

Unwary audience members may encounter productions of dramatic masterpieces by companies unprepared financially, artistically, technically, or spiritually to perform such works. Student groups sometimes attempt scripts clearly beyond their potential. For instance, few middle school speech classes could present *King Lear* or *Oedipus Rex* with much success. Students at that stage of development have rarely had the life experiences necessary for such a work; it would be as if you played Beethoven on a harmonica. Such attempts may have tremendous educational value to the performers, even to a young audience that has never experienced the script, but those are not the usual purposes of the theatre, no matter how desirable they might be to an educational institution.

To be fair to all concerned, some talented performers have made shoddy material seem better than it was. Alfred Lunt (1893–1977) and his wife and costar Lynn Fontanne (1887–1983) frequently succeeded with scripts of dubious value. When supplied with better scripts, they had even greater success (their production of *The Visit* remains almost legendary).

Evaluators of theatrical work must, therefore, try to distinguish the playwright's contribution from the quality of the production and at the same time try to judge how much the production's quality depended on the script. Theatregoers who intend to make such evaluations must also attempt this kind of distinction. This may be a skill that only experience can teach you; you might also draw on the critical preferences and explanations of various kinds of drama discussed in chapter 3. The more theatre you see, the more you'll be able to recognize skilled writing, whether it is to your taste or not. You may not be inclined to seek out tragedy, but with experience you will come to appreciate a well-written one. You may also find that your taste lies in the experimental, despite any early trepidation you may have. Knowledge and experience should be the shapers of taste and opinion, not the other way around, so give things a try. You may be surprised at what you end up loving.

Playwriting Exercises

The following are a couple of exercises for the classroom that may help you explore the complexities, difficulties, and pleasures of writing for the theatre.

Tennessee Williams (1911–1983) was one of the most successful American playwrights of the twentieth century. Such scripts as *The Glass Menagerie* (1945), *A Streetcar Named Desire* (1947), and *Cat on a Hot Tin Roof* (1955) have influenced subsequent plays and playwrights and continue to be produced in the United States and beyond. This photo shows Andy Warhol (left) and Tennessee Williams (right) talking on the SS *France*. Library of Congress. *LC-USZ62-121294*

1. OBSERVATION

(Approximate time of exercise: 50 minutes to over an hour)

Step 1: Take a silent walk around campus with a notebook and pen. Walk through buildings and outside. Use your senses to observe any details you may notice (objects, noises, patterns, rhythms, repetitions, people). Use all of your five senses. Listen. Look. Feel. Taste. Smell. As you observe, write down each item in random order on your notebook page. Don't analyze it yet; just notate it. Enjoy observing. Take your time. Don't rush. Optimally, you should do this step for at least twenty minutes.

Step 2: Return to the classroom and select your top ten favorite items. On a separate sheet of paper, write down why you selected those ten items. What made you notice them? What made them stand out from all the others?

Step 3: Pick one item out of the ten, and on another sheet of paper, write a story (a page or two) about that object. Feel free to make any leap from the item you selected to a personal memory or to another story you may have heard about. Freely associate that object with a story or image that pops into your head. Write that feeling, image, or association down.

Step 4: If you are willing, share your story with the class. Discuss how stories shared by students in the classroom might operate as starting points for a play. Some may serve as plot summaries for full-length plays, or they may look more like stories or anecdotes spoken by characters in a scene. Stories written in the first person tend to seem more like monologues; others may work better as plot outlines.

Discussion Questions

1. *Observation.* What happened to you on the silent walk? Did you feel that your sensory focus improved the longer you walked? Were you able to allow the "chatter" in your mind to slow down so that you could really take in the details of the world around you? Did you notice anything new on a route you've taken a hundred times?
2. *Selection.* Why did you pick the items you picked? What made them stand out or seem unusual? Were you already associating those items to something personal?
3. *Writing.* How easily **did** the story flow from your associations to the items on your list? Did you write in the first person? Second? Third?
4. *Reflection.* How does observation of life benefit a playwright?

2. EAVESDROPPING

(Done outside and then discussed in class)

Step 1: Go to a popular social hangout (restaurant, student union, airport, shopping center) and discreetly listen in on the conversations of strangers around you. Try not to be noticed! Otherwise, people stop speaking naturally.

Step 2: Write down conversations in notebooks. You can also record the discussions and then write them in your notebook later. It's important that you write the dialogue down, though.

Step 3: Examine the dialogue and compare it to that of an actual play script.

Discussion Questions

1. Is dialogue for the stage the same as real life? What is different? What is similar?
2. Can you tell what the people are talking about? Are their actions clear?
3. What do they seem to be trying to do to each other? Are they listening closely to each other?
4. What would happen if you tried to capture the essence of the conversation you heard by condensing it to half the length? Would it seem more like a good play's dialogue, promoting a clearer view of the character's actions, or would it simply seem false? Give it a try.

Conclusions

The script represents a stage of development between the playwright's original conception and the completed art form—the play in production. Like other artists, playwrights have infinite choice in giving form to their life response; unlike other artists, they create works that contribute to an art form rather than standing alone as distinct artistic entities. If all the theatre artists involved succeed in their collaboration, the final production may give the audience a unique insight into the human condition through art.

Perhaps the great American playwright Tennessee Williams put it best when asked during a television interview to describe the purpose of his writing or what he wanted people to realize after experiencing his plays. He thought a bit, then drawled, "Oh, I guess I want them to know that other people have been through it, too."

Key Terms

American College Theatre Festival (http://web.kennedy-center.org/education/kcactf/Home?_ga=1.221952411.2095879880.1473961724#main_content) An annual series of festivals during which plays staged on college and university campuses may advance to state, regional, and national festivals. The national festival is hosted by the Kennedy Center for the Performing Arts in Washington, D.C., with the assistance of the Association for Theatre in Higher Education. Awards are given for acting, playwriting, and scenic design.

Brecht, Bertolt (1898–1956) A German playwright associated with epic theatre whose best-known works are *Mother Courage* and *The Threepenny Opera*. Brecht strongly advocated didactic drama.

Chekhov, Anton (1860–1904) Russian dramatist of outstanding merit, most of whose work was associated with Stanislavsky and the Moscow Art Theatre. Two of his best-known works are *The Cherry Orchard* and *The Seagull*.

Churchill, Caryl (b. 1938) British playwright known for her groundbreaking plays and variations on style. Her plays (e.g., *Cloud Nine* and *Top Girls*) have met with great success.

devising A term used to describe the creation of work for the stage that relies heavily on actors to develop or help develop this work. It may include all of the rest of the production team as well and may be highly visual and choreographic—or it may be personal story–focused and visually simple.

dialogue A conversation between two or more characters.

Dramatists Guild of America (www.dramatistsguild.com) Affiliated with the Authors League of America, the guild is an organization of playwrights and lyricists.

Dramatists Play Service, Inc. (www.dramatists.com) One of the two largest and most successful publishers of acting editions of theatrical scripts, the other being Samuel French.

Durang, Christopher (b. 1949) A favorite of most young theatregoers, Durang is known for dark comedies like *Betty's Summer Vacation, Laughing Wild,* and *Sister Mary Ignatius Explains It All for You.*

Ibsen, Henrik (1828–1905) Norwegian dramatist who won international fame as one of the leaders of the realist movement in drama, although he did not restrict himself to that genre exclusively. His most highly regarded scripts include *Ghosts, Hedda Gabler,* and *A Doll's House.*

Kushner, Tony (b. 1956) Celebrated playwright of the *Angels in America* plays.

monologue A solo speech of some length from a character.

O'Neill, Eugene (1888–1953) Influential American playwright. His best-known works include *The Emperor Jones, Desire under the Elms,* and the autobiographical *Long Day's Journey into Night.*

Parks, Suzan-Lori (b. 1963) Pulitzer Prize–winning author of *Topdog/Underdog, 365 Plays/365 Days.* She received a MacArthur Foundation Genius Award in 2001.

Passion plays Ecclesiastical dramas dealing with the Passion, death, and Resurrection of Christ.

plot The organizing structure of the action in a drama. Organization by story is the most familiar but by no means the only type of plot.

Rivera, José (b. 1955) Award-winning playwright and screenwriter of plays, including *Marisol, References to Salvador Dali Make Me Hot, Cloud Tectonics, Another Word for Beauty,* and the film *The Motorcycle Diaries.* Rivera was born in Puerto Rico, and his plays, which are influenced by magical realism, are widely produced throughout the United States.

Samuel French, Inc. (www.samuelfrench.com) Along with Dramatists Play Service, one of the two largest and most successful publishers of acting editions of play scripts.

Shaw, George Bernard (1856–1950) English playwright, critic, and author. Shaw wrote brilliant didactic dramas of immense popularity, the best known of which include *Pygmalion* (on which *My Fair Lady* was based), *Arms and the Man, Major Barbara,* and *Androcles and the Lion.*

soliloquy A speech by a character onstage, usually alone and designed to reveal his or her internal thoughts. The best-known example is Hamlet's "To be or not to be" soliloquy.

Stoppard, Tom (b. 1937) Contemporary British playwright whose major successes include *Rosencrantz and Guildenstern Are Dead, Jumpers,* and *The Real Inspector Hound.*

style An aggregate of characteristics common to a person, period, nationality, or dramatic type.

Tectonic Theatre Project Founded in 1991 by Moises Kaufman, the company is responsible for the development of a system called Moment Work, with which they developed *The Laramie Project, Gross Indecency, I Am My Own Wife,* and *33 Variations.* They also train theatre artists from all over the world to use Moment Work in their own devising processes.

Vogel, Paula (b. 1951) A highly respected playwright who also teaches, Vogel received a Pulitzer Prize for *How I Learned to Drive.*

Wilder, Thornton (1897–1976) American playwright and author. His scripts include *The Skin of Our Teeth* (for which he won the Pulitzer Prize in 1943), *The Match-maker* (on which *Hello, Dolly* was based), and *Our Town*.

Discussion Questions

1. How has this chapter changed the way you think about the work of the playwright? What surprised you or intrigued you most?
2. What seems potentially most challenging to you about writing plays? Most enjoyable?
3. Spend some time with one of the plays you have read this semester and consider the ways that the story could have been told differently than the playwright chose to tell it. How would the choice of a different protagonist or a different kind of dialogue or pacing have changed the play? Discuss how the playwright's choices communicate theme, worldview, and more.
4. What kinds of plays do you think suit our current world best? Do you see life as a tragedy, a comedy, a drama? If you were writing a play about the world today, what would you write about?
5. Try one of the playwriting exercises described above. Share the results with your classmates. What was successful about these efforts?

Suggested Readings

Ball, David. *Backwards and Forwards: A Technical Manual for Reading Plays*. Carbondale: Southern Illinois University Press, 1983. A brief yet insightful overview of how to read plays.

Betsko, Kathleen, and Rachel Koenig, eds. *Interviews with Contemporary Women Playwrights*. New York: Beech Tree Books, 1987. A collection of interviews with well-known women playwrights such as Caryl Churchill and Wendy Wasserstein, as well as less famous women. This is a useful source for anyone who wants to compare and contrast playwriting approaches.

Bryer, Jackson R. *The Playwright's Art: Conversations with Contemporary American Dramatists*. New Brunswick, NJ: Rutgers University Press, 1995. A good collection of interviews with contemporary playwrights.

Cole, Toby, ed. *Playwrights on Playwriting: From Ibsen to Ionesco*. New York: Cooper Square Press, 2001. Originally published 1960. Available in paperback, this book compiles essays and observations on playwriting by the major dramatists of the past century.

Egri, Lajos. *The Art of Dramatic Writing: Its Basis in the Creative Interpretation of Human Motives*. New York: Simon & Schuster, 1960. Originally published 1942. A lively and useful how-to book for would-be playwrights.

Field, Syd. *The Screenwriter's Workbook: A Workshop Approach*. New York: Dell, 1988. Though designed for screenwriters, this book can be helpful with the process of playwriting.

Hardison-Londré, Felicia. *Tom Stoppard*. New York: Frederick Ungar, 1981. A brief but incisive analysis of Stoppard's dramas, with a biographical sketch.

Hart, Moss. *Act One*. New York: St. Martin's Press, 1989. Originally published 1959. An especially readable and insightful autobiography by a well-known American playwright.

Hatcher, Jeffrey. *The Art and Craft of Playwriting*. Cincinnati: Story Press Books, 2000. A recent take on contemporary playwriting from a well-known and well-produced author.

Matthews, Brander, ed. *Papers on Playmaking*. New York: Hill & Wang, 1957. A terrific little collection of essays by important playwrights and theorists from Western theatre history.

Needle, Jan, and Peter Thompson. *Brecht*. Chicago: University of Chicago Press, 1981. A scholarly examination of Brecht's life and work.

Plimpton, George, ed. *Playwrights at Work: The Paris Review Interviews*. New York: Modern Library, 2000. A great primary source collection of interviews with sixteen famous playwrights, including Tennessee Williams, Tom Stoppard, August Wilson, David Mamet, Sam Shepard, and Wendy Wasserstein.

Savran, David. *In Their Own Words: Contemporary American Playwrights*. New York: Theatre Communications Group, 1988. Interviews with some of the best contemporary playwrights.

Smiley, Sam. *Playwriting: The Structure of Action*. Rev. ed. New Haven, CT: Yale University Press, 2005. Smiley, himself a published and produced playwright, completely covers the process of creating drama, offering the beginning playwright excellent advice.

Wager, Walter, ed. *The Playwrights Speak*. New York: Dell, 1961. Similar to *Playwrights on Playwriting*; consists of interviews with many major playwrights.

SCRIPT ANTHOLOGIES

Coldewey, John C., and W. R. Streitberger. *Drama: Classical to Contemporary*. Upper Saddle River, NJ: Prentice-Hall, 2000. A standard collection of excellent plays paired with historical and biographical frameworks.

Jacobus, Lee A. *The Bedford Introduction to Drama*. 5th ed. New York: Bedford Books, 2005. Excellent historical and critical introductions to a wide range of classical to contemporary plays.

Klaus, Carl H., Miriam Gilbert, and Bradford S. Field Jr. *Stages of Drama: Classical to Contemporary Masterpieces of the Theater*. 5th ed. New York: Bedford/St. Martin's Press, 2002. Excellent introductions and a wide range of plays.

Worthen, W. B. *The Harcourt Brace Anthology of Drama*. 3rd ed. Fort Worth, TX: Harcourt Brace, 1999. A thorough collection of ancient to contemporary plays with insightful introductions, production reviews, and intelligent critical responses.

CHAPTER 5

The Director

We seek this: a unique perception (the director's) of a particular world (the play) expressively embodied by the means of the theatre so that others (the audience) can share it, know it, see it.

—Zelda Fichandler (1924–2016)

For the most part, theatre audiences don't think a great deal about directors, not even as much as film audiences do. Film is called "a director's medium," since the film director can, along with the film editor, recut and revise nearly indefinitely. Note Ridley Scott's 2007 final director's cut of his 1982 film *Blade Runner*. Twenty-five years after the film was released, Scott was still "directing." Stage directors, by contrast, must prepare the cast and crew for the performance and then let go. A stage manager runs the show, and directors become almost superfluous once the show is open—often retiring to the back of the auditorium to evaluate the performance, if they watch at all. Should an emergency or some unforeseen development arise, directors will usually help deal with it if they are present.

Whereas playwrights and designers offer tangible results of their labor and audiences can see the actors at work, the director's contributions seem much more difficult to distinguish, let alone evaluate. Yet the director can make or break a show.

A director supervises all creative elements of a theatrical production. Modern productions involve a multitude of complexities and decisions. Lest the endeavor of staging a show come to complete chaos (as has happened), a single person must unify the work of the others. We know this is a long chapter, but keep in mind that whatever any other theatre artist does, the director must in some way connect with, understand, and make decisions about it. Directing is a complicated job.

The modern Western concept of a director originated only about a century and a half ago, whereas the theatre has flourished for more than twenty-five centuries. But even before the emergence of the modern director, some individual usually acted as the leader: the playwright, the leading actor, the manager of the troupe, or the owner of the theatre. Unification of the many decisions required some central figure, an expert to coordinate the work of the other artists. An uncoached athletic team may win a few

Mary Zimmerman's *Metamorphoses* at Lookingglass Theatre in Chicago. Zimmerman is known for her highly physical, visually striking productions. Usman Ally in the foreground; background from left to right: Lauren Orkus, Doug Hara, and Louise Lamson. *Courtesy of Rich Hein. Photo by Liz Lauren*

games, and an unconducted symphony orchestra might garner some applause, but efficiency increases and things tend to go more smoothly with a capable individual as leader. In the modern theatre that person has emerged as the director.

Ideally, directors determine their own intentions for each production, help to hire the other artists, and guide their collaborators' creative work, welding everyone's efforts into a cohesive whole. In doing so, directors work as prophets. They try to predict audience responses to particular staging techniques, drawing on their own analysis, research, experience, and creativity, including that of their fellow artists. They function as critics in action; if they see something they don't like, they can change it. Rarely, they may even change things after the show has opened.

In many ways the director holds the most responsible position in the theatre. Often a director will:

1. Select the script
2. Do considerable analysis and research (and share it with actors and designers)
3. Cast, hire, and rehearse the actors
4. Guide the designers and approve all the design elements
5. Work with the marketing staff to draw an audience

In effect, the director oversees the entire production according to his or her own artistic and aesthetic vision. In so doing, a director shapes the artistry of others, much as a coach uses the skills of others to create something greater than the sum of its parts.

As more collaborative and devised theatre evolves, so does the actor–director relationship. However, it does not reduce (and may even increase) the need for someone with considerable skill helping to edit, guide, and shape the production. You will note that most of this chapter assumes the direction of a preexisting script, but see if you can figure out how working with a new script or in a collaborative process might reflect some of the same skills and procedures.

The Director's Alternatives and Restrictions

The nature of live theatre offers the director much freedom but also requires that innumerable choices be made. These can be understood as falling within the following categories:

1. Choice of text
2. Choice of style
3. Space
4. Time and personnel
5. Money

A new script offers challenges and opportunities for directors. Creating or helping to shape a new work takes time, which can create stress in a limited rehearsal period. However, the sense of ownership over the work can be considerable. Here, the world premiere of *Embers and Stars: The Story of Petr Ginz* at Wake Forest University. *Courtesy of Wake Forest University Theatre. Photo by Bill Ray*

Georg II, Duke of Saxe-Meiningen (1826–1914), is usually considered the first director in the modern sense of the word. His company toured and influenced many early-twentieth-century producers. *Library of Congress, LC-B2-3484-15*

1. CHOICE OF TEXT

Theoretically, directors have the entire body of dramatic literature from which to choose, plus all the available unproduced scripts they can gather. Although in the commercial theatre, the producer usually hires a director to stage a specific script, the educational theatre director usually enjoys wider choices. University directors and directors working with established companies will typically make suggestions about possible plays to produce and, with the help of a larger group—often including theatre staff, colleagues, and students—will decide on a play to direct. Because play selection is such an important part of a director's work, most directors are avid readers who as a matter of course read many plays in any given year. Once the play is chosen, many other elements shape what the audience ultimately experiences.

2. CHOICE OF STYLE

Style is the way something is done rather than the core act itself. It is concerned with form, manner, behavior, and execution. It is what the characters share with one another and how that group behaves. In short, style is the *how* of a production rather than the *what*. Style expert Robert Barton points out that time, space, place, values, societal structure, models of beauty or attractiveness, sexual mores, habits of movement, speech, and song all help in considering questions of style.

What most people forget is that every production has style—intentional or unintentional. A director's job is to make sure it is intentional, workable, and specific. Musical theatre is, for instance, not a specific style but a genre—a distinction worth understanding when considering whether to direct *Les Misérables* or *Legally Blonde*. Though both are musical theatre, the former is likely to be stylistically dark, massive, and emotional; the latter, pink, light, and fluffy.

Looking back at old science fiction movies or television shows, we may be particularly aware of *unintentional* expressions of style—specifically, insertions of what was considered physically attractive and fashionable at the time the shows were made. For instance, in old *Star Trek* episodes, the high-waisted pants and plastic-looking hair on

Directors can stage the same play in seemingly infinite ways. This production of Shakespeare's *A Midsummer Night's Dream* was directed by Sharon Andrews and designed by Jon Christman. *Courtesy of Wake Forest University Theatre. Photo by Bill Ray*

the men, the bouffant up-dos and frosty eye shadow and lipstick on the women all (probably unintentionally) betray their 1960s origins.

A director's central idea or concept for a show may lead to stylistic choices that intentionally take the show out of its original context. Sometimes these choices work; sometimes they don't. Shakespeare, for example, wrote his scripts for the theatrical conventions of his time, but later directors have selected particular ideas from these plays and connected them to other times and places, hoping to highlight certain elements of the texts. They have set *Macbeth* in Haiti, *Measure for Measure* in nineteenth-century Vienna, *The Taming of the Shrew* in modern Greenwich Village, and so on. Though not always successful, the director takes the chance and is sometimes able to reinvigorate an old text for new audiences.

For instance, Baz Luhrmann's 1996 film *Romeo + Juliet* was not universally loved, but Luhrmann made very specific stylistic choices rooted in the original work. The violence, social stratification, and unbridled passion of *Romeo and Juliet* found expression in a world of action, guns, opulence, and physicality. Whatever one thought of the adaptation, the film generated conversation and reminded audiences (again) of the contemporary relevance of this four-hundred-year-old play. Ultimately, whether one approves of a given concept (leading to a specific style) or not, the written text remains. To be sure, a bad production can cause audiences discomfort or irritation, but the play can always be revisited afresh by another director.

3. SPACE

Beyond the text, the restrictions of the live theatre shape what the director can do. Stage productions take place in a relatively small space, which would seem to prohibit some effects. Theatrical producers have put some astonishing things onstage, such as the chariot race from *Ben-Hur*, complete with live horses, but the effect could not compare with that of the film version. Film can capture spectacle, a traditional theatrical element, far more impressively than can the stage; the live theatre relies on a different sort of spectacle and on the imaginations of audience members.

Battle scenes, for example, trouble most modern directors, but they occur often in Shakespearean scripts. An Elizabethan audience with no cinematic experience would accept the convention of a few actors representing two armies, but modern audiences might find such staging ludicrous. Even Shakespeare found it necessary to apologize for his stage's limitations in the prologue to *Henry V*:

> But pardon, gentles all,
> The flat unraised spirits that hath dar'd
> On this unworthy scaffold to bring forth
> So great an object. Can this cockpit hold
> The vasty fields of France? Or may we cram
> Within this wooden O the very casques
> That did affright the air at Agincourt?

Here, *Midsummer* gets quite a different treatment, with a 1960s "counterculture" treatment at the Oregon Shakespeare Festival. *Courtesy of David Cooper*

The Utah Shakespeare Festival's elegant take on *Midsummer*. *Courtesy of Bruce Lee of the Utah Shakespeare Festival*

Directing Film and Directing Theatre: A Few Differences

Rehearsals. In film, these mainly consist of what, in the theatre, is known as "table work": Actors and the director sit at a table, read through the script, and discuss and analyze it. In theatre, directors get actors on their feet, often from the first day, learning to deal with space, physical impulses, acoustics, and their fellow actors. To be sure, many theatre directors also use table work, but it's only a starting point. In the theatre, rehearsal is necessary to allow actors to function on their own, sustaining long scenes and plays that last for several hours rather than scenes that last for only a few minutes.

The final cut. Spontaneity is important in both theatre and film, but film directors can cut out flubs and poor choices in the editing room. A theatre director helps the actors to work freely within a structure and must be able to trust the actors to do the play they've rehearsed. What's more, in the professional theatre, the actors must be prepared to do it well eight times a week. In many ways, actors have the "final cut" in the theatre, but with good direction a well-shaped yet spontaneous performance is possible.

Focus. One reason that film is called a director's medium is that the film director decides so much about where you look and what you see. Film and theatre writer/director Neil LaBute has said that film is inherently more manipulative than theatre for this very reason: "In the movies you can grab [the audience] by the back of the head and tell them where to look." In theatre, focus is shaped but not forced. If a director has every person onstage look at a woman standing upstage center, you, in the audience, will probably look at her, too—but you don't have to. In the theatre the choice is always yours. This makes focus in the theatre less manipulative but also more difficult to control.

Technical concerns. The timing of the incorporation of technical elements is different in theatre and film. While film directors must continually concern themselves with cameras, lenses, angles, and lighting in order to get each shot in the can, theatre directors have a rather different process. They work with actors in rehearsal separately while sets and costumes are being built, lights are hung and focused, and sound is being recorded. All the elements are gradually introduced and are pulled together during technical week, once the actors are (presumably) ready to perform. Technical rehearsals are discussed later in this chapter, but in some ways shooting a film is always like a highly concentrated technical rehearsal.

Then, too, rapid shifts of locale involve enormous expense and difficulty if attempted realistically in the theatre. Suggested or minimal scenery often seems to work better for plays that require fast changes, but turntables, flown scenery, and wagons may also solve such problems. Pacing a show is part of the director's job, so he or she must carefully consider any design decisions affecting continuity, speed, and rhythm.

4. TIME AND PERSONNEL

Like all theatre artists, directors must realize and deal with the limitations of rehearsal time and production companies. Not all casts, designers, and production staffs are equally skilled or motivated. With an extended rehearsal period, a director may be able to coach stronger performances out of young actors, and with more time a designer may be able to execute a more ambitious design with a less-skilled group of technicians. Conversely, a brilliant group of actors, designers, and technicians can make difficult things possible in very short order. However, directors rarely have full control over the casting or staffing pool; they can only choose the strongest people available and work hard to bring out the best in them.

5. MONEY

The theatrical director typically works with a smaller budget than a film director and usually for a smaller salary. No amount of money can buy artistic excellence, and live theatre can make up for lack of extravagant spectacle with the intimacy and impact of live performance. However, because of fewer sources for revenue and smaller potential audiences, the live theatre cannot usually invest as much money in a production as can television and film.

Requisites for Excellence in Directing

As the director's influence on the modern theatre has increased, so have the qualities essential for the director. Along with curiosity, adventurousness, excellent communication skills, patience, and a collaborative spirit, the director requires some other key qualities. As one might suspect, these qualities overlap:

1. The desire for excellence
2. Executive ability and leadership qualities
3. An understanding of humanity
4. Creativity and imagination
5. Skill in the craft of directing
6. Formal training: a liberal education

1. THE DESIRE FOR EXCELLENCE

It may seem obvious to say so, but if one is to achieve excellence in any human endeavor, one had better want to, and directors must be willing to invest months—in some cases years—in dedicated preparation and rehearsal. We can all find hundreds of reasons we don't succeed with a project. However, a successful director needs a passion for the theatre and a drive to produce the best show possible, even under circumstances that may be less than ideal. As Georg II, Duke of Saxe-Meiningen (1826–1914), known as the "first director," said, "There are no excuses in the theatre."

2. EXECUTIVE ABILITY AND LEADERSHIP QUALITIES

The director must guide, support, evaluate, and edit the work of others. Good directors are good communicators who listen carefully and express themselves clearly, who work through conflict well, and who learn to deal with many different types of people. If insurmountable difficulties arise, the director may dismiss a member of the company, but good directors rarely need to do so. They do their best to draw the best work possible from every member of the company and thus also function as teachers and leaders.

The actual guidance of the cast in preparing their roles is an obvious directorial function, but the director must simultaneously coordinate the work of the designers and artists while adhering to a limited budget and finite time schedule. Such activity demands the best qualities of leadership. Great directors can elicit excellent work from their colleagues while paying strict attention to mundane details. Although the old show business axiom "The show must go on" does not in all cases hold true (the theatre may have burned down), the show *should* go on as scheduled, lest the audiences be disappointed and the credibility of the producing agency plummet.

Virtually everything ends up on the director's desk, and that's one reason that a director must prepare carefully before rehearsals begin. If, for example, the company is staging *Inherit the Wind*, a dramatization of the 1920s Scopes Monkey Trial, the director must do extensive research on the specifics of the time period and the trial

Though dress rehearsals often turn a director's attention to design concerns, they can be a good time to make important adjustments with actors, as well. Here, Sharon Andrews gives notes before a dress rehearsal. *Courtesy of Wake Forest University Theatre. Photo by Bill Ray*

and make specific decisions about what's needed for the show—for instance, whether to use the organ grinder and monkey called for in the opening scene. If the director decides to include them, someone has to find a monkey tame enough to use onstage; the cost of renting, housing, feeding, and caring for the monkey has to appear in the budget; and someone must arrange for the monkey's safe return after the show closes. (This is a very practical example; later you'll find more on the research and analysis that drives production choices—nearly all of which the director must ultimately contend with.)

Leading people toward any communal goal demands the ability to communicate clearly and efficiently. A director with magnificent but unarticulated ideas contributes little and succeeds only in frustrating all concerned. Even in the commercial theatre with trained actors, directors function very much as teachers, sharing with the other members of the company their conceptions of a particular production and professing their theatrical philosophies. In educational and amateur theatre, the teaching responsibilities of the director are more obvious. And in a larger sense, the director uses the production, as does the playwright, to instruct or edify the audience.

3. AN UNDERSTANDING OF HUMANITY

The director deals with human understanding in two ways:

- Through collaboration with live human beings in an artistic endeavor
- Through the fiction of the drama via research and analysis

Collaboration

The director leads a company of artists and support personnel, all of whom have strengths and weaknesses, frailties, fears, and misconceptions. Moreover, they are usually working under the pressure of deadlines and their own professional reputations. As artists, they are often pushing the outer limits of their abilities, going beyond their previous work into risky realms. Directorial coordination of this work and these people demands sensitivity and an ability to bring out the best in each individual, at the same time welding them into an ensemble. At the heart of this "welding" is the receptive aspect of a director's work. Directors take in ideas from at least a dozen people on every production; they mediate conflicts, make sure team members feel heard and appreciated, and spend most of their time in rehearsal watching and listening. Without a leader who focuses well and listens extremely well, collaboration cannot really take place.

Research and Analysis

The director must also come to a deep understanding of the script as a depiction of human beings in action, sometimes in unusual situations. Some of this understanding comes from doing *research*. The prompt book that a director creates includes this research, which can be shared with curious designers and actors. A director may have little experience in dealing with English kings from the medieval period, for example, but in staging Shakespeare's *King Lear*, he or she will need to know and understand a great deal about medieval monarchies, as well as about fathers, daughters, jealousy, madness, sibling rivalry, paternalism, excess, greed, Shakespeare's language, verse speaking, and the like. This requires some intellectual awareness, to be sure, and the director will profit from doing scholarly research.

Analysis, which you might most closely connect to the close readings of texts you have done in English classes, is also included in the prompt book and is another crucial step in the director's preparation. We cover this later in the chapter, and you may take a directing class while in college, where you'll learn the complexities of this kind of analysis. It is certainly time-consuming work, but a director who has a thorough understanding of the script will be able to make decisions and enter rehearsals with confidence.

4. CREATIVITY AND IMAGINATION

Artists of any kind must possess creativity—the ability to combine elements into hitherto nonexistent forms evocative of human emotion. Artists bring to bear all their

American director Robert Wilson (b. 1941) is one of the world's foremost experimental theatre directors. This is a shot from *Einstein on the Beach*, a work that Wilson developed with influential composer and musician Philip Glass (b. 1937). *T. Charles Erikson*

life experiences, artistic and otherwise, in the creation of their artworks. For directors this process never stops; they constantly consider alterations and improvements in the show on which they are working. Between engagements, directors continue to nurture their creative processes, stimulating them by both life and artistic experiences.

Although the creative process seems mysterious at first, certain conditions seem to encourage creativity. The suggested readings at the end of this chapter list several detailed discussions of this aspect of art and the theatre. Perhaps the best thing to realize is that the director, like most artists, may make use of nearly any life experience. Learning how to creatively draw on those experiences is part of learning the art and craft of directing.

Imagination is a related skill. Directors, like actors, must also be able to imaginatively project themselves into another personality for artistic purposes, often by using personal observations of similar situations. After the largely cerebral exercise of determining and researching the given circumstances of a script such as *King Lear*, the director must probe into what it would be like to be the king, the daughter of the king, the fool who entertains the king, and those people in that time and place. Without this imaginative ability, a director will be unable to guide actors to authentic or interesting performances or to detect choices that don't make sense for the world of the play.

5. SKILL IN THE CRAFT OF DIRECTING

Later, in "Creative Procedures for the Director," you'll see some of the elements of the director's craft. However, as in any profession, the director must acquire a unique body of knowledge, techniques, and skills. Learning to communicate with designers and actors; learning to tell a story with bodies in space; learning to guide actors toward effective realization of characters and designers toward effective designs; learning to shape, pace, and focus a production—all of these take training and practice.

The acquisition of these skills usually results from seeing a great deal of theatre, but it also comes from formal training, such as directing classes; observation of other directors at work, often while working as an actor, designer, or stage manager; study of the large body of written material on directing; and personal creative ability applied to the directing process. This process involves learning how actors, designers, and production staff work. Experience with choreography, singing, and other musical matters is important for directors of musical theatre, even though they may have plenty of support staff in the form of a choreographer, musical director, and vocal coach.

Directing involves continuous problem solving, but with experience a director will be able to predict many difficulties before they occur and thus be prepared for them. For instance, such matters as directing the movement of the actors (blocking) may be fairly simple in a show with a small cast, but if several dozen actors are to appear at once in a production, the director must have developed a detailed traffic plan before rehearsals begin. This plan will involve careful coordination with the scenic designer, and it requires flexibility once dealing with live actors.

6. FORMAL TRAINING: A LIBERAL EDUCATION

Even more than other theatre artists, directors should profoundly understand all phases of theatrical production: playwriting, acting, design, and production matters. In addition, the director should have a wide liberal education to deal with the enormous variety of scripts available to stage. These scripts may vary from Greek classical tragedy to contemporary musical comedy, with all manner of variations between. Obviously, then, the type of liberal education ideally offered by colleges and universities at the undergraduate level seems highly desirable. Directors cannot learn all they will ever need to know in four years of study, but they can learn how to learn and where to turn when they need more information.

Many directors begin their careers as actors, often in high school or college. Undergraduates do not often consciously seek directorial careers; rather they spend the four-year program working in all areas of the theatre. For this reason, undergraduate programs most commonly offer general majors in theatre without specialization. Greater refinement of the student's interest comes at the level of the master of arts (MA), master of fine arts (MFA), or doctorate (PhD). Many outstanding modern American directors received their first training in educational institutions of some sort, and many directors working today have gone on from college to earn MFAs in directing or PhDs focused on directing history, theory, and practice.

The director's training ideally ought to cover a broad humanistic range with an artistic orientation. Potential directors would do well to study dance, sculpture, painting, music, architecture, poetry, and literature, both to widen their aesthetic insights and to familiarize themselves with different artistic techniques and contexts. Politics, history, philosophy, critical theory, religion, languages and cultures other than one's own, economics, psychology, sociology, and even the physical sciences may also become useful in the work of a director. In many ways, directing is the ultimate Renaissance person's job.

The Contemporary Situation for the Director

The director's relationship with a producing agency often distinguishes the commercial theatre from the noncommercial theatre. In the commercial theatre, the producer, who organizes the production financially, perhaps with an artistic director, decides to present a particular play. He or she then hires a director for the production. The director, the producer, the artistic director (if there is one), and sometimes the playwright then select the cast and the remaining staff. The director has the freedom to refuse a contract, but commercial directors do not commonly enjoy great latitude in selecting scripts. However, they usually deal with scripts from commercially successful playwrights and enjoy the excitement of staging world premieres. The Off- and Off-Off-Broadway theatres seek commercial goals to a degree (some are nonprofit operations partially funded by foundation grants) but tend more toward experimentation and experimental works.

Regional professional companies—such as the Oregon Shakespeare Festival in Ashland, the Guthrie Theater in Minneapolis, the Actors Theatre of Louisville

(Kentucky), or the Alley Theatre in Houston—hire directors, actors, designers, and other staff members on a yearly basis, assigning them to work on several productions per season.

A director in the educational theatre has more autonomy; the government of the state or the institutional administration "produces" the play in that it hires the directors and other staff, supplies the facilities, and pays the bills. Production goals include both artistic merit and theatre education at the level appropriate to the school.

Directorial rewards include artistic merit and popular success—ideally, combined. The satisfaction of watching a successful and exciting opening night compares with that of coaching a successful athletic team or any similar cooperative effort. Salaries for directors range from nothing for volunteer directors in some schools and community theatres to $60,000 per show or more for leading commercial theatre directors. Profit sharing in a big hit musical can raise that number significantly, as commercial directors' contracts often stipulate that they receive a percentage of the box office income.

College or university theatre directors receive a salary. Their responsibilities usually include teaching, administration, and research. Teaching loads often involve twelve or fifteen hours of student contact per week, but many departments consider that directing a major production is at least the equivalent of teaching a three-credit course and release the professor-director from the classroom for that time. In secondary schools, theatre direction often constitutes a part of an overall teaching position. Community theatres, as noted earlier, may hire directors by the year or draw them from volunteer members of the company.

Directors need to stay aware of all pieces of the puzzle, including the somewhat invisible work of pit musicians and their conductor. *Courtesy of Wake Forest University Theatre. Photo by Bill Ray*

Creative Procedures for the Director

Directors approach their work in many different ways, depending on their specific situations and their preferences and resources. Often, however, they follow a definite pattern, usually based on the following sequence:

1. Script selection
2. Script analysis and staging demands
3. Design conferences
4. Casting
5. Rehearsals

1. SCRIPT SELECTION

As suggested earlier, the script to be produced and the director meet in different ways in different theatres, depending upon the nature and intentions of the producing agency. In the commercial theatre, the producer hires a director for a specific project. In repertory theatres, the producers might consider a specific script in light of its relationship to the other scripts being produced that season. Most companies attempt to stage a variety of scripts in a single season.

Educational theatres obviously have an educational mission. They tend to consider a variety of types of shows; some even try to stage one play from most major periods of dramatic literature every four years, thus exposing students to most major forms. Schools also seek to offer their theatre students a variety of production experiences. Primary and secondary schools have fewer scripts from which to select but seek a comparable variety. Audiences also like variety, so a balance of comic and serious, old and new, is generally part of creating a "season" of plays.

Fundamentally, though, theatre happens in time and space, so—whatever the context—organizations and directors must ask, "Why this play? Why here? Why now?" Determining what the script has to offer a given audience can deeply affect the focus of a production.

2. SCRIPT ANALYSIS AND STAGING DEMANDS

However the script gets chosen, the director must begin preparation long before casting or rehearsals. As mentioned in "Requisites for Excellence in Directing," careful script analysis forms a crucial foundation for everything the director will do. In fact, all other aspects of the production depend on this analysis—casting, staging, design, and marketing. The director must spend long hours with the script to gain a profound knowledge and understanding of it. This will provide both an artistic goal and a method of dealing with the multitude of practical problems involved in staging. Such analysis involves unearthing and coming to understand:

- What actually *happens*, moment to moment, in a script
- *Themes, images, and ideas* that drive the play and that may form the basis for the production's concept
- The *mood* or emotional qualities of the play
- *Character behavior and psychology* that will help in coaching actors
- *Use of language* and other elements that clue us in to the style of the piece
- *Careful attention to all clues of context*—historical, social, economic, religious, geographical, educational, and philosophical (and more)

Staging Demands

As readers will by now have deduced, the director, during the analytical stages of preparation, begins to envision the total production. The director may approach the script traditionally, or his or her approach may be utterly nontraditional, stressing values of the script previously unimagined. Whatever the director's intention, the demands of the script as the director envisions the production must be of prime concern. The following are among the considerations of basic importance.

The theatre itself. Will the available stage be able to house the production as intended? Are the facilities sufficient for shifting the scenery? Is the theatre of a type appropriate for the intended production? In the minds of some directors, a specific script or intended production might be more appropriate to a proscenium, an arena, or a three-quarter thrust stage (definitions of these terms appear later).

Especially in the commercial theatre, budgetary considerations force the director to consider the theatre's seating capacity. A small theatre probably cannot support a lavish production, even if the box office sells all the seats for every performance.

The cast. Are appropriate actors available to produce the play as intended? In the commercial theatre, as mentioned earlier, a production may require a star performer to help cover production costs. Stars attract people who buy tickets. In the educational or avocational theatre, the cast usually comes from a limited group of people of varying experience and ability; hence the director must examine the available resources carefully.

Scenery and lighting. If the company plans a lavish production, as for many modern musicals, the director must know that the facilities available can house the required scenery. Some scripts involve many complex lighting effects; some need almost none. A director who is unaware of the capabilities of the available equipment may encounter rude surprises during conferences with the lighting designer.

Costumes, properties, sound, and makeup. During the early stages of preparation, the director keeps a wary eye out for unusual demands in costuming, properties, sound effects, and makeup. Theatre people refer to some shows as "costume dramas" because of their heavy demands in that area when staged traditionally—for example, Restoration comedies (British scripts written between 1660 and 1700) and Elizabethan scripts. Some directors and costumers choose to set period plays in modern times; others use period costuming. Directors and designers have to make their choices early, considering the available financial and personnel resources.

Similarly, some shows require extensive properties—items used by the actors onstage, excluding scenery and costumes. Kaufman and Hart's *You Can't Take It with You*, for example, requires a pair of pet snakes, among other exotic items. Sam Shepard's *A Lie of the Mind* requires a bloody deer carcass, and *The Hot L Baltimore* by Lanford Wilson calls for an old-fashioned telephone switchboard. Such items can be difficult to locate or build, and the director must be aware of such demands from the beginning.

Although no one can predict all the challenges of a production in the early planning stages, the director tries to ferret out the most likely problem areas. At the same time, the director is making aesthetic choices that will dominate all decisions about the show as it nears opening night. Some directors prefer, as pilots say, to "fly by the seat of their pants," improvising answers to problems as they arise. Some succeed with this approach, but the potential for disaster is obvious, especially with complex scripts. The sign one sees backstage sometimes, "No amount of planning can substitute for blind, dumb luck," is an amusing but dangerous concept.

To illustrate all this planning, consider a director hired to stage *Hamlet*. The title role is one of the most complex ever written in the English language; analyses of the Danish prince fill entire library shelves, one critic or scholar often contradicting another as their perceptions vary. Surely the director should examine the major analyses done by previous surveyors of the script, but the ultimate choice must be his or her own. Hamlet's age, as mentioned earlier, is a problem, as is the central question of whether Hamlet is a vacillating intellectual or a man of action who sweeps to his revenge when he is certain of his uncle's guilt. And what about the ghost who precipitates the action of the play? Is this in fact the spirit of Hamlet's father, come from the grave, or merely a figment of Hamlet's imagination? If the guards and Horatio can see the ghost in act 1, why can't Hamlet's mother see it in act 3? No matter that Elizabethan audiences would have accepted the ghost at face value; what will a modern audience do? What is technically and aesthetically possible and desirable in portraying the ghost for the production at hand, and what meaning does each potential choice make? A veritable flood of such questions arises at every turn when one picks up a copy of *Hamlet* with an eye to production.

Even if the director has answered all these questions, more problems arise in connection with staging. The script calls for a variety of sites in and around Elsinore Castle; should the director seek to distinguish them individually, as some late-nineteenth-century directors did, or employ a more neutral "unit" setting, thus reducing the amount of scenery to be shifted and the time needed for such shifts? Most choose the latter course, which would seem to focus attention more on character, language, and the action of the play than on spectacle.

Costuming offers the same sort of problem. If one uses period costumes for *Hamlet*, which period should they represent? Shakespeare set the action in tenth-century Denmark, but he wrote it for Elizabethan England; his company would have used costumes of their own time period. One might feel that what was good enough for Shakespeare should be good enough for us, but that argument has no real meaning. Others suggest that Elizabethan audience members are unlikely to show up in the twenty-first century and that we must consider each script in terms of modern tastes and conventions. The director, along with the designers, must make these basic choices.

Properties for *Hamlet* include swords, crowns, daggers, and the like. Whether the weapons should be correct historically (Elizabethan or tenth-century Danish?) is ultimately the director's decision and should probably bear some relevance to the scenic and costume choices. Directors have, in fact, staged *Hamlet* in modern dress with revolvers, but ordinarily the climactic duel scene requires either actors who can fence brilliantly or the services of a fight choreographer—yet another complication with which the director must deal.

Sound effects, such as cannon fire and musical flourishes, require design, location, and execution; the director must work with the sound designer to determine the precise nature of these. Makeup plots require directorial approval. If a young actor plays Polonius (Ophelia's father and Hamlet's enemy), a rather elaborate makeup plot must be devised, tested under lights, and executed for each performance.

The director thus approaches the text of the script as something of a map. Not only do different directors find different destinations in the specific map/script, but also they usually find different courses to their destination. But in each case they should plot the route in advance rather than just blundering along.

3. DESIGN CONFERENCES

After script analysis, conferences with the various designers may occur at any time, preferably before the director casts the show. The director and designers must resolve the multitude of concerns in staging a script, described in the section on script analysis. See chapters 7 and 8 for detailed discussions of these conferences. However, it's worth noting that whatever research and development a designer does, a director participates in, though sometimes only as an observer. Whatever design decisions are made, a director oversees, has the option to question or modify, and ultimately approves.

4. CASTING

Directors have said that 80 percent of a production's eventual success or failure is due to the casting of the performers who will appear in it. Many considerations affect this matter, some of which are listed here.

Considerations

1. *Appropriateness to the role in question.* "Type" may come into play here or may be something to fight against. However, casting always involves finding someone who can make the characters work for the important ideas and relationships in the play. For instance, Philip Seymour Hoffman, brilliant actor though he was, would have been an unlikely candidate to play Mary Poppins. Less blatant distinctions concern

Character Considerations

Human beings are complicated, so character analysis is, too. Directors have to take into consideration a whole host of concerns, including chemistry between actors. However, their decisions about who to cast begin with considering many of the following elements in both the character and the actor. Note that many of these are not prescribed in a script, and interesting things can happen when a director is willing to move beyond the obvious!

Physiology

1. Sex
2. Age
3. Height, weight
4. Color of hair, eyes, skin
5. Posture
6. Appearance: good-looking, over- or underweight, clean, neat, pleasant, untidy, shape of head, face, limbs
7. Defects: deformities, abnormalities, birthmarks, diseases
8. Heredity

Sociology

1. Class: lower, middle, upper
2. Occupation: type of work, hours of work, income, conditions of work, union or non-union, attitude toward organization, suitability for work
3. Education: amount, kind of schools, marks, favorite subjects, poorest subjects, aptitudes
4. Home life: parents living, earning power, orphan, parents separated or divorced, parents' habits, parents' mental development, parents' vices, neglect, character's marital status
5. Religion
6. Race, nationality
7. Place in community: leader among friends, clubs, sports
8. Political affiliations
9. Amusements, hobbies: books, newspapers, magazines character reads

Psychology

1. Sex life, moral standards
2. Personal promise, ambition
3. Frustrations, chief disappointments
4. Temperament: choleric, easygoing, pessimistic, optimistic
5. Attitude toward life: resigned, militant, defeatist
6. Complexes: obsessions, inhibitions, superstitions, phobias
7. Extrovert, introvert, ambivert
8. Abilities: languages, talents
9. Qualities: imagination, judgment, taste, poise
10. IQ

Source: Lajos Egri, *The Art of Dramatic Writing: Its Basis in the Creative Interpretation of Human Motives*, rev. ed. (New York: Simon & Schuster, 1972).

an actor's temperament or personality. Directors often speak of an actor's "quality," that is, the total impression given by the performer, summing up physical and psychological characteristics as perceived by an audience. This "quality" is not a value judgment but rather the impression the actor gives from the stage. Ten people reading the same line aloud will yield ten different impressions, as may be readily demonstrated in a classroom.

2. *Talent.* This troublesome term indicates a potential for success or achievement. In the theatre, when applied to actors, it involves *the ability to convincingly embody and reveal a character onstage.* Directors may discover an actor's talent through various casting and audition methods, through seeing the actor in previous productions, and/or by speaking with trusted colleagues who know the actor's work.

3. *Experience.* A director can assume that a professional performer has a substantial backlog of experience, but in educational and community theatres, a director may well encounter people who have literally never set foot onstage before. In such cases the director must be wary, no matter how talented or appropriate a newcomer may appear to be. By the same token, in most theatre groups, the director should be aware of the need to develop talent as well as to utilize it. This growth process—and the value of shared experience—in part helps account for directors' propensity for casting certain actors again and again. Directors learn what an actor can do, and a shorthand can develop between the two that is enjoyable, economical, and productive. Many companies are formed to capitalize on such collective experiences. For instance, French director Ariane Mnouchkine has worked with her company, Théâtre du Soleil, since 1964. Many other examples abound. However, directors who consistently cast the same actors in a college situation, for example, may find themselves starting from scratch when that group graduates or departs.

4. *The actor's status.* The actor's status concerns the director less frequently in the educational than in the professional theatre. Most Broadway productions include one or more stars in their casts in order to attract an audience or to help raise the money to finance the production in the first place.

5. *Growth potential.* Growth potential—most commonly a consideration in educational and community theatre—relates closely to the matter of experience. Artists should ideally work at the outer limits of their range, a bit beyond where they feel safe. Although this kind of stretching is desirable in the commercial theatre, it is almost mandatory if a performer is to improve. The director, basing an opinion on past experiences with the actor, must frequently consider the student's potential for artistic growth rather than merely exploiting his or her current abilities. Misjudgments are common, but when a director takes a risk and a student actor or designer succeeds, theatre's educational mission is at the top of its game, helping students learn and grow while also creating good art.

6. *Versatility.* The ability to play a wide variety of roles is less of a concern for a director casting only one show, unless the actor needs to play several small roles in one production. If, however, the director or a team of directors is assembling a company for a series of shows, the more versatile actor has a definite advantage, especially if the season includes musicals. Regional companies often demand such versatility of

their actors. What's more, a versatile actor is likely to make more surprising and interesting choices than an actor who treats every role as if it were the same.

7. *Relationship with the rest of the cast.* Two concerns emerge here. In any production, professional or amateur, the director must consider the entire cast as a unit, not just a series of individuals, although one-person shows are an exception. Often the physical relationships of the roles (height, weight, coloration, and the like) concern the director. Similarly, vocal qualities should blend appropriately; a cast composed entirely of baritones would soon prove monotonous. Another relational matter can emerge—the actor's professionalism and attitude toward his or her work in the theatre. Disruptive behavior in the commercial theatre can lead to canceling a contract for all but the most essential stars, and sometimes even for them, but no such possibility exists in educational or community theatre. An actor's reputation from previous productions may be a factor, but if performers, no matter how appropriate for their roles, are not dependable, a director will and should hesitate to cast them. Finally, the entire company should ideally "get along." Most actors will work with anyone to secure a role, but in some cases, since actors are human beings, personalities will clash. The director must be sensitive to potential difficulties of this sort. One might hesitate to cast, for example, two ex-husbands of the leading lady in the same show. They might work together beautifully, but then again they might not.

Casting Techniques

Given all these matters to juggle, a director proceeds to cast a show. Methods vary, but most directors use some combination of the following techniques.

1. *Interviews.* Interviews are a common form of auditions in the commercial theatre and are often the only opportunity for actors to present themselves to the producing agency. Since Actors' Equity requires producers to hold two-day open calls for all shows, commercial directors often use brief interviews as an initial screening technique. Directors can thus see several hundred actors in only a few days and eliminate most of them very early in the process.

2. *Prepared auditions.* In addition to the interview, a director might ask a performer to present material he or she has prepared earlier. This technique is useful for directors of repertory companies, such as summer stock theatres, who may be looking for performers to play a series of roles over a season. Educational and community theatre directors often use this form of audition as well. Most actors, therefore, have a number of one- and two-minute monologues memorized and prepared, as well as songs.

3. *Cold readings.* In this form of audition, the actor reads from the script that the company intends to produce. Because performers' abilities to sight-read vary widely, directors rarely rely on this technique alone. More commonly, directors use this method in conjunction with interviews and prepared auditions. A director might even coach an actor during auditions, trying to see how well the actor takes direction.

4. *Improvisations.* Improvisations have become increasingly popular in the last few decades; some directors use them for auditions. The director may call upon the actor

to improvise a scene, perhaps with another performer, perhaps from a situation in the script. The director does this hoping to learn more about the actor's potential and how well he or she handles an imaginary situation. Several of the volumes in the suggested readings contain detailed descriptions of such techniques.

5. *Theatre games.* Akin to improvisation is the growing use of theatre games or exercises. Again the director hopes to penetrate the actor's façade and observe the essential humanity beneath. Your instructor can probably lead you through a few theatre games to give you a feel for what these are like. Through such games and exercises, the director can observe actor concentration, energy, spontaneity, teamwork, and openness.

By whatever techniques the director has found most useful, he or she eventually selects a cast. Certainly auditions afford a director an opportunity to exercise compassion and humanity; auditioning can make the most confident person feel vulnerable, and most actors auditioning for a role don't get cast. The audition scenes from *A Chorus Line* or *All That Jazz* in no way exaggerate the process. When a cast list goes up, however, there is no turning back; good or bad, directors have to live with their choices for months. Thus, directors should cast carefully.

REHEARSALS

Rehearsals involve interactions between people in the act of creation. Directors, faced with different scripts and different personnel, use a wide variety of methods during the rehearsal period. No two directors are quite alike. Few are rigidly despotic, dictating every line reading and every piece of business from their predetermined analysis. Most encourage freedom to the actors during this period, allowing them to experiment as they pursue the nature of their characters. The most effective directors balance structure and experimentation, allowing the cast relative freedom within prescribed limits.

Whatever the director's methods, he or she must have an overall plan with clearly defined goals to make sensible progress. The following sequence typifies a standard rehearsal schedule.

Reading Rehearsals

During reading rehearsals, directors hope to share both their vision and their enthusiasm for the production with the cast. Most commonly, the cast, the stage manager, and the director sit around a large table and read through the script, considering it as a complete entity before beginning to dissect it in later rehearsals. The director may share research, his or her own interpretation of the script, how the script works, and the specific problems of staging it. During these first meetings of the cast with the script, the director tries to make sure the cast begins to work together toward a common goal. In some cases, the designers may be present to describe their contributions and share renderings or models. Beginning with a strong vision of the whole can be valuable throughout the rehearsal process.

What Does a Stage Manager Do?

If the director is the person most responsible for the concept and focus of a show, providing leadership throughout the creation of the production, the stage manager is the one who makes sure it actually happens the way it has been designed to.

The rehearsal phase. The stage manager (SM) is with the director every step of the way. The SM acts as a liaison between director and designers and keeps everyone informed. She schedules and runs production meetings, takes care of scheduling, and attends every rehearsal. There, she makes sure the stage is clean and safe and that everything needed for a rehearsal is there and notes all blocking, all plans for cues, and all ideas to be communicated to designers and theatre management. With the help of a good stage manager, directors can therefore concentrate on directing.

The dress/tech phase. During technical and dress rehearsals, the stage manager gradually takes the reins from the director, becoming expert at the timing of all lighting and sound cues and all scenic shifts. She makes sure the backstage crew has a clear sense of what needs to happen and that board operators (sound and lights) are ready to perform their jobs.

The performance phase. You might think of the stage manager as the director in performance. She makes sure everyone shows up for the production, oversees light and sound checks, and makes sure actors get their "calls" (updates on time before curtain and—sometimes—during the show). She makes sure all sets and props are ready to go before she allows the house manager to open the doors for the audience to enter. During the performance, she calls all cues, which have been meticulously detailed in her version of the prompt book (which also includes all blocking). In the professional world, the stage manager is also responsible for rehearsing in any replacements and understudies, teaching them their blocking and helping them with interpretation.

The stage manager may also have assistants (assistant stage managers, or ASMs), who take on whatever tasks are needed, in performance often taking charge of backstage crews stage left and right and communicating any backstage problems to the SM.

Much happens backstage, but the work of a good stage management team is essential yet virtually invisible.

Blocking Rehearsals

After reading through the script, the cast moves to a rehearsal hall or to the stage. Construction of the scenery has usually just begun, so the stage manager uses colored tape on the rehearsal floor to indicate the location of the scenery. Experienced actors are used to working this way, and inexperienced ones usually pick up the technique quickly. The actors use substitute furniture and properties: three folding chairs may represent a sofa, or a Styrofoam coffee cup may become the Holy Grail.

The blocking rehearsals coordinate the actors' locations and movements during the play. Many directors work out this movement in advance by various means, most commonly recording it in a prompt script by drawing the traffic patterns on small floor plans of the scenery.

The director can thus dictate movements to the actors, who record them in pencil in their scripts. They can make changes later; directors often find that stage arrange-

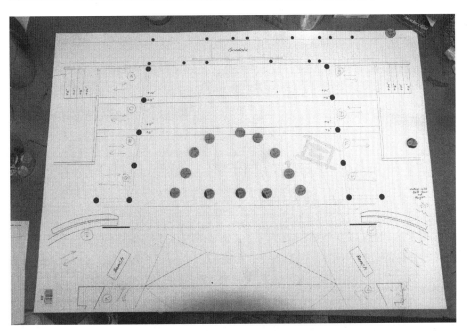

British director James Dodding's penny blocking for a production of *The Gondoliers*. The director can use any number of things to represent actors, but here Dodding has taped actors names onto individual pennies and moves them about on a ground plan, tracking each person in preparation for a blocking rehearsal. This is particularly useful when dealing with complicated movement and/or large groups of people. *Courtesy of Wake Forest University Theatre. Photo by Bill Ray*

ments that seemed good on paper do not work with live actors on a stage. The company must remain flexible.

Directors may dictate where they want the actors or give motivation to the movement, as in "You cross left to get a drink" or whatever makes sense in the situation. They may also encourage actors to experiment, discovering the blocking "organically," as they feel compelled to move. In addition to revealing the conflict and the psychological life of the characters, blocking also helps highlight important moments, structures the pace and rhythm of the show, and communicates style and mood. Unless the cast is unusually large or the action unusually complicated, a director can generally block an act of a realistic play and then have the actors walk through it in about three to five hours. A three-act play will thus require about nine to fifteen hours of rehearsal to establish and check the blocking.

Again, scripts and directors vary widely in this regard. For instance, if a script requires any choreography—of fights, dancing, or other synchronized movement—more time will be required. Working organically, with actors experimenting and exploring movement, also takes more time than the director coming in with a relatively established plan, since eventually the blocking will need to be edited and certain elements fixed. Style plays a large part in this as well, dictating all kinds of vocal and physical choices.

A good director knows how to compose a stage picture to tell the story and also help focus audience attention. In this Lyric Theatre of Oklahoma production of *Oklahoma!* note how the two center actors have their arms stretched above them and are looking straight out, while the attention of the downstage actors on the two in the center "tells" us to focus on them, as well. *Courtesy of Keith Rinearson*

Directors vary in regard to degree of control or choreography, as well. Director Robert Wilson, for instance, treats each moment of his productions as a choreographed moment, while some directors prefer to set as little as possible, hoping for greater spontaneity and flexibility in performance. You might discuss with your classmates the relative advantages of these approaches.

Whatever the technique, directors try, through blocking, to illuminate relationships, communicate conflict, highlight important structural moments, and develop the style and mood of the play through the quality, content, and amount of movement.

Characterization and Detail Rehearsals

Detail rehearsals usually make up the bulk of the rehearsal period. Although procedures vary, many directors divide the script into sections called "beats" or motivational units and rehearse them, preferably sequentially. Depending upon the play, the cast, the director, and the circumstances, much discussion may follow; the company dissects the script into its smallest components. Here the cast and director must retain their vision of the entire show while working with the most minute matters.

Here, too, the director should make clear to the cast the precise goals for any given rehearsal, a courtesy too often overlooked. Some actors work with minimum direction; some require close supervision and continual reinforcement from a director in order to work well. The director and the actor bring their own unique humanity, experience, and vision of the production to bear toward a shared goal. Rehearsals at this point must blend all the points of view into one, a process requiring the utmost in openness, sensitivity, and directness.

Run-Throughs

As the company progresses, the director usually begins to have the cast perform increasingly larger portions of the script without interruption; the show is becoming theirs. After the dissection stage, the cast begins to acquire a sense of the show as a whole. At this point the director often takes notes during the rehearsal of an entire act, then discusses matters of concern after the run-through of that act. Eventually the director has the cast run through the entire script, after which they may rehearse troublesome scenes and/or discuss portions of the script that offer special problems.

Technical Rehearsals

Technical rehearsals, perhaps a week before opening night in the educational theatre, involve the addition of the technical elements—scenery, costumes, lighting, properties,

The idea that directors are dour and bossy has been propagated for too long. Note how director Nicholas Martin and playwright Christopher Durang are enjoying the actors' work in Durang's funny play *Vanya and Sonia and Masha and Spike* at the McCarter Theatre in Princeton, New Jersey. *T. Charles Erikson*

When lighting, props, costumes, scenery, staging, and the focus of the actors all work together well, even a simple moment can be beautiful. Director Rosetta Cucchi updated the action of the opera *La Bohème* (upon which the musical *Rent* was based) to the days surrounding violent student uprisings in Paris in May 1968. Boston Lyric Opera, October 2015. *T. Charles Erikson*

sound effects, and so on. Some producing agencies prefer to add all elements in one rehearsal; others add them more gradually, allowing the cast to grow accustomed to some elements before adding others.

These are times that can try all concerned, and the director sometimes has to adjudicate clashes of will. The company usually works against a tight time schedule: nerves frazzle, tempers shorten, and reputations as well as considerable money may be at stake. The director's organizational skills and experience should minimize the pressures, and with luck, no unpleasant surprises will arise to complicate matters. But when they do, the director must coordinate spot decisions for the good of the production and all concerned.

Some problems can be solved when they appear; others require work between rehearsals. Any experienced director has horror stories to relate about this stage of rehearsal—sound or light effects that don't work, scenery that collapses, costumes that fall off, all manner of disasters. Directors must find their own means of coping with this period, and a good many actually enjoy technical rehearsals. This is the time when all one's planning comes together; the designs near completion and can be seen and heard together. In short, the show finally begins to look, sound, and feel as it will on opening night.

Tryouts or Preview Performances

Eventually the show has to perform for an audience. As described earlier, Broadway producers used to take shows out of New York to such cities as Philadelphia, Washington, or Boston for out-of-town openings. The local critics would review the shows there, and the company could experience audience response. The company could make adjustments—scenes would be removed or rewritten, tempos adjusted, costumes refitted, and so on. This practice became prohibitively expensive, so producers have largely abandoned it, preferring to preview performances in New York. In the educational and avocational theatre, which operate with lower budgets, directors will sometimes invite audiences to attend dress rehearsals before an opening. The director and cast must judge responses carefully. Friends and acquaintances may or may not give objective reactions, and invited audiences may respond rather more positively than the theatregoing public. Still, an audience is an audience, and audiences tend to be more alike than different.

The Opening and the Run

After the show opens, the cast continues to refine it. During a run in a regional theatre, the director or stage manager may hold additional rehearsals of troublesome scenes or the entire show. In the Broadway theatre and some other operations, the stage manager takes charge of the production after it opens and calls additional rehearsals at his or her discretion. In some cases the director may return to tighten up a show during a long run. In the educational and avocational theatre, schedules do not often permit such additional rehearsing, though directors may continue polishing a production through the final performance via notes to the actors.

Evaluating the Director's Contribution

Evaluating a director's contribution is complicated because, as many theatregoers come to realize, much good directing is nearly invisible. As in the case of the playwright, audience-critics may well have great difficulty distinguishing the director's contributions from those of the other theatre artists. Efforts and results merge, and distinctions blur between the actors' art and the director's guidance, the scenic artist's design and the director's concept. A director may stage a superb script and fail to achieve its potential; inexperienced directors rarely do Shakespeare well, for example. A director may take a mediocre script and inspire a brilliant performance, or an exceptional cast may bring a script to a life and artistry far beyond that envisioned by the playwright—or the director, for that matter. But if in the modern theatre the director selects the script, defines the concept for the production, casts and rehearses the actors, and approves all design elements, he or she must carry the primary responsibility for the overall production's success or failure.

Judgment of the director's work reveals the interdependency of theatre audiences and artists, a relationship sometimes overlooked but inescapable in the theatrical transaction. No one has yet written a definitive history of theatre audiences, but theatre history reveals a few periods when artist and audience operated on the same wavelength, nurturing one another, stimulating each other to heights neither could achieve alone. In the modern theatre, audience and artists can still achieve a momentary oneness, transcending reality and approaching some sort of truth. The director leads the quest for such experiences.

Although the audience rarely has any direct awareness of it, the director's personal relationships with the other artists affect the production in fundamental ways. A harmonious working situation usually produces freer, more inventive, and more efficient work, and the director assumes the responsibility for the creative atmosphere. Directors who vent their frustrations with fits of rage and shouting rarely produce anything except jangled nerves and hostility, with a corresponding loss of the show's full potential. Groups of people working toward a common goal usually profit from positive, visionary leadership.

In assessing the director's work on a production, then, one might return to the things we've discussed as the director's goals over the course of this chapter—though some of these questions may apply more easily to some productions than others:

1. Did the production tell the story clearly and dynamically?
2. Did the style work? Was it stylistically coherent and communicative?

Internationally acclaimed theatre director, choreographer, and video and installation artist Ping Chong was one of the earliest proponents of media in the theatre. He has made theatre all over the world. This is a scene from his and Talvin Wilks's piece, *Collidescope: Adventures in Pre- and Post-Racial America.* Courtesy of John Solem

3. Was it cast well? Were characters and relationships clear and appropriately complex?
4. Was the production creative and imaginative? Did it stimulate and surprise you?
5. Did it generate a meaningful response, intellectually and/or emotionally?
6. Did it feel coherent? Did it have its own logic and work structurally, visually, aurally, thematically?

If you can say "yes" to all of these big-picture questions, you can be fairly sure someone skilled was at the helm.

Conclusions

The theatre will always need insightful and innovative directors; the need for excellence never diminishes. Many of the old traditions of staging and directing are fading into disuse; new rehearsal techniques constantly emerge. Multimedia productions call for skills undreamed of by directors in the past. And the collaborative nature of devising work is helping disrupt the idea of a top-down structure of authority. Above all, the director's work—whether as collaborator, analyst, researcher, choreographer, innovator, problem-solver, or communicator—demands qualities rare in any profession.

Key Terms

blocking A term referring to the overall traffic patterns of actors on a stage: entrances, exits, movements, and so on. *See also* business.

Brook, Peter (b. 1925) Outstanding British director whose most famous production was the world-acclaimed *A Midsummer Night's Dream* in 1970. Author of *The Empty Space*, a highly regarded treatise on theatrical theory.

business All stage movement and action. As more commonly used, the term refers to smaller actions, such as lighting a cigarette, reading a book, or drawing a weapon.

Clurman, Harold (1901–1980) A highly successful director and author of several important theatre books. In 1931, he helped found the Group Theatre, which, even after disbanding in 1941, continued to have an influence on the American theatre.

composition The way bodies and movement are arranged to create stage "pictures" that, among other things, communicate story, power dynamics, and relationships.

cue A signal for a technician or an actor. An actor's cue to enter the stage setting, for example, is often a line from another actor; the cue for a lighting technician to adjust stage lighting may be an actor's touching a light switch.

French scenes A term referring to the habit of the French dramatists in times past to mark the entrance or exit of a character with a scene division. Still used by some directors in script analysis.

previews Tryout runs of Broadway productions in New York City prior to the official opening (usually attended by the critics), usually for some weeks.

prompt script or prompt book Usually the director's script, containing his or her notes, the blocking and cues for the show, detailed analysis of the script moment by moment, and any other relevant material. Such a script was originally used to prompt actors during rehearsals, hence the name.

Reinhardt, Max (1873–1943) Austrian actor/manager and an outstanding director whose most famous productions included *Oedipus Rex, Jedermann, The Miracle*, and *A Midsummer Night's Dream*. Reinhardt is credited with inventing the prompt book—what he called the *regiebuch*.

run-through An uninterrupted rehearsal of a scene, an act, or an entire production, as opposed to rehearsals during which directors or technicians stop the action to make adjustments.

Saxe-Meiningen, Georg II, Duke of (1826–1914) German director whose company toured widely and with considerable influence between 1874 and 1890. He is generally considered the first director in the modern sense.

Stanislavsky, Konstantin (1865–1938) Russian actor, director, teacher, and author. Cofounder of the Moscow Art Theatre and originator of the Stanislavsky system, an internal, psychological approach to acting.

subtext A term associated with Konstantin Stanislavsky's and Lee Strasberg's approaches to acting, referring to the line of internal thought that an actor discovers in analyzing and delivering his or her lines and actions.

typecasting The casting of roles in a play by matching the most obvious characteristics of the actors to the characters.

Discussion Questions

1. What makes a good director? A bad director?
2. Discuss what types of training are required to be a director. Where does one go to get such training?
3. Why does script analysis matter to a director? Use the various topics for analysis outlined in this chapter, and apply it to something you've read for class.
4. Why does style matter to the director? How does one determine style in a script and apply it in a production? Choose a play you've read for class, and discuss the effect that various styles might have on your perception of that play. *Hamlet*'s Elsinore Castle is usually dark, foreboding, and heavy. What if it were a place of frivolity, bright colors, and rapid speech and movement, with only Hamlet all in black? How do these stylistic changes affect meaning?
5. How does a director *prepare* to cast a production? What methods are used in the actual casting process?
6. Discuss the function of a director during the rehearsal process. How does a director prepare for blocking rehearsals? Name the other kinds of rehearsals and what happens during those. Do you think longer or shorter rehearsal periods are more beneficial? Why?

7. What is the director's role once the show has opened? How do you think this changes the relationship between the director, cast, and crew?

8. What seems to you the most challenging aspect of directing? The most appealing?

Suggested Readings

Ball, William. *A Sense of Direction*. New York: Drama Publishers, 1984. Ball's book has become a standard in directing courses around the country. He tackles some difficult issues with clarity and grace.

Bartow, Arthur, ed. *The Director's Voice: Twenty-One Interviews*. New York: Theatre Communications Group, 1988. A superb collection of interviews with important late-twentieth-century directors.

Boal, Augusto. *Games for Actors and Nonactors*. New York: Routledge, 1992. A superb collection of cutting-edge games from one of the contemporary masters of world drama.

Bogart, Ann. *A Director Prepares: Seven Essays on Art in Theatre*. New York: Routledge, 2001. Bogart sketches out some brilliant ideas in this brief edition. She is considered by many to be one of the greatest stage directors of our times.

Cohen, Robert, and John Harrop. *Creative Play Direction*. 2nd ed. Englewood Cliffs, NJ: Prentice Hall, 1983. An excellent introduction to how directors work. Includes history as well as practical advice.

Cole, Toby, and Helen Krich Chinoy, eds. *Directors on Directing: A Source Book of the Modern Theatre*. New York: Bobbs-Merrill, 1963. Available in paperback, this volume contains a series of essays about and by the most famous directors of the past century. The first essay, "The Emergence of the Director" by Chinoy, is especially lucid. An excellent bibliography is included.

Dean, Alexander, and Lawrence Carra. *Fundamentals of Play Directing*. 5th ed. New York: Holt, Rinehart & Winston, 1989. An amplified edition of Dean's original 1941 work, long considered a standard text for beginning directing classes. Nicely illustrated, with a useful glossary of terms.

Hodge, Francis, and Michael McLain. *Play Directing: Analysis, Communication, and Style*. 6th ed. Englewood Cliffs, NJ: Prentice Hall, 1994. Perhaps the most widely used college directing text today. Hodge, a professor emeritus from the University of Texas, is held in high regard by colleagues and students alike.

Logan, Joshua. *Josh: My Up and Down, In and Out Life*. New York: Delacorte Press, 1976. In his autobiography, Logan describes in a readable style how he rose to the top ranks of Broadway and Hollywood directing. A scintillating glimpse backstage.

Mitter, Shomit. *Fifty Key Theatre Directors*. New York: Routledge, 2003. Mitter highlights some of the most important directors in history via source material, including Brecht, Stanislavsky, Barba, and Vakhtangov.

Monta, Marian, and Jack Stanley. *Directing for Stage and Screen*. New York: Palgrave Macmillan, 2007. Monta and Stanley have created the rare text, a book that draws smart parallels between directing for live theatre and for film. Highly recommended for those with dual interests.

Shapiro, Mel. *The Director's Companion*. Boston: Wadsworth, 1997. A terrific and brief book that outlines the basics of stage directing.

Spolin, Viola. *Theatre Games for the Classroom.* Evanston, IL: Northwestern University Press, 1986. An excellent collection of games from one of the pioneers of theatre games and improvisation. Any of Spolin's works is highly recommended.

Stafford-Clark, Max. *Letters to George: The Account of a Rehearsal.* London: Nick Hern Books, 1989. A fascinating rehearsal log, in which British director Max Stafford-Clark records his thoughts and experiences during the course of rehearsing George Farquhar's *The Recruiting Officer* and preparing to direct Timberlake Wertenbaker's *Our Country's Good.*

Sterne, Richard. *John Gielgud Directs Richard Burton in Hamlet: A Journal of Rehearsals.* New York: Random House, 1961. Includes the prompt script of Burton's *Hamlet.* Sterne kept a detailed description of rehearsals, offering an inside look at the show's preparation.

CHAPTER 6

The Actor

Bullfight critics ranked in rows
Crowd the enormous Plaza full;
But only one is there who knows—
And he's the man who fights the bull.

—Domingo Ortega, translated by Robert Graves;
favorite poem of John F. Kennedy

All the contributions of the other theatre artists notwithstanding, the actor alone "fights the bull." Once the performance begins, the actors' work literally makes the play happen. The performers have the most direct and immediate interaction with the audience, and they alone can respond and adjust to audience reactions during the performance. Perhaps the audience's traditional fascination with performers stems from the directness of this relationship. Actors work with and for each audience, stimulating a response that is, ideally, appropriate for the play, the place, and the audience.

Despite this close connection—one we have all felt at some time—actors' work is poorly understood by the general public. Everyone seems to think they know what good acting is, but few people have ever stopped to examine their misconceptions. Hopefully you will be ahead of your friends after reading this chapter. If, on the other hand, this all seems obvious, please forgive us; you might be surprised that this is new information for many people.

First, a few myth busters:

1. Acting is not about ego. Good actors subsume themselves to the characters they play, work collaboratively with others every single day, and derive pleasure from the give and take of the highly charged personal connections they form. Master teacher Konstantin Stanislavsky famously said, "Love the art in yourself, not yourself in the art," and most actors believe and practice that.

2. Good acting is not "faking it." Notice how obvious it is to you when someone you know is faking enthusiasm or laughing falsely. Ferreting out falsehood and finding ways to believe as strongly as possible in the context and needs of the character are absolutely foundational tasks in most actor training. Similarly, acting is not about putting on facial expressions or "showing" emotion. Rather, by believing in (or, if you like, pretending) fully, actors *allow* feelings and reactions to bubble up out of their interactions with each other.

3. Memorization is not the primary concern of actors. Certainly this can be a challenge at times, but it is simply groundwork—more like planting the seeds in a garden than harvesting the veggies. So you might want to avoid going up to your actor friends and saying, "How did you memorize all those lines?" It's the least of their worries.

4. It's not about "saying it right." Good actors are not fixated on making sure they put the emphasis on the right words. (This is called a "line reading.") Having done their analysis, they are instead focused on affecting the other actors/characters with their words, just as you are when arguing with people or trying to make them laugh. So it's not about controlling emphasis, just as, in performance, it's not about being loud enough or clear enough. All that gets worked out in actor training and—if need be—in rehearsal.

In a paper about a production, you might therefore avoid talking about an actor's facial expressions and such things. Actors make choices, as we discuss later, that give form to the character, and those are certainly good fodder for discussion. However, in performance, the actors' focus is not on how to create a facial expression or how to say a line, any more than Roger Federer has to think about how to hit a backhand in the middle of a match.

We discuss what actors *do* think about later in the chapter. However, please remember that their work is intricately woven with that of the other theatre artists. Actors rarely improvise their lines; the playwright predetermines their words, just as the director and/or choreographer supervises their actions. Lighting and sound design choices may control the timing of certain moments and set a mood within which the actors work. The designers create the scenic and costume environments, thereby affecting the performers' choices of movement. The actor must further adjust to the architecture. The size, acoustics, and arrangement of an auditorium affect vocal projection and the size of gestures.

Actors interact most directly, however, with each other and with the director. The director requires each actor's living presence to create the actual performance, and the actors look to the director for objective evaluation of their work, for guidance, and for leadership during rehearsal and performance. Without actors, a director has nothing to direct; without a director, actors could perform but would risk losing the cohesiveness and unity required for excellence.

The Actor's Alternatives and Restrictions

No artist encounters more obvious limitations of self than the performing artist. Most other artists work with some material or some sort of instrument—a painter with pigment and canvas, a musician with an instrument, and so on—but the actor operates simultaneously as both artist and instrument, both creator and the thing created. The playwright puts limits on the actor's characterizations, to be sure, as does the director, but during production and much of rehearsal, actors rely on themselves and their fellow actors to create a living performance in which their physical, vocal, and "psychic" reserves are constantly taxed.

We are often introduced to actors as movie stars, but most great actors began in the theatre. Here, Lupita Nyong'o plays Kate (with her classmate Max Gordon Moore as Petruchio) in Shakespeare's *Taming of the Shrew* at Yale. *T. Charles Erikson*

A Confederacy of Dunces at Huntington Theater Company with Nick Offerman as the iconic and ridiculous Ignatius J. Reilly. Adapted by Jeffrey Hatcher from John Kennedy Toole's novel. *T. Charles Erikson*

Physical limitations restrict actors; they cannot play all roles, at least not sensibly, partially because of physical characteristics. Maggie Smith is a wonderful Professor McGonagall in the Harry Potter films; she would make a strange Ron Weasley. Even mimes often suffer frustration because they cannot turn themselves into any person, animal, or object desired. As one mime said, "The bones keep getting in the way."

Directors must consider an actor's *vocal equipment* when casting a role. Any audience properly demands to hear and understand an actor, and although film or television actors always have the advantage of electronic amplification, stage actors may or may not; they face the problem of projection and articulation at every performance. Vocal stamina becomes a major consideration. If a film actor grows tired, the director can call a rest; a stage play stops only for intermissions.

Vocal quality also modifies any performance. Viola Davis and Amy Adams have rather different voices, as do Jon Cho and Robert DeNiro. Directors must consider what they are trying to communicate with a given character and take into account how an actor's voice may enhance that character choice. For instance, in *Star Wars*, Mark Hamill's tenor voice worked very well for Luke Skywalker, but James Earl Jones's deep bass sound was probably a more appropriate choice for Darth Vader.

The actors' *psychic limitations*, their intellectual and emotional ranges, are harder to describe but are of equal importance. Limitations aren't permanent or absolute, and actors who limit themselves to what they are easily good at rarely grow, but the ability to see one's strengths and weaknesses is also important in facilitating growth. Usually, artists continue to develop as they age and experience more of life and of their craft.

Although the physical and vocal aspects of acting make up the immediately perceived craft of the art, the actors' use of their spiritual resources can lead them to genius or doom them to mediocrity. Like all arts, acting emanates from the artist's total psyche: life experience, emotional and physical reserves, intellectual flexibility, aesthetic philosophy, physical and sensory awareness, relationships with other artists and with the audience, and more. In short, the total makeup of the actor's personality comes into play. Politicians sometimes speak of a candidate's being "big enough for a governorship but not for the presidency"; athletes speak of heart; singers mention soul when describing another singer. Some critics analyze an artwork's aesthetic size. Scholars consider *Macbeth* a "bigger" script than *As You Like It*. Aesthetic size in this regard does not mean spectacle or the numbers of actors or scenery used; it rather implies the depth and breadth of the depiction of the human condition. Some playwrights perceive and articulate a more thorough or striking depiction of humanity, and such scripts make greater demands upon the artists who choose to stage them. Not every actor has the internal resources to achieve brilliant success as Hamlet, Medea, or Oedipus. Some actors may have the psychic depth to understand and feel these parts but lack the skill and confidence to tap into and communicate these feelings at will.

The use and expansion of psychic limits is a concern of actors, acting teachers, and directors. Although actors from the very beginning have struggled to understand this aspect of their art, the work of Konstantin Stanislavsky (1863–1938), a Russian director of the late nineteenth and early twentieth centuries, typifies modern acting theory, and his contributions to the training of contemporary actors have had major impact. No theatre artist of the twentieth century stimulated as much controversy as

Konstantin Stanislavsky—or Constantin Stanislavski—(1863–1938) may have had a more profound impact on modern acting theory than anyone else. His "system" for realistic acting has influenced acting teachers, actors, and directors for the last one hundred years. *Library of Congress, LC-DIG-ggbain-35320*

Stanislavsky; theatre students hear very soon of "the system" or "the method." This was never Stanislavsky's intent. (See the "The System versus the Method" box for more.) Other approaches to acting are plentiful, as well. Philip Zarrilli's *Acting (Re) Considered* is a phenomenal source for those interested in pursuing this further. However, for the purposes of this introductory text, an investigation of Stanislavsky seems to us a good place to start.

The System versus the Method, or Doing versus Feeling

You might ask an acting teacher to more thoroughly explain the differences between the American "method" and Stanislavsky's "system." However, the action-focused "system" that Stanislavsky developed was changed by Lee Strasberg at the Actors Studio in New York to an almost exclusively psychological and internal approach. To a great extent Strasberg focused on the idea of "emotion memory." As Jean Benedetti points out in his preface to *An Actor's Work*, such an approach foregrounds "each actor's personal feelings that correspond to the character, a technique which Stanislavsky expressly rejected." Instead, Benedetti continues, "in the 'system' each section of the play contains something an actor has to *do*, [whereas] in the method it contains something he has to *feel*." For Stanislavsky, action and interaction, textual analysis, and his "method of physical action" are central—not mere subjectivity and emotion. This does not mean that action and emotion are unrelated. Rather, emotion comes from understanding and connecting to the "given circumstances" of the play, which *include* emotion, and then pursuing the character's goals, in relationship with the actors on stage with you. If you find this at all confusing, ask your teacher about it, or even better, take an acting class.

Born to progressive art patrons and introduced at an early age to theatre, Stanislavsky became frustrated with the artificiality of the Russian stage. With the popular playwright and teacher Vladimir Nemirovich-Danchenko, Stanislavsky founded the Moscow Art Theatre and dedicated himself to the following goals:

1. *The development of an acting system* that would create "a favorable condition for the appearance of inspiration by means of the will, that condition in the presence of which inspiration was most likely to descend into the actor's soul." Toward this end, he developed exercises and training techniques to foster the creative state in actors during their work onstage. Scholars note that Stanislavsky based most of his system on his observations of great actors. Although some of these actors achieved a somewhat systematic approach to their art, it remained for the Russian director to develop a system that would help actors bring the subconscious into conscious view and into conscious control. This emphasis on unearthing subconscious impulses was obviously not unique to Stanislavsky; his contemporary, Sigmund Freud, is best known for his attention to this aspect of human psychology.

2. *Productions with an artistic process as well as a professional product.* Stanislavsky believed the rehearsal process needed to be a focused artistic experience dedicated to creating quality art rather than the copious quantities of mediocre theatre he saw all around him. He also demanded high standards of professionalism from actors, realizing that discipline was needed to create the kind of acting ensemble he desired: one in which actors worked together for the benefit of the production and the company, not for the glorification of themselves as stars. Physical and vocal training were part of this discipline, as Stanislavsky and his collaborators knew that,

in order to communicate the subtleties of a character's inner life, an actor required a sensitive and robust personal instrument.

3. *A commitment to developing actors* who could more fully realize the characters being created by the new realist playwrights of the time. This meant helping actors to move beyond performances based on tradition to spiritually and physically free, personally connected, and psychologically coherent characterizations that flowed from the actors' choices as well as from those of the playwright. Remember that Freud's ideas were becoming popular around the same time and that the idea of personal psychology was new to people then. Realist plays, psychology, and modern acting theory are, therefore, interwoven.

With these new ideas in mind, actors could move beyond the stereotypical, beyond the idea of one "correct" interpretation, to an art form that embraced each actor's life experience, each particular company of actors, and each production's demands. Though Stanislavsky's system has sometimes been criticized as actors and teachers continue to seek new ways to illuminate the plays of our time, his was important work and certainly changed the actor's craft. It created the first practical approach to actor training, script analysis, and the building of a character. See the suggested readings for related material.

Contemporary American acting has been shaped by followers of Stanislavsky and by those who recognize the need to go beyond the early interpretations of his work. Acting teachers, such as Sonia Moore, Stella Adler, Lee Strasberg, and Sanford Meisner, each interpreted Stanislavsky's work differently, and each has contributed meaningfully to the training of thousands of American actors whose names are familiar to you. Name a favorite actor, and he or she has almost certainly had some training based on Stanislavsky's teachings.

At its best, acting is teamwork of the highest caliber. Certainly technical reliability is part of a superior group effort, but a kind of psychic "communion" can also take place between actors, energizing them, supporting their commitment to the performance, and ultimately translating to the audience as great acting.

You should know that you, as an audience member, have an impact on the actors, since you inevitably modify the actor's work with your energy, attention, and responsiveness. Acting at its highest levels seeks to stimulate oneness of spirit between performers and audience; some audiences accept this connection more easily than others. Such emotional oneness depends on the interactions of many complex factors, such as the quality and subject matter of the play, the background of the audience, their theatregoing experience, what the audience has been led to expect in the play, the specific choices made in the production, and much more.

If actors face many limitations, they also have the potential for some unique rewards and satisfactions beyond fame and fortune. Stage actors receive immediate response to their work; the audience sends unmistakable signals through laughter, silence, physical posture (as well as restlessness or stillness), and even their breathing. Not all actors love the curtain call at the end of the show; some depend on it. But beyond such external approval, the experience of having acted well with one's fellow actors can be exhilarating and deeply satisfying.

An Early Experiment in Personalizing a Role in Ancient Greece

According to legend, Polis, an Athenian actor of the fifth century BCE, once played a Greek monarch anguished by the loss of a son. The production circumstances had nothing to do with realism: Athenian actors then wore masks covering their entire heads, heavy body padding, and richly ornate costumes. Yet Polis brought onstage with him the ashes of his own dead son, trying to stimulate something within himself to lead to greater honesty in his performance. For centuries, therefore, actors have known that powerful psychological stimuli can greatly benefit them.

If the work goes badly, stage actors have another chance to modify, correct, or improve their roles in the next performance. This opportunity has its price, however; the actor who achieves a brilliant evening of rapport with an audience faces a new audience at the next performance. Inexperienced actors often err by trying "to play last night's show"; few succeed. If we can believe a theatre legend, Laurence Olivier experienced such a problem during his 1965 *Othello* in London. Fellow actors reported that Olivier reached undreamed-of heights one night as the Moor, stunning audience and cast alike. After the audience's ovations, Olivier stormed into his dressing room, slammed the door, and raged about furiously. When one of the cast finally got up the nerve to ask the great star why he seemed so disturbed when the show had gone so brilliantly, Olivier snarled a reply: "Yes, it was brilliant, but I don't know if I can ever do it again!"

Above all, the actor's art is intensely personal. Successful actors truly lead and shape the imagination of an audience. Fulfilling such an endeavor is not about ego satisfaction; it may offer a chance to reach beyond the bounds of mundane experience to explore the language and imagination of characters written by great playwrights. Such transformation can be enormously liberating. Further, like sport, acting provides a chance to explore the limitations of one's own personal reserves and offers the pleasure of connecting strongly to other people. Acting alone in a room might help an actor in training, but performing includes fellow actors and demands the attention of an audience.

A starring actor can obtain stunning commercial rewards (the economics of acting appears later in this chapter). Also, the bonding and sense of oneness that develops in a play's cast, while not unique to the theatre, can create a deep sense of connection. People who share an intense interest in a common activity may sometimes seem to present a closed front to outsiders; their togetherness grows from shared experiences and interests.

In college and university theatre, the educational aspects of production can offer the student-actor remarkable opportunity. Everyone seeks new experience; actors seek not only their own experiences but those of a created personality, the character, and a created world with one's fellow actors. When properly approached by actors, directors, and teachers, the study and exercise of acting amplify a person's self-awareness and add insight into humanity. Education at all levels seeks precisely the same goals.

Audience Judgment

Who is a "good" actor? Audiences can make mistakes and change their minds—and actors can become more skillful! Many writers and painters who later developed into masters found only rejection from the public at first, and the same sort of thing happens in the theatre. Audiences hissed Henry Irving (1838–1905) off the stage in the English provinces when he first tried acting; he became the first actor knighted in England. When Laurence Olivier (1907–1989) appeared as Romeo in New York, a critic described him as resembling a belligerent sparrow. When Edmund Kean (1787–1833) made his first London appearance as Hamlet, he prompted a reviewer to call him "one of the vilest figures that has been seen either on or off the stage. . . . As for his Hamlet, it is one of the most terrible misrepresentations to which Shakespeare has ever been subjected." A few years later, Kean had become known as the greatest actor in the world.

For a different slant and a more contemporary look at this subject, you might compare the early work of Tom Hanks in the TV sitcom *Bosom Buddies* to his performance in more recent work, such as the film *Bridge of Spies*. Has Hanks grown as an actor? Might the quality of the writing and the skills of the director and his costars also have something to do with our perception of his work as an actor? What factors drive your evaluation of an actor's skills?

Requisites for Excellence in Acting

The concept of talent, a word bandied about in most of the arts and sciences, leads to confusion; everyone talks about it, but almost no one defines it. Talent for an actor, however, seems related to the following:

1. Vivid imagination
2. Strong access to emotion
3. An expressive voice and body
4. Physical and mental stamina
5. Bravery and self-confidence
6. Flexibility/improvisational spirit
7. Love of the craft

Taken all together, these connect to the ability to create a reality onstage—a theatrical truth based on the given circumstances of the character and the situations depicted in the script.

1. VIVID IMAGINATION

Actors require active imaginations and the bravery to expose and embody even the most painful and ridiculous sides of human nature. Without imagination, actors cannot lift themselves into the given circumstances that each playwright dictates; they will never be able to move beyond their own experience. In the theatre, where the extraordinary is the rule, bravery and boldness of execution are needed. Bigger-than-life actors, such as Nathan Lane, Jonathan Pryce, and the diminutive Kristin Chenoweth, can electrify even an enormous audience through the power of their imaginations and their courage to take a creative choice to its limit.

2. STRONG ACCESS TO EMOTION

As mentioned earlier, our culture frequently misunderstands actors' craft, suggesting that actors *fake* emotion. The extreme of this is to equate acting with hypocrisy or lying. However, good actors develop their imaginations and easy access to their own emotions—something directors may refer to as an actor's "emotional availability." The goal matters: Actors create their realities within a characterization for an artistic rather than an opportunistic goal. Similarly, children pretend to be superheroes for their own pleasure, not to fool anyone. An actor does not truly believe that he or she has become the character—we call that mental illness—but like the audience, the actor must willingly and temporarily suspend disbelief. This ability to control one's imagination in order to create an illusion marks the beginning of acting talent. It's doubtful that Thespis truly thought he had become Dionysus, unless he had dipped heavily into the festival wine.

(Left) Junius Brutus Booth (1796–1852) was a London-born actor who spent most of his career in the United States. His children included John Wilkes Booth, the assassin of Abraham Lincoln, and (right) Edwin Booth (1833–1893), perhaps the most outstanding American Shakespeare actor of the nineteenth century. *Library of Congress, LC-USZC4-6711*

3. AN EXPRESSIVE VOICE AND BODY

Only through what an actor *does*, vocally and physically, do we know what is happening with the characters in a play. If they lack responsive voices and bodies, audiences are left confused, perhaps even in the dark about what has been said or has occurred. As an analogy, pianists may have superb skills, but without an adequate piano, they cannot succeed. Actors must develop their instruments, as well as the concentration to control body, mind, and voice. Such control results from diligent exercise and practice; we find no shortcuts to these qualities, and we cannot overestimate their importance.

4. PHYSICAL AND MENTAL STAMINA

Consider a role like Hamlet, in which the central character is onstage for three hours with few breaks besides intermission. The nonactor can scarcely imagine the stamina needed for such work. The old truism "Art conceals art" applies to most theatrical endeavors. What appears easy, natural, and graceful in production usually results from rigorous effort both in and outside rehearsal. The actor with a substantial role must sustain it through long rehearsals and performances. Even with a short role, the actor must be ready after long and enervating periods of waiting to expend his or her energy at the proper moment. In either case, performers soon realize that good acting demands both physical conditioning and mental stamina.

For those readers who have never acted, even in an amateur setting, imagine a class speech or presentation you have given and take away any notes you might have used. Then add detailed imaginary circumstances of place, time, weather, manners (and more), as well as complicated physical and emotional demands; enlarge your audience to several hundred spectators; and—as a final challenge—multiply the length of that presentation to several hours. This may give you some idea of the challenge required.

5. BRAVERY AND SELF-CONFIDENCE

Given these demands, most actors are aware of the risk of screwing up. Like athletes who risk losses in front of their fans, actors must put aside their anxieties and self-doubts and commit to the task at hand. Director William Ball called great actors "heroes" because of their ability and willingness to do so. Confidence is integral, as well, and contributes mightily to actors' willingness to make bold, imaginative choices, and trust in the moment.

6. FLEXIBILITY/IMPROVISATIONAL SPIRIT

A parallel exists between the actor's work during rehearsal and that of a jazz musician. Musicians can prepare to play improvisational jazz, but they cannot execute it except at the moment of creation. Jam sessions popular with jazz musicians are merely rehearsals during which the performers play for one another; they thus serve as their own audience. Much the same condition would exist if actors performed together for an empty auditorium. But performing for an audience with an improvisatory mind-set requires immense trust and—again—confidence in oneself and one's fellow players.

7. LOVE OF THE CRAFT

Loving what you do and continuously working toward improvement is essential in all the arts. Given the challenges we've outlined here, sticking with acting means a love of the craft of acting and of improving one's skills. Great actors tend to love language, love movement, love rehearsal, love making discoveries and decisions, and truly enjoy a challenge. When one comes to the theatre every day with that kind of spirit, the possibility of great work getting done is exponentially increased. These kinds of actors are also more likely to be cast repeatedly and to build great relationships and reputations because working with them is a joy.

Other factors contribute to an actor's excellence. Physical appeal, a distinctive personality, and attractiveness all have marketable potential, especially in Western theatre. These qualities can prove valuable to the actor, especially in productions stressing the actor's uniqueness and charm rather than artistry. Such productions seem somewhat more decorative than substantial, but they have diverted and entertained millions and

Dennis Krausnick as Lear and Michael Huie as Gloucester in the enormously challenging (and exciting) *King Lear.* **Directed by Cindy Gendrich.** *Courtesy of Wake Forest University Theatre. Photo by Bill Ray*

thus hold a definite place in the theatrical spectrum. Sadly, when such a performer's physical appeal fades (and fade it will), so does his or her career, as exemplified by the hundreds of child stars and sex symbols who fail to deal well with growing older.

Professional performers frequently mention luck and connections as major factors in their careers—not surprising in any profession so oversupplied with talent. An aspiring actor trudging around the agencies and casting offices of New York or Los Angeles has to realize that he or she is simultaneously not only an artist but also a one-person small-business operation. Such an actor is literally the product, the public relations officer, the packager, the package, and the board of trustees, all at the same time. As we all do to some degree, actors must sell themselves to the available market. Such commercial circumstances may alienate a young idealist, but actors need a strong shot of pragmatism. Their creativity may burn with a hard, gemlike flame, but they also have to pay the rent.

College theatre sometimes protects the student actor from the hard, cold facts of getting a job in the commercial theatre. Conservatory programs can neglect the education of the total person while concentrating only on theatrical skills. By experiencing both types of training, students can gain a sort of overview, but often they have to put it together themselves. Institutions are striving to alleviate these unfortunate circumstances, but in the ever-changing world of theatre and other entertainment media, flexibility and self-motivation may be some of the best career skills that colleges and universities can teach.

Actor training is thus complex and never-ending, and right now no place exists in the United States where an apprentice actor can enroll in a long-term, comprehensive training program leading to employment. MFA (master of fine arts) degree programs are sometimes affiliated with regional theatres, and these associations can provide welcome exposure for aspiring actors. Nevertheless, they do not guarantee employment. Most actors receive their earliest experiences and training in undergraduate educational institutions, perhaps gaining further training in conservatories; MFA programs; master classes in New York, Chicago, LA, or other large cities; and actual professional work.

The Contemporary Situation for the Actor

Actors Equity Association (AEA) functions as the stage actors' professional union in the United States. Horror stories regularly emanate from New York City about how many Equity members actually earn a living at their profession. At any given time, about 80 percent of Actors Equity members have no work as actors; this explains why much of the food in New York restaurants arrives at your table carried by aspiring thespians.

Figures from Actors Equity may discourage anyone from considering an acting career. In 2013–2014, for example, Equity says that the 17,522 members in good standing worked an average of 16.7 weeks over the course of the year. In the course of the year, 41.3 percent of the membership worked at least one week under an Equity contract. Eighty-one of those members made over $200,000 in Equity jobs, and 1,626 (or about 9 percent) earned more than $50,000. But four times as many earned $5,000

Actors need to be flexible in many ways. Every play has its individual style, which actors must embrace; they must be able to work with (and play) a variety of people with openness; and they must be physically and vocally flexible. August Strindberg's *A Dream Play*, here at Rutgers University in 2016, requires all of the above. *T. Charles Erikson*

or less doing Equity work. Complicate this by the fact that stage managers are hired under Equity contracts. They make up about one-sixth of Equity membership and are much more likely to have steady work than most actors are.

Compare these figures to the federal government's definition of the poverty level (in a one-person household $11,490 was the 2013 threshold), and it's obvious that most commercial actors must work in film and television as well as theatre or require some other skill or profession to pay their expenses. In addition to holding down a "day job," many actors find that much of their time is spent looking for acting work, networking, and reminding their agents of their existence. These unhappy circumstances may explain some of the desperation involved in the profession or the elation an actor may express when hired for a television commercial.

If one is lucky enough to get one of the higher-paying contract jobs for, say, a Broadway show, Actors Equity members can make over $130,000 per year—a decent salary in New York City. But even if one's show runs for a year or longer (a rarity), there are often long dry spells between big-ticket jobs, so stage actors can rarely count on that high an annual salary.

The long-running Broadway hit (later a motion picture) *A Chorus Line* dramatized the circumstances of working dancers. In it, the director/choreographer selects eight dancers from thirty finalists drawn from hundreds of applicants. Most performers face rejection most of the time. You may be able to empathize, but few of us would choose to face rejection so frequently. Gender also plays a role. There are more actresses than

The Golden Age at College of Wooster, 2013. Marisa Adame, left, and Summit Starr, right. *Courtesy of Matt Dilyard*

actors yet more roles for men—and women are more subject to type-casting based on physical appearance. Faced with this situation, many young performers grow discouraged and leave the profession. Many thousands, however, remain, even though only a few will rise to the top, through talent, training, persistence, love for their art, connections, and sheer luck.

Regional theatres may offer a bit more security and artistic satisfaction than a New York career, although circumstances vary widely. Professional companies outside New York often offer contracts on an annual basis, sometimes renewable if justified by the company's demands and the actor's work. Performers in regional companies rarely receive national exposure, however, and their salaries tend to be somewhat lower (about $928 per week on average for large Actors' Equity Association's League of Resident Theatres [LORT] in 2013). The lower cost of living outside New York helps make those lower paychecks livable.

The increasing affiliations between professional and educational theatre groups offer a possible hope for the future. Universities offer greater security, and professional groups often possess greater experience and expertise; alliances can combine the best of both.

Student actors seldom receive payment from universities, though some may attend college on talent scholarships. Student actors' work constitutes a means to an end. They perform to increase their theatrical understanding through practical experience. Often plays are chosen to stretch the students, so many contain difficult material and characters well outside students' age and life experience. The quality of the acting in university theatre, therefore, varies considerably, but some is excellent.

Community theatre actors usually perform as a sort of hobby, though they may also achieve a high degree of excellence. Some, indeed, bring considerable professional or university experience to their work, and the festivals of the American Community Theatre Association often present good theatre by any standards. The Little Theatre movement of early-twentieth-century America, essentially a collection of community theatres, achieved a dramatic renaissance in this country, giving opportunities to theatre artists then in the early stages of development.

Creative Procedures for the Actor

Actor training in nearly all traditions involves the preparation of the instrument—body, voice, and imagination. This tradition goes back to one of the earliest actor-training schools in the world, China's eighth-century establishment of the Pear Garden—a rigorous school in which actors learned acrobatics, pantomime, dancing, singing, and martial arts. In the West, training has come to focus not only on physical and vocal training but also on concentration, sensory awareness, interpersonal relationships, sensitivity, and related techniques. Such training typically begins early and should continue throughout an actor's career. Though the process of growing as an actor is extremely fluid, the actor's work may be broken into two categories: first, the general work of self-improvement and, second, the specific work of preparing a role for production.

SELF-IMPROVEMENT: DEVELOPING THE VOCAL AND PHYSICAL INSTRUMENT

General self-improvement includes voice, acting, and movement classes and the like, usually under the tutelage of professionals. The skills acquired in singing and dance classes may also prepare the actor for roles in musical comedies, an important part of the modern theatre.

Voice

Vocal exercises for an actor are like instrumental practice for a musician. The best performer can always improve, and all players must exercise their skills just to stay at a current level. Pablo Casals, probably the greatest cello player of all time, practiced his usual four hours, even on his ninetieth birthday. Vocal work seeks to improve all aspects of sound and speech, through attention to:

- Freedom and relaxation
- Breath control
- Resonance
- Articulation
- Placement

- Volume and projection
- Interpretation

Your professor can probably lead you through a basic vocal warm-up, or you can consult some of the sources listed at the end of the chapter. Kristin Linklater, Arthur Lessac, and Cecily Berry provide some of the most widely used and effective techniques, and each focuses on a different aspect of vocal development. Linklater stresses freedom, Lessac emphasizes precision, and Berry primarily works with textual demands. Daily exercises to address these concerns will almost certainly improve an actor's instrument and yield a competitive edge over others who do not devote themselves this way. Such dedication will not ensure employment, let alone success, but it does improve an actor's expressiveness and flexibility.

Actors in musical theatre obviously must be able to sing, and this generally means their training also includes specialized individual voice classes for singers. All of the previously mentioned vocal concerns are doubly important in musicals because singing is pitch- and volume-specific, requires proper placement and breath control, and tends to tax the voice even more strongly than stage speech. However, there are numerous roles in the "straight" theatre requiring actors to speak for hours with little interruption. As mentioned earlier, the actor playing Hamlet, for instance, is onstage almost constantly for over three hours, speaking for much of that time. Few singing roles require such stamina.

Body

Most actors in musical theatre are also strong dancers. The intense physical energy of most musical comedies requires that they remain fit and flexible. Strength, flexibility, and balance are traits we, therefore, associate with dancers, but successful actors in any genre benefit from regular work on their physical development. Each person moves in a distinctive way, and some actors seem to handle themselves exactly the same way for every character they play. Since this can be a real range limitation, it follows that actors benefit from training that expands their physical choices.

Although unusual muscular development may or may not be necessary for a particular performer, all actors need muscle tone, stamina, and a flexible body. Actor movement classes often begin with exercises and activities designed to increase students' physical awareness as a first step toward economical movement and relatively "neutral" alignment. By acknowledging their own tensions and quirks, actors can begin to relax and reorganize the way body parts relate to one another. Again, this neutralizing work allows them to *choose* the peculiarities of each character's physical behavior rather than always being stuck in their own. Actors, therefore, benefit from work on:

- Relaxation
- Flexibility
- Strength
- Agility
- Balance

Actors are athletes, rarely more so than in musical theatre. Here, the cast of the Guthrie Theater's *The Music Man* prepares for a dress rehearsal. *T. Charles Erikson*

Basic stretching exercises, or more specific attention through yoga, Pilates, tai chi, or other exercise systems, can be extremely useful. Many actors also improve their expressive range further through mime and mask work. Additionally, they may go through combat training and dance classes, which build strength and provide specific skills needed in a wide variety of plays—not just Shakespeare and musical comedy.

Rudolf Laban and Creating a Character

We all have habitual ways of moving, but the characters we play have different histories, different social customs, and different psychology, so they probably shouldn't all move the same. Getting a handle on how to change the way you move can be aided by understanding the work of movement expert Rudolf Laban. Laban is widely known for his development of dance notation but also as an influential force in movement for actors, separating it into four components that can be combined in almost limitless ways:

1. Weight (heavy/strong/firm or light resistance)
2. Time (speed: quick or slow; duration: long or short)
3. Space (mass and line: direct or indirect)
4. Flow (fluid or interrupted, sudden or sustained, bound or free)

Experiment with these components, exaggerating each, then thinking of them on a continuum (e.g., for weight 10 = a feather; 1 = a giant boulder). Now become aware of how changes in (and combinations of) movement generate physical and emotional feelings. They may even, to an outside observer, begin to convey character or personality.

SELF-IMPROVEMENT: DEVELOPING INTERNAL RESOURCES

Acting is a lifelong pursuit, and with any effort, actors' internal resources grow as they age, simply through the process of living. However, there are specific things that help maximize an actor's development, some of them quite pleasurable. Watching great actors is a wonderful way to learn (and be entertained in the process), so actors should attend the theatre whenever possible.

Actors also profit from exposure to and study of the other fine arts to develop their own artistic sensibilities. The mind-expanding experience of some modern art may well stimulate a sharpened sense of innovation in the modern actor; what's possible in one art may well initiate something in another. Experienced performers read avidly and tend to follow theatrical developments, just as professionals in any field do to keep informed. Reading acting books can be an enjoyable opportunity for artistic self-exploration, just as reading widely about theatrical traditions can help one make richer, better-informed choices. And keeping abreast of industry trends by reading *Variety* and other theatrical publications can prepare the actor for informed career decisions.

Perhaps most important, actors' training should lead to a lifelong study of nature, the life from which they draw their art. What may seem to the onlooker—the theatrical civilian—as mere egocentricity or eccentricity in performing artists may be the essential study of themselves and other human beings. For example, many actors, including some of the greatest ones, have made notes on their reactions when overwhelmed by personal grief in order to use them later onstage. Each of us contains in microcosm the totality of human qualities; since Everyman is in every man and woman, such seemingly callous self-observation is invaluable for the artist. Actors must carefully study the varieties of human action and reaction from the heights to the depths in order to obtain an understanding of and empathy with the spectrum of characters they may attempt.

Finally, actors should pursue their craft by the continued study of acting itself. Studios and conservatories exist for students, of course, but dozens of institutions exist for working professionals. The Actors Studio in New York and Los Angeles was developed for just such a purpose, as were the William Esper and the Hagen-Berghof (HB) Studios—both in New York. Cities with theatrical communities of any size inevitably have classes available—often through well-established theatres.

To facilitate personal and artistic growth, modern acting instructors have devised a vast number of techniques, including improvisations and theatrical games. These serve as either warm-up exercises for rehearsal or performance, or as general techniques for freeing the actor from inhibition or blocks to creativity. Chicago teacher Viola Spolin (1906–1994) and Brazilian director Augusto Boal (1931–2009) are particularly popular sources for such improvisatory exercises. Classes at the Groundlings in Los Angeles or at Second City in Chicago, as well as multiple iterations of the Upright Citizen's Brigade (UCB), are all good places to go for crash courses in both improvisatory acting and sketch-comedy writing.

In the song "Nothing" from the musical comedy *A Chorus Line*, a young actress named Morales, browbeaten by an acting teacher, fails to "feel the motion" of an imaginary bobsled in acting class. (Morales suspects that her failure may be genetic, since they had no bobsleds in San Juan, Puerto Rico.) Improvisation can nevertheless prove immensely useful to actors, expanding their imaginations, improving confidence and willingness to trust themselves and each other, and improving their ability to understand how specific circumstances can affect human behavior. If an actor swathed in furs when the stage temperature rises over ninety degrees seeks to present an illusion of bitter cold, the value of Morales's imaginary bobsled may seem less idiotic and more practical.

Those who have never acted (and many who have) often find such mental and physical gymnastics highly amusing; an actor vigorously imitating a wave or a piece of frying bacon can be ludicrous, if not grotesque. But such exercises can free actors physically and mentally. A performer may approach a character more efficiently for having played a cigar butt; indeed there may be a certain area of commonality between a cigar butt—wet, soggy, raveled, gross, nasty—and a character such as Fagin in the musical *Oliver*. Farfetched? Perhaps, but if a person thinks something helps, it does.

The same is true with exercises and games. A simple example is "Mirrors," an exercise in which actors pair off, face to face. One initiates actions, usually very slowly at first; the other person tries to reflect the actions as exactly as possible. When the performers do the exercise very well, an onlooker cannot tell which player initiates and which reflects. Such activity may cause the giggles in young performers, but it can help an actor achieve nonverbal communication with another person, an obligatory skill for successful acting. Mirroring also improves concentration, may refine physical control, and can focus powers of observation.

Sanford Meisner, an influential acting teacher whose work also grew out of Stanislavsky's teaching, takes this kind of simple observation as a foundation for all good acting—especially his repetition exercises. Today, William Esper's New York studio is one of the most well-known places to learn this kind of technique—one that demands emotional honesty and intense connection between actors.

Some actors do not connect to this kind of approach to acting, which has only been with us for about a century and a half. In fact, actor Willem Dafoe says, "I'm not attracted to naturalism, I'm not attracted to behavior. I'm attracted to dance. I'm attracted to gesture. I'm attracted to singing with your voice, as opposed to having a natural manner." Perhaps because of this different approach, Dafoe's characterizations tend to be wild, free, unpredictable.

Many other acting techniques are available to train body and mind and to unleash that kind of freedom. Biomechanics, an athletic training and performance technique developed by a contemporary of Stanislavsky, Vsevolod Meyerhold, develops concentration and physical specificity. Even in the West, increasing attention is being paid to non-Western theatrical forms and actor training, such as Japanese Noh and Kabuki, Indian Kalarippayattu and Kathakali, and others. Physical-emotional connections are also being sought. One such approach is called Alba Emoting, which examines the physical bases of emotion in terms of breathing, posture, and eye focus/tension.

Actors and acting teachers will continue to seek new techniques for training, and though some will disappear, others will win approval by bringing substantial gains to artistic development.

It's easy to think that acting is all about realism, given our exposure to so much film and television. Not every play asks for that, however, and not everyone loves realism. Theatre that is infused with strong poetic choices in design and movement can lift your experience beyond the everyday and move you in ways you didn't expect. Here, a dance/theatre production of José Rivera's *Sonnets for an Old Century* blends monologues and dance. *Courtesy of Wake Forest University Theatre. Photo by Bill Ray*

PREPARING FOR A SPECIFIC ROLE

The second aspect of the actor's work varies widely from person to person but usually follows a three-part pattern, though these are not followed in a chronological way, but tend to overlap.

1. The actor analyzes the script and his or her role in it to find personal connections to the role, to determine an approach, to understand the script and character deeply, and to make choices about his or her goals within the production.
2. The actor finds the means to apply these discoveries and achieve those goals.
3. Finally, the actor seeks the means of retaining those achievements and keeping the performance fresh during the run of the show.

Analysis, Approach, and Making Choices

Script analysis by the actor parallels that by the director but with a narrower focus on one role alone. The actor must study the entire script and relate his or her portion of it, no matter how small, to the goals of the overall production.

Actors generally begin by carefully reading and rereading the script to discover the given circumstances of the role: where and when the action takes place, what information about the character the playwright has delineated, relationships with other characters, the character's goals, what complicates the achievement of those goals, and so on. Here, consulting chapter 5 under the director's work on character analysis will prove helpful. Actors must obviously do this kind of close analysis on any role they play.

Playwrights rarely supply all the necessary details, so the actor and director often find it useful to deduce or create them. A few major matters of concern would include the character's parentage, education, religion, relationships and experiences, physical qualities, and economic status. Some actors try to determine the circumstances of a character as far back as his or her grandparents and seek to create a character's history leading up to the first entrance. Some even find it helpful to speculate about what the character does after the play's end. For example, what will happen to Horatio after the Danish court has cleared off the bodies of Hamlet, Claudius, Laertes, and Gertrude? How will Horatio fare under King Fortinbras? Any investigation may lead to a more three-dimensional characterization and hence increase audience appreciation.

At the same time, many actors try to find in their character some aspect of themselves, some point of connection. Every characterization will vary; by the very nature of acting, the actor's own personality will modify the role. Therefore, Hamlets performed by Laurence Olivier, Mel Gibson, Richard Burton, and Kenneth Branagh differ markedly, partly because of the different intentions of the actors and directors and partly because of the different qualities and personalities of the performers.

Actors must find a spark of sympathy or indeed love for each character they present. They must find, even in the most hideous and despicable of personalities, the understandable motivation that generates the character's action in his or her circumstances. The ancient Greek playwright Terence famously said, "I am a human being. Nothing human can be alien to me."

Brooklyn-based company Colt Coeur is known for its youth and for visceral, deeply felt work. This 2015 production of Ruby Rae Spiegel's *Dryland*, directed by Adrienne Campbell-Holt, was praised for the commitment of the acting by Tina Ivley and Sarah Mezzanotte, shown here. *Courtesy of Adrienne Campbell-Holt*

Actors must experience life before they can illuminate it, so each individual actor must experience—if not always widely, then certainly deeply—to enrich his or her supply of creative resources. Most actors try to find within their own personalities qualities useful in preparing and playing a role. Playing villains illustrates this process especially clearly. Human beings rarely think of themselves as villains; villainy as a concept represents social evaluation from an external point of view. Medea, Iago, a torturer of the Spanish Inquisition, Saddam Hussein, and Stalin all in some way or other justified their actions to themselves. The actor's responsibility includes finding the germ of truth in the character's self-justification, even though the actor himself may not personally condone the character's reasoning. This willing suspension of moral disbelief calls for a wide and sympathetic understanding of human behavior. In fact, actor Richard Dreyfuss has said, "There's a little bit of Hitler, and a little bit of Jesus, in each of us."

Actors use many different means of preparing a role for the stage. Some may work internally, seeking a psychological basis for the role. However, not all plays are realistic plays, and therefore not all acting strives for realism as its highest goal. Musical comedies, high comedies, farces, and satires require that the actors identify the world of the play just as carefully as their realist brothers and sisters, but the techniques required once inside that world may be different. British actors Maria Aitken, Simon Callow, and Athene Seyler have all written at length about playing high comedy, and they all, in some way or another, touch on the need for heightened energy, agility, and vocal and physical precision, as well as a special awareness of the audience's role in what one is doing. This is not a matter of manipulation but of responding to the audience's needs. Callow remarks, "The job of the actor is not to *make* the audience laugh, but to *let* them laugh." Despite a preference for serious drama by most groups giving awards for great acting, most actors know that comic plays are at least as difficult to execute well. The old saying goes, "Dying is easy; comedy is hard."

Still other nonrealistic styles, such as those in productions by auteur directors like Robert Wilson or Richard Foreman, require unusual treatment of movement and voice; these productions can be difficult for inexperienced actors and even more challenging for novice audiences. Actors who work in these and other postmodern plays, as well as in epic, surrealist, or absurdist works, which don't rely on the psychological progression of character, can run up against the Stanislavsky system's limitations. Actors and audiences may find these other styles more difficult to penetrate because they have been so conditioned by realism's pervasive influence. However, as you will undoubtedly discover during trips to the theatre, each production creates a different world. And theatrical choices, including acting style, must be carefully made to illuminate that world and communicate it to the audience.

Since each play requires specific physical and vocal demands, some actors prefer an external approach, beginning with the physical aspects of characterization as a basis for development. Laurence Olivier, for example, suggested that he constructed his characters from the outside, with the role traveling inward as he worked. Johnny Depp says he allows various images to inspire his character choices, and many other actors find that a combination of internal and external elements help them define a character. Few actors would deny that shoes, glasses, and other elements of a costume can help tremendously in slipping into character. Similarly, specific physical choices can help an actor define how a character presents himself or herself and therefore help the actor inhabit the character more fully. (See the sidebar on Rudolf Laban for one approach.)

Debate has raged for centuries about various approaches to creating character—especially with regard to emotion—with no resolution in sight. Actors need an external technique when they perform so the audience can see and hear the events taking place. At the same time, the actors must remain open to emotional responses. In so intensely personal an art as acting, all artists will seek their own methods of combining their individuality with the demands of the role. Perhaps Joseph Jefferson III (1829–1905), a highly successful American actor, came closest to putting the problem in proper perspective when he said he tried to keep "his heart warm and his head cool," combining the emotional and the intellectual approaches. Increasingly, techniques from the East and West have cross-pollinated and blended, with Asian actors increasingly using Stanislavsky-based approaches and Americans experimenting with the techniques of Tadashi Suzuki and other Asian teachers. What matters most is what works for a given actor and a given play.

Application and Rehearsal

The second step in role preparation seeks the most effective means of enacting the character. As exploration continues, the actors rely upon the director to watch their efforts and guide their work. One of the things actors diligently seek is freedom of expression, so though they may evaluate themselves and their work while acting, this kind of "monitoring" can keep them from wholeheartedly throwing themselves into their roles. Just as one cannot write and edit at the same time, actors require a director to edit their work. Creation comes first, then criticism. The late, great Philip Seymour Hoffman described his own process as one of "allowing things to be out of control within a structure." He noted that the script provides a path that must be followed but that the actor has to find a way to maneuver within that structure and "make room for chaos." This chaos might be understood as responsiveness to the moment, a willingness to let in and even embrace the unexpected—a far cry from the idea that actors are just trying to memorize their lines and say them "right"!

To help build structure and thereby some confidence in allowing that chaos in, during working rehearsals, actors seek a pattern of action for their roles. This does not simply mean learning the blocking; it also refers to the internal action that shapes movement. Actors trained in the realist tradition will often use three questions to help them define that action: (1) What do I want? (objectives), (2) What am I willing to do to get it? (tactics), and (3) What stands in my way? (obstacles). By answering these questions with information from the script, actors can make internally motivated physical choices that communicate to other actors/characters and therefore to the audience. This does not mean every moment is pinned down exactly. Good performances can and do shift and change as actors continue to find new things.

Other basic areas of actor concern are well described in Michael Shurtleff's book *Audition*. He focuses on defining, in auditions, the specifics of character. But these guideposts, as he calls them, are a good distillation of the kinds of questions realist actors work with all the time. Shurtleff asserts that, to create a good audition, the actor must define all of the following:

1. Relationships
2. Conflict: what is at stake?
3. The moment before: what drives the character into the scene?
4. Humor (which, according to Shurtleff, good actors find in every good play)
5. Opposites, the emotional poles of the scene
6. Discoveries, or how the characters change
7. Communication and competition
8. Importance: what matters in the scene?
9. Events, marking what actually happens in each scene
10. Place, or the entire physical nature of the scene
11. Game playing and role playing
12. Mystery and secret

These are only some of the areas of inquiry for actors, who seek to make specific and palpable the lives of their characters. Often the only thing actors need to do is identify the answers to the questions they ask. If their training is good, their flexible imaginations, bodies, and voices will reveal, through words and actions, much of what they have thought about.

Billy Elliott **at the Lyric Theatre of Oklahoma. Big musicals require a strong ensemble that works as a unit. Long runs can erode concentration, so actors must work hard to stay fresh and focused.** ***Courtesy of Keith Rinearson***

Of course, character development and the internal and external concerns of actors in other traditions tend to be somewhat different. In Noh drama, for instance, physical form, movement, and a traditional style of speech that's more like singing or declamation all create a sense of character that is not personality- or psychology-driven. Nevertheless, a sense of place, time, events, character traits, mystery, and conflict are still defined in Noh, as in Western acting.

Whatever the acting tradition, actors must develop characters that communicate through the space between stage and audience member. Intelligible speech and song, clear physical choices, and a rich internal life all contribute to this communication.

Staying Fresh

The third step in acting a role involves keeping the performance fresh and spontaneous after the show has opened. In rehearsals, stage action fluctuates markedly. During the first week or so of performances, the cast responds to audience reactions and can easily concentrate on the relative novelty of the performance. But after a few weeks, a few months, or in some cases a few years, performances can grow stale and tired, and actors must find ways to keep a sense of vitality and life in their work.

American actor William Gillette (1855–1937) coined the phrase "the illusion of the first time" to describe this problem for the actor. An actor may repeat a role hundreds of times through rehearsal and performance and so faces the danger of "walking through the role"—that is, mere mechanical repetition. Actors may, therefore, vary their performances. Good actors like Meryl Streep positively thrive on being surprised. Streep is purported to have told Kevin Kline during the filming of *Sophie's Choice*, "Don't be afraid to hurt me; you won't. And do whatever you want, go wherever you want with it; I'll go with you. I love to be surprised."

In order to keep a performance fresh, actors may also continue to study their roles over and over, trying to find fresh insights and nuances in a character. Mrs. Sarah Siddons (1755–1831), an outstanding English actress, played Lady Macbeth intermittently for thirty years, yet she spent the morning before each performance studying the part and reading the entire script. She usually found something new in it—as she said, "something which had not struck me as much as it ought to have struck me." Continuing exploration of this sort enables an actor not only to survive but also to grow during long runs.

In summary, actors are faced with a process that asks them to discover, role by role, what it is to be human. In developing a given character, this means a complex (and widely variable) interaction with text and collaborators. Training (both internal and external), research, analysis, and experimentation all contribute to the actors' ability to help a text to live and breathe. Once rehearsals are over, actors must then determine how to keep the play alive and fresh through a series of performances. Considerable individual variation exists, but actors of all times and places have faced comparable problems in creating their roles.

Evaluating the Actor's Contribution

Because the actor's work merges so completely with that of the playwright, the director, and the designers, precise evaluations can be difficult. The powerful or clever lines spoken by an actor usually come from the playwright, although the actor must deliver them well. Effective, funny, or unusual movement may represent an actor's contribution, but these choices may have been the director's idea or both the actor's and the director's. The clothing the characters wear represents a costumer's efforts. Even the performer's physical appearance may reflect the skills of hair and makeup technicians.

Looking at an actor's work is also complicated by the fact that roles vary and actors change and grow. We can begin to assess the quality of their work by looking at both individual performers and the larger scope of a career.

AN INDIVIDUAL ROLE

Given that so many things are not under the actor's control, returning to things that are under the actor's control may be a good place to start in evaluating an actor's work. Michael Shurtleff's guideposts, mentioned a few pages ago, provide a nice template for evaluating any given performance. After you go to see a play, answer these questions—and try to be as specific and detailed as an actor must be:

1. *Relationships.* Were the actors clear, nuanced, interesting/surprising, and believable within the style of the production? How did you know how the characters felt about one another *by what the actors did and how they did it* rather than by what words they spoke?

2. *Conflict.* Was it defined and explored clearly and vigorously by the actors? See if you can give a specific example or two.

3. *The moment before.* Did there seem to be a context within which the characters were operating? That is, did there seem to be a life outside the confines of the set that informed actor/character choices onstage? Think of Kramer on *Seinfeld,* whose strange inner life made every entrance a window into his life outside Jerry's apartment. Did the actors in the play you saw seem to have a sense of their life outside each scene that helped invigorate the scenes of the play?

4. *Humor.* Did the actors find the humor and use it? Shurtleff claims that humor exists in every play and that good actors will find it. See if you can describe a specific moment—maybe something hilariously funny but perhaps something that simply illuminated the actor/character's awareness of the absurdity or silliness of the world.

5. *Opposites, the emotional poles of the scene.* Did the actors find variation, change, an emotional journey, surprises?

6. *Discoveries.* Was the performance fresh? Did the characters make discoveries, or did the actors seem to already know what was going to happen? Did their discoveries change their behavior, add energy, help you stay engaged? See if you can describe the discoveries in a scene, or chart three or four of a character's big discoveries over the course of the play.

7. *Communication and competition.* Were the actors/characters invested in each other? Did they listen and respond to one another fully? Or did they seem like people walking around in their own little bubbles, unaffected by each other in any true sense? See if you can describe specific moments that revealed the intensity of connection between them (or the lack thereof).

8. *Importance.* Did the actors seem to know what mattered in the scene? Did they understand the characters' goals and work strongly to achieve those goals? Be specific about how you knew that. What did they *do*?

9. *Events.* Did the actors' choices help you to follow the events of the play, or did they seem to muddy the storytelling? If it got muddy, can you explain what the actors did that allowed it to fall apart? If the events seemed clearly defined, choose some specific moments that stood out, and describe how the actors helped you follow the characters' journey.

10. *Place.* Did the actors understand, believe in, and use the physical context of the play, including not only the specific confines of the set but also the larger world of the play? What did they *do* that let you know if they'd defined this world and invested themselves in it imaginatively?

11. *Game playing and role playing.* Did the actors understand the characters' specific roles and the games they played within those roles? In a production of *Hamlet,* you might see our hero playing the game of "being crazy" or the role of the lover to Ophelia. Ask yourself if the actors in the play you saw seemed to have a sense of role? Can you give a similar example to illustrate this?

12. *Mystery and secret.* Pick someone in the production and ask yourself, "Was there something indefinably interesting about this actor?" Did the actor seem to know more than he or she shared? Were you intrigued to know more? This is a difficult thing to pin down, but what did the actor *do* that caught your attention and pulled you in?

THE SCOPE OF A CAREER

In looking at an actor's career, these criteria still apply. However, other elements also come into play, including the demands of a role, the actor's flexibility or range, and your expectations of an actor based on his or her reputation and your previous experiences watching the actor.

THE DEMANDS OF THE ROLE

Roles vary widely in their demands upon the performer playing them. The title role in *Hamlet* exhausts the talents of most actors, whereas the role of Reynaldo in act 2, scene 1, of the same script makes minimal demands and offers minimal rewards; indeed, directors usually cut the role. But considerations other than length come into play. Hamlet has more lines than Othello, but experienced actors usually find Othello more difficult to perform and King Lear still more demanding.

However taxing the role, evaluators should consider how well an actor integrated his or her efforts into the entire production. That is, how good an "ensemble player" was the actor? Such roles as Hamlet, Cyrano, Oedipus, Hedda Gabler, or Medea necessarily dominate productions of those scripts but must not do so to the exclusion of all others on the stage. An overpowering star may succeed commercially, but artistically he or she is suspect. Ensemble playing is thus one factor to evaluate.

Similarly, we may examine how successful each actor is in integrating his or her choices with the world of the play. John Gielgud is famous for saying, "Style is knowing what kind of play you are in." We all connect more or less easily with certain playwrights' views of the world; actors are no exception. Some actors are, therefore, very good in emotionally demanding roles but fail miserably in comedy. Each production makes particular demands, a factor that any critic should consider in evaluating an actor's work.

FLEXIBILITY

Over the course of a career, actors play many roles. The variety of roles offers a possible index to their worth, assuming they succeed in more than a few. Meryl Streep, who has acted onstage and in film for over four decades, is a good example of an actor able to nearly disappear into her characters. She is an excellent stage actor of enormous energy

Al Pacino's long and varied career has included theatre as well as film. His spontaneity and willingness to make strong choices have served him well in both mediums. Here, Pacino plays Hughie Long in *Hughie* at the Long Wharf Theatre. *T. Charles Erikson*

and range, having received acclaim for performances in plays as varied as *The Seagull, Mother Courage and Her Children,* and *The Taming of the Shrew.* She is also equally good onstage and in film. Watch her in any three films—say, *The Devil Wears Prada, Sophie's Choice,* and *The Iron Lady.* Note the physical, vocal, rhythmic, emotional, and intellectual variety of choices, and it is clear that she is an actor of rare flexibility.

THE ACTOR'S REPUTATION

Other matters, some irrelevant, may affect the theatregoer. The actor's reputation is one of these. Only stars have this "problem." Having watched an actor succeed in earlier roles, the audience may expect the same actor to achieve brilliance in every performance. In some cases this expectation works to the actor's advantage; audiences may prove predisposed to accept and applaud an actor in a mediocre performance. Such an advantage fades rapidly, however; last year's press clippings and reviews have little effect on this year's work.

Actors, like other citizens, are sometimes quite active politically, and some audience members have taken them to task. Susan Sarandon and Sean Penn, for example, have alienated some of their fans by their political liberalism. Charlton Heston and Scott Baio have done the same with their conservatism. An actor's personal life may also add to or detract from his or her following, and this can become an important box-office consideration. That such matters color a performance may seem artistically idiotic, but life as a performer makes strange demands.

Conclusions

The future for professional actors remains somewhat grim, as supply will continue to exceed demand. However, actors remain the most direct connection audiences have to the theatre. It is therefore worth understanding what they do and how challenging it can be.

An actor is an artist. By now you should be aware that theatre can consist of far more than mere show biz, although it is an art that functions in an industry. Michael Chekhov—an actor, director, and teacher—described the qualities of the ideal theatre artist in *To the Director and Playwright*. These ideals certainly apply to actors. Ideally, to be a theatre artist, one should:

1. Have the ability to open oneself to something higher than most people are capable of envisioning
2. Have the capacity to see and feel things, psychologically as well as physically, that are normally hidden to others
3. Develop the ability to express what is thus revealed to oneself
4. Have an individual way of interpreting what one sees and feels
5. Be able to find one's own original *form* to express one's thoughts and state them so that the largest number of people will understand
6. Be an emblem of one's higher self, a guiding light and clarion voice to humanity's blind, inarticulate search for the meaning and mission of life
7. Primarily be a creator and an innovator in word and deed—and with them

Key Terms

Actors' Equity Association (www.actorsequity.com) Founded in 1912, this organization serves as a union for professional actors, determining minimal contracts, rehearsal conditions, and so on.

Actors Studio (www.actors-studio.com) Founded in 1947, this actors' training institution bases much of its work on the Stanislavsky system as modified by the late Lee Strasberg.

backstage.com and *Back Stage* **magazine** An actor's lifeline to casting and current happenings in the New York City theatre business.

beat The smallest unit of a dramatic action, often marked by the entrance or exit of a character, a new approach to a goal by a character, or the seizing of initiative by a character.

blocking A term referring to the overall traffic patterns of actors on a stage: entrances, exits, movements, and so on. *See also* business.

Booth, Edwin (1833–1893) Considered by many theatre historians as the finest actor ever born in the United States. See Eleanor Ruggles's *Prince of Players* for his biography.

business All stage movement and action. As more commonly used, the term refers to smaller actions, such as lighting a cigarette, reading a book, or drawing a weapon.

cue A signal for a technician or an actor. An actor's cue to enter the stage setting, for example, is often a line from another actor; the cue for a lighting technician to adjust stage lighting may be an actor's touching a light switch.

Dench, Dame Judith (b. 1934) One of the few actors to excel onstage, in television, and in film. Her popularity grows with age.

Diderot, Denis (1713–1784) French man of letters whose contributions to the theatre include several plays of the *drame larmoyant* ("tearful drama") type. His essay "*Paradoxe sur le comédien*," which addressed the degree to which an actor should feel actual emotion while performing, is still relevant today.

Esper, William Famed New York acting teacher. His William Esper studio is probably the best-known place to study the Meisner technique. *See also* Sanford Meisner.

Garrick, David (1717–1779) One of England's greatest actors, responsible for many reforms on the London stage and changes in acting styles. In 1769, he held a Shakespeare Jubilee in Stratford-upon-Avon that increased interest in Shakespeare's works.

Gillette, William (1885–1937) American actor and dramatist, whose greatest successes were in his role as Sherlock Holmes and his own Civil War spy dramas, *Held by the Enemy* and *Secret Service.*

HB Studio (www.hbstudio.org) One of the more highly regarded actor training schools, founded in 1946 by Herbert Berghof. Berghof was joined by his wife, the highly successful actress Uta Hagen, the following year.

Irving, Sir Henry (1828–1906) The outstanding English actor/manager at the turn of the twentieth century, highly regarded in several Shakespearean roles. Irving was the first English actor to be knighted.

Kean, Edmund (ca. 1787–1833) An outstanding English actor whose debut in London in 1814 marked the beginning of Romantic acting on the British stage. His flamboyant acting reflected his tempestuous life.

Lane, Nathan (b. 1956) Lane's performances in musical theatre and nonmusical theatre in New York City have always landed him top praise from critics and fans.

McKellan, Sir Ian (b. 1939) One of the greatest actors of our time. McKellan came up through the ranks of the Royal Shakespeare Company. He's best known to Americans for his roles in the *Lord of the Rings* films.

Meisner, Sanford (1905–1997) Brooklyn-born "Sandy" Meisner was a member of the Group Theatre. He developed his own approach to Stanislavsky's work, in which he emphasized "the reality of doing."

Olivier, Sir Laurence (1907–1989) English actor, director, and producer, knighted in 1947 and in 1970 created a baron, the first actor to receive this honor.

Siddons, Mrs. Sarah (1755–1831) Widely considered the greatest tragic actress of the English stage. Her most successful role was Lady Macbeth. Her brother, John Philip Kemble, was also a leading performer of the time.

Smith, Dame Maggie (b. 1934) One of the greatest living stage actors today. Recognizable for her role in the Harry Potter films.

Strasberg, Lee (1901–1982) American actor, director, and teacher. One of the founders of the influential Group Theatre, later a leader of the Actors Studio, and a major if controversial influence on American acting.

Streep, Meryl (b. 1949) Considered by many to be the greatest living actress, she is known best for her film work, but she began in the theatre and continues to perform there from time to time.

subtext A term associated with Stanislavsky's and Strasberg's approaches to acting, referring to the line of internal thought that an actor discovers in analyzing and delivering his or her lines and actions.

Discussion Questions

1. Who are some actors you like? Why do you think they are good actors?
2. What constitutes acting "talent"?
3. What are the rewards and hazards of being an actor?
4. What is character analysis, and why do you suppose such a thing is worthwhile?
5. Who was Stanislavsky, and what were some of his goals with regard to acting?
6. What is the difference between Stanislavsky's "system" and the method?
7. What is the "illusion of the first time," and why is it a useful idea?
8. Playwrights, designers, and directors are often called "artists" of one sort or another, yet in the United States, actors are often considered "personalities" rather than artists. What is the difference between a personality and an artist when it comes to acting? Is training the only difference?
9. Which, if any, of the facts about acting (what it entails, what percentage of actors work, and so on) surprised you?

Suggested Readings

ACTING THEORY

Aitken, Maria. *Style: Acting in High Comedy*. New York: Applause, 1996. This conversational book on the particulars of acting in high comedy is an excellent introduction to acting in general. Aitken, an accomplished comic actor herself, is lucid, writes well, and offers real-life insights into the challenge of comedy. The Applause Acting Series is, in general, accessible and practical.

Alberts, David. *The Expressive Body: Physical Characterization for the Actor*. Portsmouth, NH: Heinemann, 1997. First-rate actor training always includes some treatment of the physical life of the character. This is a straightforward, readable introduction to actors' physical concerns. Excellent exercises and good organization make this an especially fine book on actor movement.

Barton, John. *Playing Shakespeare*. London: Methuen, 1984. An advanced treatment of acting Shakespeare by the associate director of the Royal Shakespeare Company, an exceptional director.

Benedetti, Robert. *The Actor at Work*. 10th ed. Boston: Allyn & Bacon, 2008. A lucid approach to the basics from a fine directing teacher. Other Benedetti books are also available.

Berry, Cicely. *The Actor and His Text*. New York: Macmillan, 1987. Berry uses Shakespearean verse as a jumping-off point for examining vocal production and actors' use of language to communicate what is in their minds and imaginations. Unifying the need for vocal freedom and for precision, Berry is one of the best teachers writing on voice today. Her *Voice and the Actor* is also a standard text.

Caine, Michael. *Acting on Film: An Actor's Take on Movie Making*. New York: Applause, 1990. Although restricted to film acting, this is a fascinating and informative examination of actors at work. A companion videotape is available and recommended.

Callow, Simon. *Acting in Restoration Comedy*. New York: Applause, 1991. Based on televised master classes in Restoration comedy, this book offers considerable insight into all acting assignments.

———. *Being an Actor*. London: Methuen, 1984. A brilliantly honest assessment of the profession on the modern stage from a British viewpoint. Highly recommended.

Chekhov, Michael. *To the Actor: On the Technique of Acting*. New York: Harper & Row, 1953. Written by the nephew of the great Russian playwright Anton Chekhov, this volume, although somewhat advanced for the beginning student, clearly delineates some of the more mystical and psychological aspects of acting.

Cohen, Robert. *Acting One/Acting Two*. 5th ed. New York: McGraw-Hill, 2007. One of the best introductions to the techniques of acting; a standard in many educational and training programs. Cohen's *Acting Power* and *Acting Professionally* are also recommended reading.

Cole, Toby, and Helen Krich Chinoy, eds. *Actors on Acting: The Theories, Techniques, and Practices of the Great Actors of All Times as Told in Their Own Words*. 4th ed. New York: Three Rivers Press, 1995. A key work in any study of acting theory and practice, this volume selects from the pivotal works on the subject from Plato in ancient Athens to Joseph Chaikin of the Open Theatre. The meticulous scholarship by the coeditors concludes with an outstanding bibliography.

Goldman, Michael. *The Actor's Freedom: Toward a Theory of Drama*. New York: Viking Press, 1975. One of the more exciting publications on this subject, in which the author examines the actor in performance with perception and lucidity.

Hagen, Uta, with Haskel Frankel. *Respect for Acting*. New York: Macmillan, 1973. A book widely admired by actors at all levels of development, written by an outstanding actress and teacher. Highly recommended.

Harris, Julie, with Barry Tarshis. *Julie Harris Talks to Young Actors*. New York: Lothrop, Lee, & Shepard, 1971. Harris has achieved the highest pinnacles of theatrical success; in this volume, she recalls her early frustrations and imparts to the would-be performer the enormous benefits of her experience. This book is a must for anyone considering a theatrical career.

Shurtleff, Michael. *Audition: Everything an Actor Needs to Know to Get the Part*. New York: Walker, 1978. A classic in actor training from the Broadway casting director of *The Sound of Music*, *Gypsy*, and *Jesus Christ Superstar*.

Stanislavsky, Konstantin. *An Actor's Work*. Trans. Jean Benedetti. New York: Routledge, 2008. A contemporary translation of Stanislavsky's *An Actor Prepares* and *Building a Character*. Widely regarded as much clearer, more faithful translations of Stanislavsky's ideas than those previously available. A must-read for any serious student of acting.

Tucker, Patrick. *Secrets of Screen Acting*. 2nd ed. New York: Routledge, 2003. One of the best discussions of the differences and similarities in film and stage acting.

ACTOR BIOGRAPHIES

Archer, Stephen M. *American Actors and Actresses: A Guide to Information Sources*. Detroit: Gale Research, 1982. An annotated bibliography of books and magazine articles about American performers, cross-indexed.

———. *Junius Brutus Booth: Theatrical Prometheus*. Carbondale: Southern Illinois University Press, 1992. A thorough glimpse at early American theatre though the lens of the famous Booth family.

Leach, Joseph. *Bright Particular Star: The Life and Times of Charlotte Cushman*. New Haven, CT: Yale University Press, 1970. Cushman was the first American actress to achieve an international reputation for excellence. Leach did immense amounts of research in the preparation of this excellent volume.

Moody, Richard. *Edwin Forrest: First Star of the American Stage*. New York: Knopf, 1960. In chronicling Forrest's life, Moody set a standard of scholarship and writing that has seldom been equaled.

Prideaux, Tom. *Love or Nothing: The Life and Times of Ellen Terry*. New York: Scribner, 1975. Ellen Terry was England's most popular actress at the turn of the twentieth century. Tom Prideaux, for decades theatre editor and critic for *Life* magazine, has written an outstanding evocation not only of Terry but also of daily life in the theatre in England at that time.

Ruggles, Eleanor. *Prince of Players: Edwin Booth*. New York: Norton, 1953. Edwin Booth is considered by many to have been America's greatest actor. Ruggles captured the spirit of this tortured artist in one of the outstanding theatrical biographies of all time. Although the volume is out of print, it is easily found in libraries and used bookstores, as it was a popular Book-of-the-Month-Club selection.

Part III

THE DESIGNERS

Skilled designers and technicians contribute richly to the success of a production. In modern theatre the design and execution of scenery, lighting, costumes, properties, makeup, projections, and sound have grown into fully developed professions and specialties. Examination of each can expand the theatregoer's understanding and appreciation of the various designers' contributions. First, however, we should take a look at issues of collaboration, the design process, and the goals of theatrical design.

Collaboration

As noted in chapter 5, designers work closely with the director. They must share a mutual vision of the production, ideally from their first meeting through the opening performance. Their relationship is not based on mere courtesy; the designer's arrangement of scenic elements will program the actors into specific patterns of movement; the costume, hair, and makeup designer's choices will affect how audiences perceive a character and—in some cases—how the actors can and cannot behave; lighting and sound designers profoundly affect rhythm, mood, and more. Directors and designers should, therefore, confer until they agree on the basic interpretations of a script. Their conscious decisions should then permeate all elements of the production, from casting to selection of costumes and properties. If the staff disagrees on such points, the final production runs a considerable risk of being an uneasy compromise. Certainly it will lack unity and coherence.

Similarly, if separate designers create the scenery and lighting plans, only close coordination can achieve unity. The color filters, or gels, used on lights can substantially enhance or destroy scenic and costume designers' color schemes. The costume designer must also coordinate color, line, and period with the other designers, as must the personnel in charge of furniture and other properties. Lighting and sound designers (as well as projection designers, when applicable) should also confer because they are so time oriented and so often coordinated with each other. That is, sound and light cues very frequently get "called" at the same time.

Looking Glass Alice at the McCarter Theatre, Princeton, New Jersey. *T. Charles Erikson*

In the end, the director must arbitrate any conflicts and make the final decisions. Though a director's vision may place definite limits on the designer's creation, within those boundaries the designer finds enormous creative opportunity. Designers and directors who work well together will ask questions, challenge assumptions, share ideas, and come up with insights that lead to a product better than either could have achieved without the other.

The Design Process

Theatrical designers work for years creating a process that yields the best results during performance. Though the design process may differ from artist to artist and production to production, most designers agree there are a number of distinct phases. J. Michael Gillette describes seven steps in the design process:

1. Engagement
2. Analysis
3. Research
4. Incubation
5. Selection
6. Implementation
7. Evaluation

As you work your way through these, you might think about one of the plays you have read or seen this semester and try to imagine the details of creating the design for it.

1. *Engagement.* The designer is approached with the possibility of engaging the project. A host of issues play out in the final decision, but the main influences on this decision tend to be both financial and artistic. If the designer decides to accept the challenge of the position, that designer must commit all energies to the project.
2. *Analysis.* The designer examines the text for information on the world of the play. Production style, concept, and thematic concerns also come into play as the designer evaluates what will be useful to the decisions that must be made.
3. *Research.* Research is important in order to create a complex and living stage production. This step in the process usually involves much reading and many trips to libraries, archives, and museums, along with research on the Internet. Even when designing for a contemporary play, research will help designers to discover the multiplicity of options available.
4. *Incubation.* After the designer has worked intensely on collecting materials, a cool-down period is helpful. This period allows the designer to gain some distance on the design in order to see its shortcomings and its strengths.
5. *Selection*: Here the designer must decide what is appropriate for the production and what should be edited out. The director will often enter this process with the designer to help solidify choices to fit the production's conceptual framework. Sound designers are collecting music to listen to during this period. Projection designers

are finding images. Lighting looks are discussed. Thumbnail sketches of costumes and scenery, pulled costumes, and props can all be a part of this stage as the design is being pinned down.

6. *Implementation*. Models, plots, sketches, and all other types of paperwork are finished during this step, and the design is built. This means not only building sets but also costumes, props, lighting, sound, and (if used) projections. For projection and sound designers, this is when the projections and sounds are created and edited. Lights are hung and focused; colors are chosen. Speakers are placed and cabled. "Implementation" usually takes weeks or months, not days. Adjustments are made during this process as unforeseen problems and insights arise.

7. *Evaluation*. Though evaluation is a major component of each previous step, a final period of evaluation is beneficial to any designer's growth as an artist. While immersed in the project, a choice might seem appropriate. However, once the designer has gained emotional and intellectual distance, it may appear awkward or uncommunicative. As Gillette observes, back-patting is not the main goal of the final evaluation. The designer should critically evaluate the methods and materials used during the process, as well as the end product.

These seven steps can be used by all of the different production designers, but the process is not completely linear. The designer continually looks back at the previous steps to check progress and maintain the integrity of the overall production concept.

The Goals of Theatrical Design

All theatrical designers work toward similar goals:

1. Definition of the world of the play (time, place, economics, etc.)
2. Evocation of mood (atmosphere, feeling)
3. Reinforcement of style
4. Support and amplification of the dramatic action
5. Focus of audience attention

Despite these similarities, there are considerable differences (a) in the materials with which designers work and (b) on which aspect of the production they focus. Lighting designers, for instance, have a particularly strong relationship with the theatrical event in time—with helping to define rhythmic elements, pacing, and shifting focus. Costume designers are most involved with expressing character and character relationships within a certain set of circumstances. Certainly both kinds of designers do their work with the goals listed here, but they do so in different ways.

Many people execute the work of the designers, all in the service of a well-made and seamlessly executed production. We have mentioned the importance of the stage manager (or SM) in chapter 5, but during the run of the show, the SM is in charge of all cues going smoothly, of reporting needed repairs, and (among many other things) acting as a liaison between the director and everyone else on the team—and there are typically a lot of people backstage on that team. We will therefore spend some time discussing the people who make it all happen (pay especially close attention to the sidebars):

- Tactile designs, chapter 7: "Scenic, Prop, and Costume Designers" (and in the sidebars, technical directors, drapers and stitchers, hair and makeup artists, carpenters, and IATSE—the International Alliance of Stage Employees)
- Temporal designs, chapter 8: "Lighting, Sound, and Projections" (and in the sidebars, information about lighting and sound technology)

Scenic, Prop, and Costume Designers

Stage designing should be addressed to the eye of the mind.

—Robert Edmond Jones (1887–1954)

According to an old theatrical legend, a small, second-rate theatrical company once toured Ireland with a production of Christopher Marlowe's *The Tragical History of Doctor Faustus*. The script involves a medieval scholar who sells his soul to Satan for twenty-four years of power and earthly delights. In the last scene, time has run out for Faustus, and the jaws of Hell gape open before him. In a small town one evening, the play limped to its conclusion as the actor playing Faustus thundered through his last speech:

Ah, Faustus,
Now hast thou but one bare hour to live, And then must be damned perpetually!

And so on to the closing lines:

My God, my God, look not so fierce on me! Adders and serpents, let me breathe awhile!
Ugly hell, gape not! Come not, Lucifer!
I'll burn my books! Ah, Mephistophilis!

During the last four lines, Faustus started to sink below the stage floor, by means of an elevator-like trap, into red lights suggesting Hell. Unfortunately the trap stuck about three feet down, leaving Faustus's upper torso above stage level with no place to hide. The audience greeted this development with stunned silence; then a beery voice from the top balcony roared out, "Hallelujah, boys, Hell's full!"

Anyone working in the theatre will amass a storehouse of such anecdotes about stage doors not opening, mustaches dropping off, costumes splitting, scenery collapsing, curtains refusing to open or close, lighting or sound effects coming at the wrong time or not at all, properties missing, and the like. These moments may offer great hilarity in retrospect, but they seldom amuse those involved. The cast sees hundreds of hours of work sullied, and audiences feel uncomfortable as the company loses control of its production. Everyone anticipates a certain number of accidents during rehearsals, when the people responsible can remedy them, but the live theatre allows for no outtakes.

Such accidents underline the importance of designers and technicians in modern productions. However, designers' work goes far beyond simply avoiding mistakes. Each element in a well-executed production is designed, intentional, and geared toward creating a coherent environment, or "world of the play." Scenic, props, and costume design are the most tangible of the design elements, and we begin with them.

Scenic Design

The scenic designer's work produces effects both massive and subtle. If we regard scenery in its widest sense—as those visual elements that define the space in which the theatrical event takes place—the following purposes commonly apply to most production situations.

THE PURPOSES OF SCENIC DESIGN

1. Definition of space
2. Reinforcement of style and evocation of mood
3. Focus of attention
4. Amplification of the theatrical event

1. Definition of Space

The scenic design, or set, often delineates some specific locale in which the action of the play occurs. Many plays take place in living rooms, for example, but playwrights have set their scripts almost everywhere: a bank of clouds in heaven, Golgotha, Delphi, Cleopatra's throne room, bars, brothels, bedrooms, Graceland, back alleys, meadows, Mars, or Hell. Even scenic designers who do not attempt to delineate such locales in a naturalistic way must evoke an awareness of the site's essential nature if they wish to depict them scenically.

The scenic designer must usually define the space in which the actors perform. In an arena production with the audience surrounding the action, the designer ordinarily uses very little traditional scenery, and thus the floor, hanging elements, and other minimal pieces take on even greater importance than in a proscenium configuration. In some cases the designer will use no scenery at all; if the production takes place in some "found" space, as some experimental productions have, traditional scenery would seem superfluous. Nevertheless, someone selects the space for production, and that selection determines much of the production's eventual form.

An imaginative designer can throw away clichéd ideas and reimagine what even the most well-known play looks like. Here, the space for *Romeo and Juliet* is transformed into a beautiful (and climbable) wall of flowers, with a simple opening as Juliet's balcony, giving us a design that is fresh, young, and modern. Direction and scenic design by Darko Tresnjak. Hartford Stage, 2016. *T. Charles Erikson*

2. Reinforcement of Style and Evocation of Mood

The space designed for a production should be visually appropriate to the events contained within it. In the simplest cases—living rooms—the characters' nature and circumstances and the audience response sought by the designer determine the room's specific characteristics. For example, *Who's Afraid of Virginia Woolf?*, a savage critique of marriage and society, requires a very different type of living room than *Hay Fever,* a comic romp, or *The Glass Menagerie,* Tennessee Williams's heartbreaking script about leaving home. The space in which an event happens should visually reinforce that event. Otherwise, designers might construct a single living-room set for all such plays, saving considerable money and effort.

Designers seek to achieve these necessary distinctions and thus the appropriate audience response by using the traditional elements of visual art: color, line, texture, mass, and space.

- *Color.* Designers rarely conceive of *Hamlet, Oedipus Rex,* or *Death of a Salesman* in pastel pinks and greens; other color choices seem more appropriate to those scripts, although pink and green might serve admirably for a Restoration comedy or Oscar Wilde's *The Importance of Being Earnest.* Color psychology constitutes an important tool of the designer.
- *Line.* Likewise, variations of line can support a production's central concept. Traditionally, crossed lines imply conflict (basic to almost every script, if not always central); circles and quick curves support comedy (polka-dot clown costumes, for example); long, slow curves tend to suggest the sensuous lines of the human body; and tall verticals lead the eye toward the heavens, as exemplified by a Gothic arch.
- *Texture.* For example, rough- or smooth-looking forms.
- *Mass.* Big, bulky, heavy set pieces vs. light, wispy ones, for instance, make different statements to the audience.
- *Space.* Volume, shape, and the closed or open feel of the set.

Use of these elements can have an emotional impact upon us, usually below the level of awareness. They can also reinforce style, support the definition of mood, and thus help create a coherent, communicative, and enjoyable production.

3. Focus of Attention

By the very definition and selection of the playing space, the designer focuses the audience's attention on that space. Selective lighting, described in the next chapter, further leads the audience to concentrate its attention upon a specified area. But within the defined space, the designer, by the arrangement of elements, can give subspaces visual priority, especially in proscenium or three-quarter staging. The director often uses down center (the area of the stage closest to the audience and in the middle of the stage) for a play's most important scenes, those which he or she wishes to have the most impact. A designer often tries to assist by leaving this area uncluttered or by grouping furniture in such a way as to allow the director to emphasize specific actors and scenes. The director and designers must obviously coordinate their efforts.

Simple solutions that reinforce each other can tell us where we are and how it feels. Winter clothes, "snow" on the ground, and cool light here combine in John Friedenberg's production of *Almost Maine* to create a cold winter night. *Courtesy of Wake Forest University Theatre. Photo by Bill Ray*

4. Amplification of the Theatrical Event

By defining space, evoking mood, and focusing attention, the scenic designer intensifies your understanding of—and emotional response to—the theatrical event. We should therefore evaluate the scenery's contributions in these terms. Good scenery for one production might well appear absurd for another, even another production of the same script. Scenery's value emerges only as it contributes to a production's total concept and execution.

The Scenic Designer's Alternatives and Restrictions

As mentioned in the introduction to part 3, the scenic designer must have a close relationship with the director. Designer and author Darwin Payne has called the scenic designer "the first director," since the designer may arrange for potential traffic patterns that the director has overlooked or ignored. In the negative a designer may restrict potential patterns that the director had hoped to use. For a production of *Hamlet*, the director and design staff must decide early whether the script depicts a weak-willed and vacillating young prince thrust into a situation he cannot handle or whether it is the tale of a man of action who only seeks to confirm his suspicions before he sweeps to his revenge. Consider how one might design a set differently with those competing

Design and acting ideally work hand in hand, as in this production of *Ghosts of Versailles*, 2009. Opera Theatre of St. Louis. Projections by Wendall Harrington, sets by Allen Moyer, costumes by James Schuette. Directed by James Robinson. *Courtesy of Wendall Harrington*

concepts. As you will see, concept is not an intellectual choice removed from practical choices but something that leads to specific decisions that affect what actors and directors can do and ultimately what an audience experiences.

Modern scenic designers face almost unlimited options when confronted by the current varieties of design styles, script demands, and directorial visions. Theorists and critics have again categorized the various approaches. As with the other elements, these categories merely attempt to describe; they cannot cover all possibilities or options. Nevertheless, we can illuminate some of the major options for the scenic designer.

Representationalism versus presentationalism, as in the case of the playwright, offers a point of departure. The designer first decides whether the setting should be immediately recognizable to the audience by way of offering the illusion of an actual place. The scenery may be completely nonrepresentational or merely suggestive. Few designers attempt complete realism, finding it neither desirable nor feasible. After all, audiences suspend their disbelief about what they see onstage; they do not imagine they actually look into someone's living room during a production. Designers may work in various styles, such as selective realism, expressionism, surrealism, and so on, but usually their work falls along a spectrum between the realistic and the abstract.

A representational set need not be an interior. Here, Jeffrey Hatcher's *Smash* asks for the lawn of a girls' school in England, and Mary Wayne Thomas delivers this charming space. *Courtesy of Wake Forest University Theatre. Photo by Bill Ray*

TYPES OF STAGES

The kind of theatre in which you design a play makes a bigger difference than one might expect. Stage equipment such as elevators; trapdoors, or "traps"; flying equipment; lighting positions; doorways; and the like often determine whether a particular design can function on a specific stage. The size of the house (where the audience sits), the size of the cast, the acoustic demands (whether it is a musical with mics or an intimate two-person drama), the requirements of the play, and much more influence design choices and whether they can work in a given space. Designers must check sight lines from the auditorium to ensure that patrons cannot see into the backstage area but can see all of the acting area. No matter what sort of configuration the theatre has, the designer must consider such matters as storage, especially if a production requires more than one setting. Not all theatres are created equal, and therein lies the challenge. Plays may be done anywhere, but here we consider the configuration of theatres specifically designed for that purpose: proscenium, thrust, arena, and flexible spaces.

Proscenium Staging

Since the Renaissance, the proscenium stage has emerged as the most common form of theatre architecture. This "picture-frame" staging originated in Italy during the Renaissance—specifically, with the Teatro Farnese in Parma, Italy, built in 1618—when

Rob Eastman-Mullins's model for *Twelve Angry Men* (top) and the realized design for *Twelve Angry Men* in production (bottom). *Courtesy of Rob Eastman-Mullins*

architects, graphic artists, and theatrical designers grew fascinated with perspective. The proscenium configuration facilitates scenic displays: behind the curtain of a well-equipped theatre, technicians can shift enormous amounts of scenery on and off the stage, dazzling the audience with spectacular effects. The disadvantage lies in the relatively small proportion of the audience who can sit near the stage and the subsequent dilution of a production's impact for those farther away. In addition, the presence of the architectural frame sometimes inhibits interaction between the performer and the audience. The proscenium configuration most resembles film; the presentation occurs visually within a rectangular frame.

Thrust Staging

Modern theatre artists often prefer the thrust, or three-quarter, stage. The upstage wall still offers considerable scenic potential, and because the seating arrangement extends to 180 degrees or more around the sides of the acting area, large audiences can be close to the action. In fact, the two greatest periods of dramatic production, those of fifth-century-BCE Athens and Elizabethan England, used approximately the same arrangements, although audience capacities varied considerably. Thrust staging leads to some problems in blocking; audiences may have to look at an actor's back more often than in proscenium staging, but directors have found ways to minimize this potential difficulty.

Arena Staging

The arena configuration, or theatre-in-the-round, obviously puts more people closer to the playing area than any other arrangement, since the audience surrounds the players. (Modern sporting arenas usually employ this arrangement.) Unfortunately, however, some actors always have their backs to some part of the audience. Moreover, designers can offer only the most minimal scenic support to the action. For these reasons arena staging has seemed more appropriate to plays not especially reliant upon depiction of locale. An arena usually offers the cheapest form of staging and the simplest means of converting an open space into a theatrical space. These factors present advantages to companies lacking a permanent theatre.

Flexible Staging

Flexible staging (also known as a black box because it's usually a large room painted black to create a "void") allows the director and designers to choose whatever configuration they consider most appropriate to the script they are producing. Because of logistics and cost, such theatres usually have relatively small seating capacities.

Flexible staging makes it possible to redefine the arrangement of audience and performing area for each production. Theatres designed for flexibility often employ banks of seats that technicians can arrange into different patterns for different productions. Chicago's Lookingglass Theatre is particularly adept at reconfiguring their space to accommodate stylistic choices that involve pools of water, flying, circus-inspired movement, and even traditional realistic staging.

Sometimes the simplest things are all you need. Here, scenic designer John McDermott requires only a set of lockers and a bench to suggest a locker room. *Dryland,* **directed by Adrienne Campbell-Holt for Colt Coeur. Costumes by Ashley Rose Horton, lighting by Grant Yeager, and sound by Amy Altadonna.** *Courtesy of Adrienne Campbell-Holt*

Designers work with budgets; materials and labor make up much of their concern. Lack of funds may eliminate desirable but expensive materials or techniques. A professional show may have millions of dollars available; educational or community theatre productions may have only a few thousand or even a few hundred dollars to spend. Low budgets test a designer's imagination, taste, and craft.

Staff and facilities also complicate what can be done, not only in scenic design, but in all the other design areas as well. What can the people who are building the show reasonably do? Professionals' skills are, one assumes, more developed than those of students or community volunteers. Likewise, what tool, material, and space constraints does the designer face? If one wants to build a twenty-foot steel tower, a welding shop—or at least space for welding—as well as space adequate to house and move the tower will be necessary.

Within the restrictions of style, directorial vision, architecture, facilities, staffing, and budget, then, the designer sets out to create an environment for an action, the housing of an event, and a visual contribution to that event. Depending on the context in which they work, they may also have a hand in building and painting the set. Often, though, they hand their designs to a technical director (TD; see following sidebar).

The Technical Director, the Scenic Staff, and IATSI

Theatre involves physical labor, never more so than in the creation of scenery. The technical director (TD) oversees both the construction of the scenic designs and the people who build and finish them.

Scenic designers generally provide the TD with drawings of each piece of scenery, and then the TD figures out how to make these drawings work, drafting each piece of scenery for the construction crew to use. With these drawings in hand (and wood, fabric, Styrofoam, plastics, paint, and considerable skill), carpenters, welders, and painters (called "charge artists") execute the designs, most of which contain some version of these basic scenic elements:

- Flats, which are used to represent walls. These are typically made out of canvas over wood or metal.
- Platforms and wagons, which create levels and may allow scenic elements to be easily transported

Once these and other structures are built, charge artists are given paint elevations, small, to-scale painted renderings, which they then translate into full-sized painted pieces.

Traditionally, men have dominated the scene shop, since carpentry and welding have traditionally been seen as men's jobs. This has meant that the International Alliance of Theatrical Stage Employees (IATSI) has traditionally been inhospitable to women. In fact, IATSI was, for many years, a union that was dominated by father-son nepotism. Of the over three thousand members of IATSI Local One, under two hundred are women, according to sister committee chair and sound engineer Eileen MacDonald, who adds that even this is much better than it was a decade ago.

Still, some progress is being made through the union's apprenticeship program. More minorities are a part of the union than ever before, and women are joining in increasing numbers, especially as sound and lighting technicians.

IATSI, which has sometimes been vilified as too expensive and taxing to theatres' financial stability, strongly asserts its value. Former general manager of the Metropolitan Opera Joseph Volpe has said, "The case must be made that skilled labor not only has value but is essential to the successful presentation of stage productions." It would be easy to overlook the hard physical labor that making stage productions requires—and in fact this work is designed to be invisible. However, if we don't blink at the idea that investors for *Hamilton* will pull in over $13 million a year, to question the pay of the people behind the scenes may reveal, more than anything else, our cultural biases about what physical labor is worth.

Requisites for Excellence in Scenic Design

Like other theatre artists, the scenic designer profits from wide theatrical experience and familiarity with all aspects of production. Experience in acting and directing offers especially valuable insights because actors and directors must use the designer's settings. Personal experience with the problems of traffic patterns, movement potential, furniture arrangements, the deployment of crowds onstage, and similar concerns usually increases the designer's understanding of these matters.

The ability to envision a production by reading the script constitutes a major requirement for successful designers, as well as for directors. This ability stems from wide theatrical experience, from both seeing and staging many productions. It is tempting to think that set designers simply pick out furniture and paint colors, but the truth is that analysis and experience are as important for designers as they are for anyone else. The beginning reader of scripts often suffers great frustration in this regard, but designers learn to read a play with their imaginations open, translating what they imagine into both practical and aesthetic terms to create appropriate scenery.

The successful designer develops a sense of visual beauty involving harmony, proportion, color, mass, texture, line, and so on, comparable to that of the easel painter or the sculptor but employed for the unique demands of stage design. Unlike a solitary artist, the designer must always remember the communal and pragmatic restrictions imposed by the theatre. Somewhat like an architect, the designer must also be familiar with the load-bearing capacities of the various materials used, lest the scenery collapse under its own weight. And, like any builder, the designer should have a considerable curiosity about new methods and better materials.

Above all, scenic designers must willingly fit their work to the needs of the entire production. Although they must serve as their own most severe critics and must insist on excellence in their own work, they must also understand that scenic design functions only in conjunction with the other theatrical elements.

Thus training for a career in scenic design properly begins with a wide theatrical background. Designers also profit from work in the graphic arts and sculpture, which often contributes valuable craftsmanship and techniques. Working drawings and blueprints demand drafting ability, though the advent of computer-aided design (CAD) has put such skills within the reach of anyone willing to pay for and learn the software.

Designers also need research ability to ferret out information necessary for specific settings. For example, not many plays take place on or near bridges, but designers who work on such shows as *A View from the Bridge*, *Luv*, or *Winterset* will surely find some knowledge of bridge construction mandatory. Exterior scenes also demand awareness of appropriate vegetation for a given place and time. Such plays as *Oedipus Rex* and other Greek and Roman scripts may lead the designer to a study of classical architecture. Classes are taught in architecture and décor, but scenic designers' education in such matters can be lifelong.

The Contemporary Situation for the Scenic Designer

In the commercial theatre, designers hold membership in the United Scenic Artists (USA), which has offices in most major cities. Its membership includes scenic designers, scenic artists, costume designers, lighting designers, and others. The union's jurisdiction includes legitimate theatre, motion pictures, and television.

The functions of the USA include establishing fees for union designers, negotiating with employers to secure the best possible wages and fringe benefits, and represent-

Set construction takes many hours and people to get the job done. Students working on a set may learn beginning (and sometimes advanced) carpentry skills and even welding and electrical wiring. *Courtesy of Cynthia M. Gendrich*

ing union designers to obtain additional benefits. Designers obtain membership in the USA by passing a rigorous examination. Usually, depending upon the specific classification of membership, a prospective member completes a home project (much like a take-home examination) demonstrating his or her knowledge and skill. The written examination that constitutes the second part of the application may cover designing, sketching, lighting, drafting, geometry, mathematics, the history of art and drama, or scenic painting. Although many applicants fail the examination on the first attempt, they may retake it as often as they wish, and an applicant may serve as an apprentice member while gaining the necessary experience. Once the candidate has passed the examination, the designer becomes a union member and is available for professional work, and as a union member, the designer enjoys professional acceptance. For these reasons, the union has substantial initiation fees.

In the commercial theatre, designers are sometimes paid quite well. When producers and designers negotiate salary, they consider theatre seating capacity (and therefore potential income) on a sliding scale, along with the required number of settings, the number of costumes, the number of scenes, and the proposed length of the show's run. Although some observers of the modern theatre suggest that unionization has inflated production costs excessively, others point out that most of the time commercial theatre artists don't work at all (remember the statistics for actors), and therefore they must receive substantial payment to survive, let alone prosper. Another argument grows out of the relative percentage of a total production budget going to performers, directors, and designers as opposed to the money allotted to rent, stagehands, publicity, and similar expenses. Although exact figures vary from production to production, a theatre artist going from educational or community theatre into the commercial theatre will experience utter shock at the difference in budgets. For instance, the musical *Wicked* initially cost over $14 million to stage, while the budget for a small college theatre production might be as little as $1,400. Personnel and space are, in the latter instance, not included in the budget—and these are, admittedly, not small things. The range in costs is, nevertheless, striking.

Employment circumstances for designers in the educational theatre vary considerably, as one would expect. In small high schools, one person may well supervise all theatre activity, as well as have other, nontheatrical duties. Under such circumstances, the director-designer makes up the entire staff and supervises all elements of production. One person, no matter how talented or motivated, can rarely achieve excellence while spreading his or her efforts so widely. The same situation exists in some small colleges; unfortunately, the one-person department remains much in evidence, and miraculously some have produced excellent work.

Many junior colleges, some high schools, and most colleges hire a separate TD. This person may serve simultaneously as construction supervisor and designer and may also teach courses in technical theatre. Such an arrangement is obviously better than the one-person department, but if the technical director must also supervise stage lighting, sound, and costumes, the demands quickly become excessive.

Larger departments often hire multiple design specialists to facilitate delegation of responsibilities more equitably. One or more scenic designers; a technical director with assistants for various areas; and separate costume, lighting, sound, and projection designers constitute a nearly ideal deployment of personnel. Such an arrangement can foster the best work being done in educational theatre today, assuming, as always, that the operation has sufficient talent, motivation, expertise, and an adequate budget.

Salary ranges in education vary with academic degree, training, professional rank, experience, geographic location, and administrative attitudes. A beginning high school teacher might get only about $40,000 a year; a full professor at a major university might receive three times as much. Educational designers often affiliate with the Association for Theatre in Higher Education (ATHE), but they may also join an organization specifically for theatre technicians—the United States Institute of Theatre Technology (USITT)—which convenes annually and publishes a highly regarded journal.

Creative Procedures for the Scenic Designer

Like other professionals, designers work in many individual ways, but the following is a normal sequence.

1. Script analysis
2. Rough sketches
3. Floor plans and side elevatrions
4. Perspective drawings and models

5. Blueprints and working drawings
6. Erecting and striking the scenery

1. SCRIPT ANALYSIS

Designers read a script many times, first to gain a general impression and to start their creative imaginations working. They also read the script to determine the practical demands it makes: whether the scenery should indicate an interior or an exterior, the number of entrances desired, and a wealth of other details.

Having examined the script, the designer meets with the director to discuss its specific requirements, the production style, the budget, and all other relevant matters. At this point the designer may make a substantial impact on the production by offering alternative design concepts to the director. These meetings should continue until the director and the designer share a common vision of production intentions. Images and other inspiration materials are often shared in these early meetings.

2. ROUGH SKETCHES

The designer now begins to put ideas into tangible form, first as rough approximations of the possible scenery, sketched only to give overall impressions. Considerable give and take can occur as the designer and director move toward agreement.

3. FLOOR PLANS AND SIDE ELEVATIONS

The designer next refines the rough sketches into a more detailed and accurate floor plan, drawn to scale. He or she superimposes this plan on a floor plan of the stage to test whether the intended design will in fact fit on the stage and will prove capable of being shifted and stored.

A similar device is the side elevation. Designers use a cross-section view of the scenery, the side elevation, to check masking of lighting units and backstage areas and to ensure the audience will not see them during performances. In recent years many productions have left lighting instruments visible.

4. PERSPECTIVE DRAWINGS AND MODELS

Most designers convert the floor plan into one or more scale drawings. Designers use a system of mechanical perspectives, similar to those used in mechanical drawing classes, to achieve this graphic depiction of the intended scenery.

Most designers also construct a scale model, usually in one-half-inch scale, of the settings, because working in three dimensions helps them solve various problems of the design. Some models are quite complex, even for a production with only one setting.

By this time the designer should have solved most of the problems of line, color, and mass for the scenery. The perspective drawings and models will facilitate communication with construction personnel, directors, actors, and other theatre artists. For this reason, many designers prefer to prepare both drawings and models.

5. BLUEPRINTS AND WORKING DRAWINGS

All of the designer's output thus far gives only an impression of how the scenery will appear. Once the designer and director come to an agreement, the designer drafts working drawings of all the scenic elements. Blueprints, done either by the designer or the technical director, follow; these guide the construction crews in building the scenery.

In the commercial theatre, the producers usually contract the entire setting to a scenic studio. In the educational or avocational theatre, volunteers usually construct the scenery under the supervision of either the technical director or the designer; students taking technical theatre courses may construct the scenery for laboratory experience, or the department may hire the students, often in a work-study program, as construction crews. In any event, the blueprints must be accurate and clearly executed to avoid costly and time-consuming mistakes.

In larger operations the designer turns the working drawings over to the construction supervisors and confers with them if difficulties arise. In most situations the designer checks directly on the progress of construction. In a one-person technical operation, the designer personally supervises and assists in the construction.

6. ERECTING AND STRIKING THE SCENERY

Erecting the scenery for the run of a show may require the services of the designer, especially if the show has multiple sets or complex elements. If the production runs in repertory or if the schedule demands striking and resetting the scenery for any reason, the designer may wish to oversee this operation as well.

At the end of a show's run, crews clear the scenery from the stage to prepare for the next production. The educational or avocational theatre usually finds it fiscally expedient to dismantle and save many of the scenic elements. In the commercial theatre, high storage costs often demand the company simply junk the scenery—though theatre, like much of the world, is also becoming increasingly aware of the desirability of a "green" production. If a road company disbands outside New York, they sometimes donate the scenery to a company that can use it rather than pay to truck it back home. And designers are increasingly searching for ways to make their designs easier to recycle and easier on the environment.

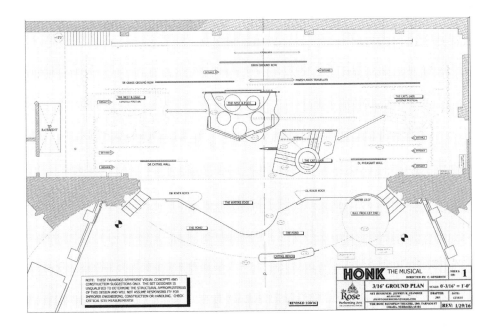

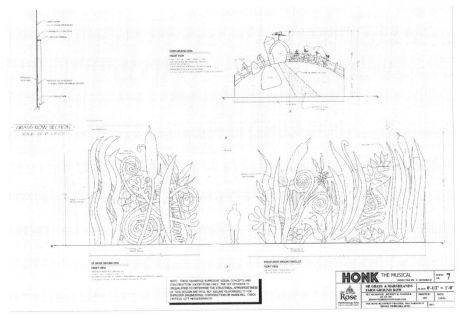

Jeff Stander's detailed—and beautiful—drawings for the Rose Theatre's production of *Honk!* were presented to both the director and the technical director for approval before building began. *Courtesy of Jeffrey Stander*

Evaluating the Scenic Designer's Contribution

In evaluating stage scenery, audience members often find that they can rather easily separate the designer's work from the other theatre artists' contributions. Scenery consists of actual objects, so audience members can feel more secure about evaluating its worth than the work of the actors, the director, or the playwright.

Audience members should, however, avoid the temptation to judge scenery in isolation, out of the context of the total production. We should evaluate stage scenery by how well it achieves the functions listed earlier but only in reference to a particular production, not as a separate entity.

Even in so seemingly simple a matter as *defining the playing space*, designers find wide latitude. In traditional theatre the production team may confine the action behind the proscenium arch, the actors making no direct contact with the audience. In such musicals as *Hairspray*, action may remain mostly on the stage, but the performers play musical numbers directly to the audience. In even more overtly presentational or theatrical productions, such as *Hair* or *Cats*, the cast may come off the stage into the audience for direct confrontation; the settings should facilitate this performer-audience interaction.

The designer for an Ibsen drama may tightly focus the action upon the stage, but the looseness of much musical comedy may blur the distinction between audience area and playing area; the designer may facilitate the looseness of the action by manifesting in the scenery the script's unconstrained nature. The production team may sometimes wish to rivet audience attention on a single performer and other times spread the focus to include the entire theatre, both stage and auditorium. Again, the director and designer must coordinate their efforts toward a goal they both support.

In *focusing attention* on a single individual, for example, intensifying the lighting on that actor will set him apart, as will a costume that contrasts with the other performers onstage. Directors have many means of emphasis, but the scenery must facilitate the dramatic choices.

So, too, with the *reinforcement of style and evocation of mood*. Let's take an example from the musical *Urinetown*, an irreverently funny play about a town with a water shortage so severe that everyone has to pay to pee. If the designer were to create a set depicting a uniformly stylish city of great wealth and resources, devoid of darkness, class differences, or humor, the set might be "pretty," but it would confuse the themes of the show, and the appropriate mood would be nearly impossible to achieve.

Scenic quality, therefore, revolves around the question of whether the scenery has *amplified the specific theatrical event* as conceived and executed. Three separate productions of *A Midsummer Night's Dream* exemplify the specificity of production intentions. Max Reinhardt's 1905 production offered a traditional approach, especially in the realistically depicted forest scenes with their almost photographic realism. In 1970, Peter Brook staged the same script for the Royal Shakespeare Company on trapezes with an all-white set and won worldwide acclaim; the show toured from London to Tokyo. Two years later the Tyrone Guthrie Theater in Minneapolis staged the same script in yet another style, also achieving a high degree of success. In three excellent productions of the same script, then, three companies used three distinct approaches.

Sometimes all that is needed to define a space is string—as in Sarah Ruhl's *Eurydice*. Courtesy of Wake Forest University Theatre. Photo by Bill Ray

(You can see three more *Midsummer*s in the section on style in chapter 5.) The scenery for each production, highly appropriate for that company, would have proven useless for either of the other two companies. One cannot judge stage scenery out of context.

Nevertheless, many of the traditional concerns of art evaluation relate to the scenic designer's work, especially in proscenium staging: balance, rhythm, emphasis, harmony, color relationships, and so on. Scenery does not always demand beauty in the usual sense, but it should attract the eye, interest the viewer, and communicate.

Stage Properties

Properties consist of all items of furniture, ornament, or decoration on a stage setting, plus any object handled or used by the cast during the production. The categories of props include the following:

1. *Trim properties* finish the look of the scenery. They include, for instance, items that give a room a "lived-in" look—ashtrays, magazines, vases, books, fireplace tools, cushions, and so on.
2. *Hand properties* include cigarettes, pistols, suitcases, coffee cups, banners, and similar items. Multiple people may use these props.
3. *Personal properties* include any prop used by a single character (a personal bag, a watch, a mobile phone).

In the noncommercial theatre, arguments frequently occur about definitions and responsibilities: Is a piece of furniture scenery or a property? Is a sword part of a costume or a property? The dismembered body parts in the *Lieutenant of Inishmore* photos are a good example of props that resist these categories but are most definitely properties, not scenery or costumes. In any case, each company must eventually define who is responsible for what. Only then can rehearsals and performances go on smoothly.

Under the direction of a prop master, a property crew gathers, builds, places, and maintains all items in this category. Scripts may demand almost anything: mummy cases, a seven-headed hydra, Geiger counters, an aquarium full of live snakes, a live monkey, or a Hindu fakir's rope trick. No theatre could hope to supply all possibilities from its storage rooms, so property acquisition often involves borrowing, renting, pur-

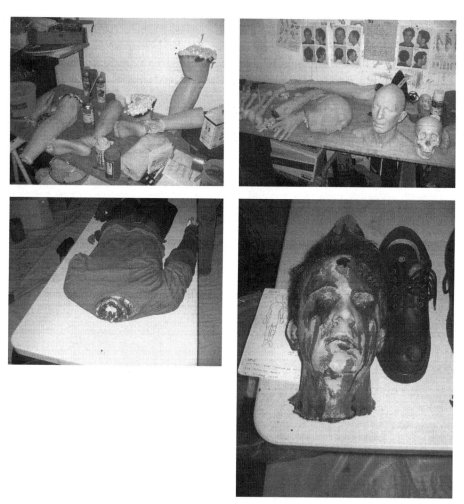

Peter Sarafin's corpse design and fabrications for *The Lieutenant of Inishmore* by Martin McDonough in its Broadway run. *Courtesy of Peter Sarafin*

chasing, or constructing items. Property rental agencies often stock items difficult to locate or build, but even their enormous resources can fail, in which case the company must either revise the script or substitute something for the property.

Careful attention to properties adds an important dimension to any show, and in some cases it can tip the scales between success and failure. Every actor or director has experienced some disaster because of a property's not being where needed or because of some other nasty surprise. Careless or stupid mistakes can nullify the concentrated work of dozens of persons over weeks of time. The careless handling of firearms has led to accidental death in a few cases, which has led to extensive rules for gun use in all productions and has even driven some states to outlaw the use of guns in amateur productions.

Costume Design

The old adage "Clothes make the man," like most clichés, contains a nugget of truth. Clothing is the scenery we wear as we go about our daily routines, and like scenery, clothing projects an image. We select that image several times a day from our available resources. No matter what you're wearing as you read this chapter, you're projecting an image. How would you describe that image? What does it say?

PURPOSES OF COSTUME DESIGN

Costumes on a stage become much more than clothing. Because a stage costume should, among other functions, express the wearer's personality, costuming becomes an important part of the overall concept of a production. Stage costuming should in fact achieve goals comparable to those of stage scenery by:

1. Expressing character
2. Visually defining relationships
3. Enhancing the actors' work
4. Reinforcing style and context
5. Relating organically to the entire production

Costume designers' most nuanced contribution to a production is usually in their connection to the actor/character—as you can see in the first three items listed here. The best costumes assist all the actors in a play in defining their characters and relationships. In *Romeo and Juliet,* the costumes should not only help us know who the characters are, but they should also help set up differences between the Montagues and Capulets. Through particular choices of colors, patterns, and fabrics, a costumer can tie individual characters to particular groups, casting them as leaders or followers, rich or poor, strong or weak. Costumes can also distinguish age and occupation and shape our view of a character, supporting and enhancing the actors' work.

Oregon Shakespeare Festival's imaginative designs for *A Midsummer Night's Dream. Courtesy of Jenny Graham*

Costumes should also tell us where and when the play is set (whether in a specific period, an invented time and place, or a combination of both), and they can even define geography and tell us the season of the year. Costumes also have to be functional. In *Romeo and Juliet*, there are sword fights, balconies to be climbed, and disguises to be donned. Every production has its own challenges for the designer—some more extreme than others. For instance, the Tony Award–winning costume designer (and director) of *The Lion King* on Broadway, Julie Taymor, was faced with a seemingly insurmountable task. She had to create a host of African animals (lions, baboons, giraffes, and many others) for a live stage production, and she did so using a combination of techniques drawn from all over the world. Not only was her production design applauded for its stunning aesthetic, based strongly in Indonesian puppetry techniques, but it also brought new audiences to Broadway.

Costumers may be asked to create angels that hover in the air midstage (Tony Kushner's *Angels in America*) or a full cast of fairy-tale creatures (Sondheim/Lapine's *Into the Woods*). Whatever the challenge, costumers must work with the rest of the production team to support the concept of the show, to communicate character and relationship, and to reinforce the style of the production with the choices they make.

The Costume Designer's Alternatives and Restrictions

A stage costumer faces unique problems in translating a production concept into costuming. The designs must fit particular actors, no matter what their size or physical distinctions, and the costumes must withstand continual, sometimes violent, action. Furthermore, costumers design groups of costumes, not just individual ones, and—as mentioned earlier—the designs should establish relationships between the characters. Costume designers employ color, line, silhouette, and texture to achieve the harmonies and contrasts that suggest relationships (e.g., Capulets in close-fitting textured darks, Montagues in looser, lighter colors and more refined textures).

The costume designer and the director may or may not choose to costume the cast in a historically accurate style, but if they do so, the costumer's research abilities become especially valuable. Research entails far more than history, however—ranging from trends in the arts, awareness of designers' work around the world, and many of the things directors must understand, such as economics, sociology, and religion. All these concerns influence the clothes people have worn and do wear today.

Production companies with limited resources or personnel may choose to borrow or rent costumes rather than design and construct them, although renting usually saves time and effort rather than money. Whether the producers borrow, rent, or construct costumes, they must make selections from the resources available, guided as always by economic considerations, artistic principles, and the production's stylistic and conceptual frame. Most productions are built and bought rather than rented because it is rare to find an entire production's designs that (a) neatly fit the concept of the current production and (b) fit the actors who need to wear them.

The Costume Shop; or, Where Do All Those Clothes Come From?

Draping, patterning, and sewing skills are important to the training of costume designers. Early in their careers, designers may spend a great deal of time executing their designs, and academic designers may continue to do that throughout their careers. However, in the professional world and in many university settings, a costume shop manager or foreman is responsible for making sure designs come to fruition.

Working for the shop are drapers, who work with fabric to create patterns based on the costume designer's sketches, and stitchers (formerly seamstresses), who actually sew the costumes—a job often far more complicated than it sounds. Wig makers, milliners (hat makers and trimmers), jewelry makers, and other accessory specialists may also do work for the shop. The smaller the shop, the more "specialties" each person needs to have.

When the actors are cast, they come to the shop to have measurements taken, and the costume designer delivers to the shop sketches (renderings) and swatches (bits of fabric) already approved by the director, and confers with the shop manager (or foreman) and potentially other members of the staff about each piece. From now on, the costume shop manager will make sure that good progress is being made toward the creation of all the garments, assigning work, budgeting time and money, and keeping track of fittings.

Sometimes there are costumes used in previous productions (kept in stock) that can be modified to work for the show. If pieces are to be built, patterns are acquired, or a draper uses muslin to figure out how to create the pieces the designer has sketched. A pattern for each is then created. At this stage, if time and resources allow—and if an expensive piece of fabric is to be used to make the final garment—a muslin mock-up of the costume is cut, sewn, and fitted on the actor. (Specialty fabrics can cost $50/yard or more. Making mistakes at this stage with $2/yard muslin is far more cost effective.) Once sure of the correct fit, the chosen fabric is cut, sewn, and fitted on the actor.

Designers visit for fittings, making adjustments to the look and choosing or approving buttons, trim, and accessories. First dress rehearsal arrives, and the director (hopefully) gets to see every garment in their finished (or near finished) state. Conversations with the designer often result in changes—some small, some large—that impact the shop.

Despite all the communication, sometimes a piece doesn't work. Perhaps someone didn't realize how closely a costume would match a wall color (thereby rendering the actor a talking head). Perhaps the lighting designer can help fix this; perhaps the scenic designer will repaint. But often it is the costume that is easiest to change—either by dyeing, adding a new layer, or creating or pulling a whole new piece from stock. Often, pages of notes from the designer and director make the final push toward opening an especially hectic time in the shop, with many people working extra hours to make each piece perfect.

Opening arrives, and things slow down a bit, or (more likely) the shop moves on to the next production. However, during the run of the show, costumes need maintenance and periodic cleaning. The costume crew takes care of the cleaning as well as any necessary repairs. Actors can be rough on clothes, and more than a few have been known to be careless about hanging things up at the end of the night, leading to extra ironing, steaming, and clean-up for crew members—not a way to breed good feeling toward yourself if you're an actor!

When the show closes in the commercial theatre, the costumes are returned to the company that built them, which will in some cases make them available to other companies. In the noncommercial theatre, someone usually returns costumes to storage after cleaning for possible use in later productions. This, along with donations, is how a theatre comes to have stock from which to pull for future productions.

SCHOOL FOR SCANDAL

LADY SNEERWELL

Designer Mary Wayne-Thomas's rendering and realized design for Richard Brins-ley Sheridan's *School for Scandal. Courtesy of Mary Wayne-Thomas*

In the modern theatre, costuming ranges from everyday clothing—frequently the only requirement for contemporary drama—to lavish and spectacular costumes for musical comedies, fantasies, or period plays. Even in productions featuring nudity, such as *Hair*, the actors must have costumes to take off.

Requisites for Excellence in Costume Design

1. Formal training
2. Imagination and creativity
3. Drawing/rendering skills
4. Sensitivity and good communication skills
5. Understanding of the human body
6. Draping, patterning, and implementation
7. Understanding of color theory

Costume design may easily be confused with fashion design, but the comparison does not hold up for long. Fashion designers focus on making an individual or group of people look their best in a given context. For example, a fashion designer may design a business suit for men that makes them look strong yet nonthreatening; the job therefore is to make the man appear professional, confident, and in control in the business world.

A costume designer's work is in service to a specific production. Not only does the actor have to look appropriate (not necessarily "good") within the character's given context, but also the character has to fit within the same world as all of the other characters. A costume designer, therefore, profits from the following.

1. FORMAL TRAINING

Analytical skills and a deep understanding of numerous historical periods require a long-gestating training period. Most costume designers study costume construction in combination with history as undergraduates at colleges and universities. Then they may apprentice in costume shops for professional companies for a time. Many will continue their formal training in graduate school, earning a master of fine arts degree before they return to professional theatre or academia.

2. IMAGINATION AND CREATIVITY

Costumes exist within a given context, limited by script, director, and design team, but often there is great freedom within that structure. For example, Shakespeare's plays were all written to be performed on the exact same stage space, and they bear the mark of the original Globe Theatre in the writing. But costume designers have no such restrictions when working on his plays. Their imaginations can run wild, with both comedies like *A Midsummer Night's Dream* (with woodland fairies, royals, and crass working-class types) and tragedies like *Macbeth* (with witches, warriors, and royalty).

Creativity also builds with time, as designers learn to connect their work with that of other practitioners. It takes time to learn to connect individual characters with strong design choices. Young designers may create a costume based on instinct or habit—and they may make some terrific choices. Seasoned designers use their intuition as well, but they also *intentionally* connect each individual costume to the total design through a complex pattern of shape, color, line, rhythm, and texture. You will see a great costume designer connecting shapes in costumes to shapes in the set the actors work on. Or you may see complementary colors in the lighting and in the costumes. In musical theatre, rhythms can be found coming both from the orchestra and the costumes. The more complex these patterns, the richer and more powerful the designs.

3. DRAWING/RENDERING SKILLS

Connected to communication skills are the visual materials costume designers use to specifically convey how they envision the final product. Through drawings—called, in their finished state, renderings—they clearly indicate to the director and the costume shop foreman how the costumes are intended to look. Rendering skills may certainly be developed in school, and as new software has developed to aid in costume design,

Designer Polly Boersig's vivid costume ideas for Shakespeare's *Macbeth*. Courtesy of Polly Boersig

more people may feel able to communicate their costuming ideas. However, with the advent of this new technology, less attention has been paid to traditional drawing skills, a fact we find unfortunate. The vivid expression of line and movement found in some costume renderings can rarely be matched by a computer program. (See Polly Boersig's zesty and unconventional drawings for *Macbeth* designs for a good example of what we mean.)

4. SENSITIVITY AND GOOD COMMUNICATION SKILLS

Costume designers obviously must communicate well with directors. However, they also work directly with actors and sometimes in the most personal of circumstances—taking actors' measurements and in fittings, they may see them in their underwear (and sometimes less). They have the power to design clothing that renders their characters thin or fat, glamorous or disgusting. Though most actors know that an appropriate costume for a character may not be the most flattering thing they've ever worn, sometimes the process can be difficult. We all have opinions about what looks good on our bodies, and actors are no different. Costume designers must therefore be sensitive, not only to what the director and the production require but also to the human beings they work with. They must stick to the prescribed design but also engender actor trust and confidence. Clarity of communication, a supportive costume-shop environment, and a sense of camaraderie go a long way toward making everyone accept and enjoy the costuming process.

5. UNDERSTANDING OF THE HUMAN BODY

No two bodies are alike. If you've ever tried to rent a Halloween costume, you've probably realized this. A costume must be built to fit your body if you are to wear it for months on end in a long theatrical run. A costume designer, then, must learn each actor's shape, proportions, and variations and design and fit the costume appropriately to that particular actor's body. Not only that, no two actors will move exactly alike. One actor may want more pants room for an affected walk based on a new interpretation of the role, while another might focus the physical characterization in the upper body.

Some years ago, the actor Antony Sher famously decided, in consultation with his director, Bill Alexander, to play Richard III as a spider-like man on crutches. William Dudley, the designer, helped bring this concept to life, giving him a silhouette like a spider but also clothes he could move in. Each costume must therefore work on the actor's body but also create for us the image of the *character's* body.

6. DRAPING, PATTERNING, AND IMPLEMENTATION

Most costumes must be built rather than bought or pulled from stock (storage). Just imagine looking for the Richard III black spider with crutches and a hump in your local department store! But even purchased or pulled costumes must usually be altered, tailored, or have parts reconstructed to fit the new actor's body and use. Whether pulled, bought, or built, somehow a costume designer's idea must move from idea to execution. Complicating this situation is the fact that plays are set in every time and place imaginable, and unfortunately there are no special pattern sections at your local fabric shop for Restoration fops or medieval princesses. This means that designers must either (a) create their own patterns, draping fabric on a form to determine how to best create what they have drawn; (b) modify patterns they find in pattern books or stores; or (c) create a pattern from a piece of already existing clothing that closely matches what they are trying to make.

Knowledge of fabric becomes extremely important as well, as the choice of denim, silk dupioni, or broadcloth will completely change the look of a design. Though professional designers may simply hand their renderings and fabric swatches to a costume shop foreman to execute, their designs will be better (and more practical to realize) if they understand the techniques and limitations of actually building costumes. Most great designers therefore possess strong draping, patterning, cutting, and sewing ability.

7. UNDERSTANDING OF COLOR THEORY

Like many other designers, costume designers can often be found with a color wheel in a pocket or on a desk. A color wheel is a circle with slices of color spread in pie shapes around the wheel. Colors that appear on opposite sides are referred to as *complementary* colors because they resonate with or complete each other.

A costume designer needs to know how to select the right fabric color to fit within the overall design scheme. Or the costumer must learn how to use dyes in order to accomplish the right hue or shade of color. Unlike lighting, in which white light is composed of the combination of all colors, in dyes, white is the absence of any color and black is the combination of all colors. In between black and white are a staggering multiplicity of choices, and the costumer is required to have a firm grasp of how all colors do (or don't) work together. Shine red light on a beautiful green piece of fabric, and the resulting muddy mess will tell you why this is important.

Creative Procedures for the Costume Designer

The costume designer's procedures closely resemble those of the other designers but with important differences:

1. The costume designer analyzes the script.
2. The designer confers with the director to discuss the unique demands of the intended production.
3. The designer does research and continues analysis.
4. Decisions are made, resulting in thumbnail sketches—small, quick drawings to convey where the designs are headed.
5. More meetings are held with the director once the show is cast. If the director casts someone who doesn't fit with where the original designs were headed (e.g., a tall, skinny actor in a role the designer had originally designed as soft and round), then modifications will need to be made.
6. After considering any changes generated by meeting with the director, the designer then prepares final costume renderings, or plates. These often have fabric swatches attached to convey the materials to be used for each piece.
7. Renderings are presented to the director for approval. At this point the director must recognize whether something will work for characters the actors have yet to develop. Decisions to approve designs should therefore be made carefully. Designers and directors also benefit by sharing the designs with the actors as early as possible.
8. With the approval of the renderings, construction begins.
9. A "dress parade" or "costume parade" may serve as a check: The director and the costumer consult as the actors appear before them, usually in the theatre, wearing the costumes they will use in the show. Adjustments and substitutions may be required.
10. Dress rehearsals allow everyone to see the entire design in action. In most cases, if communication has been good, few changes will be needed. However, if changes are needed, this is the last chance to make them—though any requests made by the director at this point should be asked with the utmost sensitivity. Unfortunately, even after so many checks and approvals, sometimes things have to be

changed. In most cases, though, the designers and shop manager are attending to tiny details only they will ever notice.

In fact, costume designers, like all theatre artists, run the risk of overspecialization or of forgetting to put their work in perspective. The Broadway director Robert Lewis liked to tell a story about the costume designer of *Brigadoon*, which he directed:

> The show had played New Haven and we then went on to Boston to open on Monday night. With very little time to set up we were terrified that things were not going to go well technically. The curtain went up on the first set . . . and it went along all right. The curtain came down on that scene and then there was a walkover scene in front of the curtain in which the "merry villagers" come on, waking up after having been asleep for a hundred years. As they came across the stage, the crew was setting up for the next big scene behind the curtain, which was the village of MacConnachy Square. The orchestra was playing while the villagers sang as they went across the stage. It was a continuous scene; as they sang, "Come ye every-where, to the fair," the curtain did not go up; it just stayed there. It was a terrifying moment! I was standing in the back and I grabbed choreographer Agnes DeMille's arm, breaking it only slightly. The conductor couldn't stop the orchestra because it was a continuous scene; the people behind the cur-tain were already singing—you could hear them clearly. Still it didn't go up. Then, slowly, the people behind gradually got discouraged and their voices began to fade away. . . . Finally, after an eternity, with the number half over, the curtain went up, with a jerk. A few of the chorus were still singing and dancing a little, some were just standing around, still others were seated on the floor—the whole thing looked like the Edinburgh subway! In addition, at the same time that the front curtain went up, the backdrop, on which the village of MacConnachy Square was painted, went up too, revealing the back wall of the Colonial Theatre in Boston. It was at this moment that the costume designer rushed up to me, grabbed my arm and said, "That chorus girl has the wrong socks on again!" Now *that* is specialization!

This is an extreme case, and such attention to detail may sometimes be funny, but with so many things to look at, listen to, and respond to, most directors are grateful for such acute observers. Without specialists, dozens of details that contribute to a beautifully finished product would simply fall through the cracks.

Evaluating the Costume Designer's Contribution

Much like a set designer, a costume designer creates or chooses tangible objects, like clothing, shoes, and hats. Audience members are probably somewhat familiar with "reading" costumes because we costume ourselves every day. We may choose to dress up for formal affairs or dress down for informal ones. T-shirts and jeans make us feel casual, while suits reshape us to feel more confident and put together.

Evaluating a costumer's contributions fully requires a bit more training of the eyes, though. The designer must meet the expectations of

1. Expressing characters
2. Defining relationships
3. Enhancing the actor's work
4. Reinforcing style and context
5. Relating to the production as a whole

In order to see this better, it is valuable to have some knowledge of fashion in history, notice how the actors move, and watch for the ways that relationships are established through action and visual cues (color, texture, line, and mass). A costumer's choices must subtly or boldly (depending upon the style of the piece) call attention to the appropriate elements that act as markers for relationship, class, style, and more. These choices should allow us to come to a clearer and deeper understanding of each character, as well as the overall actions and conflicts of the play, within the context of a specific production.

A slim moustache and slicked back hair help transform these two college students (Laura Halsey and Michael Casby) into elegant—if rather badly behaved—adults in Noel Coward's *Hay Fever*. Costumes by Lisa Weller. *Courtesy of Wake Forest University Theatre. Photo by Bill Ray*

Makeup and Hair

Costume designers are frequently expected to cover these design elements, although in motion pictures, makeup and hair are their own specialties. Because of the need for realism in close-up photography, film has stimulated new and improved makeup techniques. Just as early film drew on theatrical skills in hair and makeup, many procedures from film are now transferring to theatre.

Hair and makeup professionals also work throughout the run of a show, executing the designs created by the costume designer or—less frequently in the theatre—by separate hair and makeup people. Great hair and makeup finishes the look of a costume and in a very personal way completes the actor's characterization.

Some Broadway shows rely heavily on wigs and wig makers. The long-running musical *Wicked* uses 140 wigs per production. Each wig used has two extra versions, since wigs can get messed up or even damaged, and restyling a wig can take many hours. Ensemble actors play multiple roles in *Wicked* (some of them as many as ten), and a change in wig and costume can render them unrecognizable from one part to the next. Exceptional skill and attention to detail is required to make and style wigs, yet in most cases the best thing that can happen is that the audience never even realizes an actor is wearing one of their creations.

In college productions, the hair and makeup specialist is often the same person. When a specialized person is brought on to do makeup, chances are it will be fairly attention grabbing. Makeup designs for shows like *Cats* and *The Lion King* require great skill and consistency. Even the actor playing Elphaba, the green witch in *Wicked*, would probably need help from a makeup artist, since every bit of exposed skin needs to be covered in green makeup.

"Prosthetics," which you have undoubtedly seen in movies, are also used in the theatre. These include false noses, swaths of burned or diseased skin—really any look that seeks to dramatically change the look and even structure of an actor's face, neck, or body. Often, pieces of latex have been molded and painted and are applied with spirit gum or other types of adhesive. This is time-consuming work, as the applied pieces generally need to be seamlessly connected to the actor's skin in such a way that allows them to move together and not come off.

Good hair and makeup artists are constantly improving their skills, and with new products and techniques being developed in Hollywood, they have a whole industry to draw on. These artists are also important in helping give the final touches to characters actors have been crafting for months—so it is helpful for them to understand the actor's process and pressures. Long hours are spent in very close proximity to one another, sometimes while the actors are feeling quite anxious, so having some empathy and genuinely liking actors is very helpful.

When done well, all of these techniques to some degree fade into the background. If you find yourself thinking about the makeup too much in a production, chances are you either have an itch to become a makeup artist yourself or the makeup has not done its job in reinforcing character and is instead a distraction. In the extreme, very bad hair and makeup can utterly destroy a lot of good work. Wigs that fall off, inept age makeup, badly applied false noses, and such can make actors look foolish, turn a

Costumes can sometimes be quite effective when treated simply. Here, Sue Gillespie Booton and Aaron Ellis wear crazy wigs and simple red jumpsuits designed by Sherri Gerdes for Kevin Ehrhart's production of *Dr. Seuss's The Cat in the Hat*. Rose Theatre, Omaha, Nebraska, 2014. *Courtesy of Matt Gutschick*

serious scene into a silly one, or simply make the audience miss important pieces of the story they have come to see. Skill matters in hair and makeup as much as it matters anywhere.

Stage makeup serves two purposes: (1) to change the actor's visual characteristics (not only the face but also often the hands, neck, or other visible portions of the body) and (2) to intensify the actor's features to overcome the high-intensity lights that may wash out features. To achieve these purposes, professionals developed a great many materials, including greasepaint, pancake makeup, false eyelashes, and prosthetics. Makeup has become a subspecialty within the theatre, demanding substantial skill and constant practice. "Street" makeup has, in recent years, also improved dramatically, giving actors and makeup designers more and healthier alternatives to the heavy paints previously used.

Similarly, hair can substantially change a person's appearance dramatically. As hairstyles change from year to year, any given period must be represented via hairstyles in theatrical productions. Hair specialists not only learn how to work with actors' existing hair, but they also learn how to style wigs and even how to make (or "ventilate") hairpieces, including wigs, beards, mustaches, and sideburns. (See the sidebar for more detail on hair and makeup.)

All actors should learn to do their own makeup for realistic characters, but complex makeup designs may require the services of a specialist. In realistic plays, the audience should generally not notice an actor's makeup under the stage lights, unless the character would normally wear cosmetics. Clowns and prostitutes are good examples of the latter. Highly theatrical productions, such as *Cats* or *The Lion King*, may require special hair and makeup as well, and in those cases skilled makeup and hair specialists will be hired to consistently execute these looks.

Poorly made-up actors and badly styled hair and wigs can disrupt any sense of believability. Therefore, some expertise in finishing an actor's look through hair and makeup is highly desirable in a designer. Evaluating the contributions of these designers corresponds to the same concerns outlined earlier in "Costume Design." In addition, we must take into account the size of the venue, the style and specific hair makeup and hair needs of the production, and whether characters have been fully realized through the appropriate, detailed application of hair and makeup technique.

Conclusions

All phases of technical theatre require expertise, craft, imagination, dedication, artistry, and responsibility. Whereas some actors and directors have thought (and some still think) that technical theatre has as its function only to enhance the confrontation between actor and audience, in recent years designers' contributions have emerged as fully equivalent to the contributions of acting, directing, and playwriting. The future seems to offer a more balanced view of the theatre, and theatre artists of all sorts as well as audiences can only benefit from this more comprehensive vision.

Key Terms

Appia, Adolphe (1862–1928) Swiss scenic and lighting designer whose innovations revolutionized stage production in Europe and America.

batten A pipe suspended from the fly space to which technicians may attach scenery and lighting equipment to facilitate shifting.

Bibienas A family of Italian scene designers of the seventeenth and eighteenth centuries who introduced many innovations and reforms into scenic design at that time.

casters Metal assemblies that contain rubber wheels that allow wagons to move easily around the stage.

counterweights Weights used with a series of ropes and pulleys to counterbalance scenery attached to battens. They make possible the flying in and out of scenic elements in a proscenium theatre.

Craig, Edward Gordon (1872–1966) English scene designer and a prolific writer on theatrical matters. Associated with the New Stagecraft and with Adolphe Appia. Although considered impractical by some theatre artists, his controversial writings have caused many to regard him as one of the leading theorists of this century.

cue A signal for a technician or an actor. An actor's cue to enter the stage setting, for example, is often a line from another actor; the cue for a lighting technician to adjust stage lighting may be an actor's touching a light switch.

cyclorama A large, usually curved cloth or plaster device behind the scenery used to represent the sky.

flats Usually wooden frames covered by cloth, built in varying sizes and used most commonly to represent a section of wall.

fly, flies In theatre construction, the flies are that area above the stage itself into which scenery or lighting may be lifted. The act of elevating scenery into that area is called *flying*. Not all modern theatres have this facility.

found space Spaces designed for purposes other than theatrical but in which productions are staged. Performances in streets, bus terminals, gymnasiums, parks, and the like are said to use found space.

gridiron (grid) The framework, usually steel, over the flies that supports the rigging for flying scenery.

International Alliance of Theatrical Stage Employees (www.iatse.net) A union for many stage technicians.

New Stagecraft A term used to describe the nontraditional staging techniques first advanced in Europe by Edward Gordon Craig and Adolphe Appia. Many of these innovations were first seen in the United States as a part of the Little Theatre movement.

platform Basic unit of scene design that the actors walk on.

properties Objects on the stage other than scenery, such as trim props (including curtains, pictures, and so on) and set props (including furniture, phones, and so on). Also includes personal or hand props (items carried by the actors).

proscenium, proscenium arch In theatres so constructed, the architectural arch that divides the audience area from the stage.

run-through An uninterrupted rehearsal of a scene, an act, or an entire production, as opposed to rehearsals during which directors or technicians stop the action to make adjustments.

strike To remove from the stage, as a property, or to dismantle a setting.

trap Short for *trap door*, a section of the stage floor that can be removed.

United States Institute for Theatre Technology (www.usitt.org) An organization for those concerned with the technical theatre at any level of production. Publishes *Theatre Design and Technology* quarterly.

wagons A platform on casters or wheels.

wings In a proscenium theatre, the areas on either side of the stage in which scenery may be stored. So called because of earlier drop-and-wing staging, with the drop hanging at the back of the stage and the wings at the sides.

Discussion Questions

1. Discuss how each designer functions as part of a whole and also as a separate entity.
2. What is collaboration? How do you approach a collaborative project as opposed to a solo project? What role does compromise play in collaboration?
3. Is collaboration more productive than a dictatorial approach? Why or why not?
4. If you were to take a job as a designer on a production, what position would you want? Why does this position appeal to you?
5. How does the process of each designer differ from that of the others? How is it the same?
6. How do the designs come to fruition (technical rehearsals/performance)? How do designers make the transition from concept to product?
7. Choose a play you have read this semester and discuss all of the things you would need to consider to design sets/props or costumes/makeup/hair for that play. Then do some basic research and come up with your own design plan. Share these designs with the class, and compare and contrast your choices with those of your classmates.

Suggested Readings

GENERAL DESIGN

Ingham, Rosemary. *From Page to Stage: How Theatre Designers Make Connections between Scripts and Images*. Portsmouth, NH: Heinemann, 1998. A terrific book that focuses on the basics of script analysis as key to great design.

Kramer, Wayne. *The Mind's Eye: Theatre and Media Design from the Inside Out*. Portsmouth, NH: Heinemann, 2004. Another book that starts with script analysis as the basis for all design.

SCENIC DESIGN

Bay, Howard. *Stage Design.* New York: Drama Book Specialists, 1974. Bay, a fine American designer, writes cogently and insightfully about the practices of his profession.

Burian, Jarka. *The Scenography of Josef Svoboda.* Middletown, CT: Wesleyan University Press, 1971. With careful scholarship and exceptional lucidity, Burian describes the work of one of the world's leading scenic designers. Profusely illustrated, albeit in black and white. Interested students should also be aware of Burian's article "A Scenographer's Work: Josef Svoboda's Designs, 1971–1975," in *Theatre Design and Technology* 12 (Summer 1976), which covers Svoboda's work through those years.

Gillette, J. Michael. *Theatrical Design and Production: An Introduction to Scene Design and Construction, Lighting, Sound, Costume, and Makeup.* 6th ed. New York: McGraw-Hill, 2007. A substantial (640 pages) and ever-expanding encyclopedia of technical techniques; highly recommended.

Mielziner, Jo. *Designing for the Theatre: A Memoir and a Portfolio.* New York: Bramhall House, 1965. Beyond the implications of the title, Mielziner describes in considerable detail how he designed *Death of a Salesman.* Many theatre artists regard Mielziner as *the* outstanding American scenic designer.

Payne, Darwin Reid. *The Scenographic Imagination.* 3rd ed. Carbondale: Southern Illinois University Press, 1993. Originally published as *Design for the Stage: First Steps.* Carbondale: Southern Illinois University Press, 1974. One of the few books dealing with design theory, this well-illustrated text is recommended for advanced students.

Pecktal, Lynn. *Designing and Painting for the Theatre.* New York: McGraw-Hill, 1995. This profusely illustrated book includes ten richly insightful interviews with American scene designers; highly recommended.

COSTUME DESIGN AND MAKEUP

Anderson, Barbara, and Cletus Anderson. *Costume Design.* 2nd ed. New York: Holt, Rinehart & Winston, 1998. A popular and fundamental approach to costume design, with a brief guide to costume history and a bibliography.

Buchman, Herman. *Stage Makeup.* New York: Watson-Guptill, 1971. Although not as widely used as the Corson book of the same title, this lavishly illustrated tome offers a variety of makeup techniques, both simple and complex.

Corson, Richard. *Stage Makeup.* 9th ed. New York: Allyn & Bacon, 2000. As the number of editions indicates, this book has won wide acceptance and is the standard introduction to makeup. Somewhat more detailed than the Buchman book, it includes excellent color plates.

Cunningham, Rebecca. *The Magic Garment: Principles of Costume Design.* New York: Waveland Press, 1994. A well-illustrated treatment of the entire process of costuming the stage play.

Ingham, Rosemary, and Liz Covey. *The Costume Designer's Handbook.* 2nd ed. Portsmouth, NH: Heinemann, 1992. Clearly outlines the process and function of the costume designer. Excellent illustrations.

Russell, Douglas A. *Stage Costume Design: Theory, Technique, and Style.* New York: AppletonCentury-Crofts, 1973. A reasonably complete "how-to" volume for the stage costumer, containing a useful outline history of costuming and a glossary of terms.

Thudium, Laura. *Stage Makeup: The Actor's Complete Guide to Today's Techniques and Materials.* New York: Back Stage Books, 1999. A cheaper alternative to the Corson book, Thudium covers all of the basics in makeup well.

CHAPTER 8

Lighting, Sound, and Projections Designers

Lights are to drama what music is to the lyrics of a song. The greatest part of my success in the theatre I attribute to my feeling for colors, translated into effects of light.

—David Belasco

Sound tells a story, and the emotion you set with sound supports that story.

—Jason Cushing

Projection is an act of transformation, more poetry than prose.

—Wendall K. Harrington

Turn on your television, or open a video on your tablet or phone. Now dim the brightness to the point where you can barely see the figures moving on your screen. Listen; you hear voices, to be sure, but what else? Music? Other sounds? And remember, you wouldn't be able to hear any sound at all if it weren't for microphones. It's tempting to think that theatre is immune from these considerations, and certainly you can do theatre outdoors with no lights, no sound reinforcement, no music, and no effects. However, that's not the way we experience theatre most of the time.

Lighting and sound designers are perhaps the least noticed and understood artists in the theatre. Their work is only fully comprehended in the context of a performance. Though you can take pictures of a beautifully lit scene or listen to a sound effect or song, sound and light both operate in far more subtle ways, perhaps best understood as functions of time. A clear expression of a production's rhythm, pacing, and flow often depends on what these designers do. In addition, because sound and light work on us rather subliminally, we often fail to recognize why our mood has shifted or how we've been led to see or hear something in a certain way. Chances are, if we've had a good night in the theatre, these two design elements have shaped our experience in ways we might be hard pressed to define.

231

The Little Prince, directed by David Catlin. Lighting design by William Kirkham. *Courtesy of Rich Hein. Photo by Liz Lauren*

Lighting, sound, and projections designers often work together because their cues frequently have to work in conjunction with each other. For example, as a show is about to begin, the designers will want to indicate to the audience that it's time to take their seats and prepare for the performance. Preshow music may be playing to set a tone or atmosphere, and you may see a projection or some "pre-set" lights on the set or curtains. The house lights that allow the audience to see their seat numbers and each other will start to dim, and as the lights come up on the stage, the preshow sound will fade and the actors will begin. These designers have thus metaphorically transported us from our personal world into the world of the play.

The Lighting Designer

The lighting designer conceives and supervises all elements of stage illumination. Like that of the scene designer, the lighting designer's work affects the production in both obvious and subtle ways. Stage lighting allows the audience to see all the visual theatrical elements: the actors, the scenery, the costumes, everything. Illumination usually covers the stage from side to side and from front to back. Lighting frequently includes effects that operate below the audience's conscious level but that nevertheless elicit considerable emotional response.

Stage lighting as we know it has grown increasingly more sophisticated since candles, then gaslights, and eventually the invention of incandescent lightbulbs in 1879. These bulbs were first used in a theatre in 1881, and their efficiency had increased considerably by 1919. Now most lighting instruments use halogen bulbs (called lamps), and technology has radically improved in the last few decades to include moving lights and LEDs, among other innovations. From a seemingly infinite combination of ef-

Black-and-white photos can't really capture the beauty of much of theatrical lighting. Here, a deep golden light spills through the rain-streaked window in *The Bluest Eye.* **Hartford Stage Company. Lighting Design by Russel H. Champa.**
T. Charles Erikson

fects, a modern lighting designer can choose the amount, the direction, the color, and the specific nature of the light illuminating the acting area.

Again, the director's overall concept unifies the production efforts. The director and the lighting designer discuss the production's goals, and the designer usually has considerable latitude within those restrictions. The scenery's nature and placement modify the lighting designer's work as well. In most theatres, the lighting designer begins work only after the scenic designer has planned the scenery. And, as previously noted, the costumer and the lighting designer must coordinate their work for the best results.

In smaller theatre operations, as we have seen, one person may direct and design all production elements. For the following discussion, we assume lighting design is separate from the other elements.

As I Lay Dying, adapted from William Faulkner's novel by Janice Fuller. Directed by Elizabeth Homan. *Sean Meyers Photography*

Types of Conventional Lighting Instruments

Ask your professor if you can see these instruments in person.

Floodlights illuminate a wide area with a diffuse light beam:

- Parabolic Aluminized Reflector lights, or PAR lights, or PARcans
- Strip lights, also known as cyclorama or cyc lights
- Scoop lights or scoops
- House lights and work lights

Spotlights produce a narrower, more controlled light beam:

- Fresnel lantern, used for down or back lighting
- Ellipsoidal reflector spotlight, used for front or side lighting (e.g., Source Fours)
- Follow spot, controlled by a person or a computer
- Intelligent lights: moving, mechanized lighting instruments, computer controlled

Strand Lighting's zoom leko, Fresnel light, and Light Pallette control board. *Courtesy of Bobby Harrell of Philips*

The Lighting Designer's Alternatives and Restrictions

Because they deal with electricity in its most practical applications, lighting designers often find that other theatre artists do not completely understand their work, any more than the average citizen comprehends applied electricity. (Can you clearly explain how a microwave oven works?) Beyond an understanding of electrical circuitry and various control devices, however, light itself carries its own seemingly mystical qualities, further complicating matters. Stage lighting weds artistic considerations with a complex and unforgiving science.

Usually the lighting designer's first restrictions emerge from the director's vision. The director should understand the lighting designer's procedures; at the very least, the director should understand the lighting designer's working circumstances. Technical operations of all sorts offer innumerable problems, and the director must know enough about the various areas to deal with difficulties as they arise.

The type of instruments available will concern the lighting designer. Spotlights are the basic units of stage lighting, but they vary from lekos, which cast sharp beams of light for considerable distances, to Fresnels, which use stepped lenses for a softer-edged pool of light and are usually used closer to the actors or scenery than lekos. Source Fours, a contemporary ellipsoidal reflector spotlight, provide very even light and, be-

Gels, Gobos, and Practicals

Gels. As far back as the seventeenth century, techniques were explored to color lights. Colored silk or liquids in glass containers were first placed in front of candles to tint the light. Later, gelatin was used (hence the name gel), but actual gelatin lost its color and melted too readily. Today, gels are actually made out of polyester or polycarbonate. They come in a huge variety of colors and arrive in sheets or rolls. Lighting designers and their assistants cut them to fit special gel frames that slide into the front of lighting instruments.

Gobos. Gobos are thin plates, usually made of metal, with holes punched in them to allow light to pass through and create patterned lighting effects. They're usually used in ellipsoidal spotlights, which, because of their lenses, allow for a wide range of focusing or unfocusing of the light—and therefore of the pattern. Since they sit between the bulb (or lamp) and the lens, their name derives from the phrase "*GO*es *B*efore *O*ptics." Lighting designers can purchase these patterned templates or make them themselves out of tin or aluminum. Almost any pattern can be created with a gobo, from the diffuse shadow of a tree to a razor-sharp swastika. Thus, a gobo can do everything from defining location (e.g., under a tree) to shaping political context and mood (e.g., the swastika). Glass gobos, used only in special circumstances, give even more variation and detail than their metal cousins.

Practicals. Practical lights are exactly what they sound like—lights that actually work, practically, as they do in everyday life. A practical lamp onstage, would therefore actually have a working bulb or bulbs. This may seem like a simple thing, but few sets are actually wired in the way your house is, and practical lights, therefore, create special problems for the lighting electrician. Still, they can add realism to a scene and, because of their strong associations for us, create mood quite readily.

cause of their design, produce a much cooler light that is less destructive to gobos or gels (see sidebar) at the front of the fixture.

Lighting designers also use general units, such as floodlights, to illuminate an entire stage or large area. Specialized units, such as scenic projectors, follow spots, and strip lights, often prove essential. Each unit varies in wattage, 250 to 1,500 watts being most common. LED (light-emitting diode) technology has become increasingly popular as well, as it is lighter in weight, more energy efficient, and in many ways easier to work with. However, like many new technologies, it cannot yet do some of the things that conventional (tungsten halogen) lighting can do very well. See the sidebar on LEDs for more details.

Arrangements for hanging lighting instruments, which may amount to a considerable weight, affect the designer's choices. Theatres vary widely in this regard; the better stages have openings in the auditorium ceiling for lighting instruments, as well as pipes called battens over the acting area to support instruments there. Many designers like to use side light from the wings, but the scenic designer must leave space for those. Whatever arrangement the designer uses, physical support and adequate current must be available for each instrument.

The Pros and Cons of LED Technology

As LED (light-emitting diode) lighting technology has developed, it has become increasingly popular. Why? First, LEDs are more lightweight and portable than conventional halogen lighting systems. Some of them even work off of batteries and can be controlled by remotes, cutting out the need for all the cable normally used for stage lighting. LEDs also use less power, last longer, and give off a lot less heat than halogen bulbs, or lamps. You can also control color (within limits) more easily with LEDs. Because they're made to mix all the light colors together in each instrument, you can designate what color you want without having to climb up and put a gel in front of the light—and that means you can also change the color coming from an instrument many times in the course of a show.

On the other hand, LEDs can't be focused in the same way that most conventional lights can, so it's harder to get a really sharp focus where you want it. And while they are bright enough for many things, their light tends to scatter, so if you're trying to light something far away from the instrument, you're better off with a conventional one. Color can also be a problem, because though LEDs can give you wide options, not all packages give the range of color (or provide a nice, clean white light) that you would have with conventional instruments and gel.

However, as of 2016, the biggest problem with LEDs has to do with dimming. With a conventional instrument, you can control the dimming of a light through the whole arc of the cue. That is, if you want a light to disappear in a 10-second fade, with a halogen light you will get a nice, even decrease in intensity. If you cue an LED to do the same thing, you can get "stutters" in the fade, and will probably find that it snaps off with one to three seconds left to go in the cue. Expensive LED systems do better with this, but even then, there are benefits to conventional lighting that LEDs can't yet match.

Special thanks to Creighton University designer Bill Van Deest for his insights.

The control system, or dimmer board, further affects the eventual design. Each light or group of lights connects to a dimming device of a limited size; this dimmer enables the operator to determine the intensity of each light. The number of circuits available determines the maximum number of instruments possible for a show.

Dimmer capacity determines how many instruments the technicians can connect to a single circuit. A 6,000-watt dimmer can control a dozen 500-watt instruments, for example. An overload in a circuit trips circuit breakers; blows fuses; or burns up a dimmer, the light booth, and possibly the theatre. Dilettantes have no place in stage lighting; safety regulations and the cost of equipment demand knowledgeable personnel. In this facet of theatrical production, an error can prove fatal.

As you may have gathered from the previous discussion, all this technology is in service of using light to control:

1. *Color.* Affects mood, completes the stage picture, and tells us about time of day, time of year, and potentially even place. (The light in Greece at midday in the summer is quite different than in London in December.)
2. *Angle.* Suggests the source of the light—sunlight, lamplight, moonlight, headlights, etc.
3. *Intensity.* Related to the light source but also affects mood and defines place and time. Think, for instance, of the bright midday sun on a hot summer day, and then imagine the nightlight in your bedroom as a child.
4. *Focus or direction* (composition). Light can tell us where to look and help us filter out what the director and designer want us to ignore. A bright ("hot") light downstage on a single person can make the rest of the stage seemingly disappear and render a large space intimate.
5. *Movement.* Light can help us follow movement, thereby helping the director to shift our attention and attend to shifting action. Follow spots, which are actually moved by a separate operator, were the only way to do this in the past. Now, however, moving lights (or movers), which are circuited in the same way other lights are, are increasingly being used. However, movement can also mean moving *us*, the audience, in our perception of space. If you take the previous example, of a single person in a tightly focused downstage light, imagine that in a moment the light opens up behind her, making the space feel totally different, bigger, maybe with a different colored light. This could suggest a movement to a new locale, even a new time, with that simple change.

Requisites for Excellence in Lighting Design

Requisites to become a good lighting designer include the following:

1. Strong visual sense
2. Sensitivity to time and flow
3. Technical expertise
4. Training

Tony Kushner's *Angels in America, Millennium Approaches*. **Lights and sets by Jon Christman.** *Courtesy of Wake Forest University Theatre. Photo by Bill Ray*

5. Knowledge of equipment
6. Sensitivity to production goals and demands

1. STRONG VISUAL SENSE

Successful lighting design requires a visual sense comparable to that needed for scenic design but with vastly different emphases. Stage lighting illuminates something already existent: actors, costumes, scenery, properties, makeup, and so on. Thus lighting designers often create in response to another artist's previous creation.

2. SENSITIVITY TO TIME AND FLOW

Although they deal with all the traditional elements of visual art, light has the quality of fluidity, which allows the designer to make unique contributions. Lighting changes regularly, altering focus and mood according to the show's demands. A successful lighting design supports the staging and the script as a sort of visual music. Sensitivity to time and flow are therefore also essential for good lighting design.

Realistic plays can be enhanced by a strong sense of mood, as in this production of *Vanities*. Lights by Kate Bashore. *Courtesy of Kate Bashore*

3. TECHNICAL EXPERTISE

Lighting designers obviously need a strong background in the technical and scientific aspects of their work. Constant concerns include basic optics, practical electricity, and the science of color. As lighting controls and instruments become more sophisticated, so must those who use them. Computerized lighting controls also grow increasingly complex and, while this has made running the lighting boards simpler, it has complicated the designer's job even as it has allowed for greater control. Whatever the advantages and disadvantages of such innovations, each one forces lighting designers to reexamine procedures.

4. TRAINING

Training for the lighting designer appropriately begins with experience in all theatrical areas. Most have worked in scene shops and understand the complexities of building and finishing sets. A good lighting design can solve a multitude of problems in scenery, smoothing out wrinkles in flats, moderating color, and helping create visual focus. Additionally, lighting designers develop a sensitivity to qualities of light at varying times of the year, in various places around the world, and under varying conditions. Many find a study of photography useful. And all good lighting designers develop a keen awareness of dramatic structure—especially plot and character development.

5. KNOWLEDGE OF EQUIPMENT

Beyond the artistic and scientific study demanded by their art, lighting designers find that they must continually examine and compare all available equipment. Continual marketing of new equipment makes this an unending study. At each convention of the United States Institute of Theatre Technology (USITT), for example, lighting companies display their latest products. Successful designers keep up with the technological innovations that make their artistry possible.

6. SENSITIVITY TO PRODUCTION GOALS AND DEMANDS

Lighting designers must above all remain sensitive to the production's goals and demands as they employ their unique creative materials to achieve and amplify those goals. Although lighting tools and methods may seem purely scientific, lighting designers have artistic goals, and their contributions must support and amplify the work of their fellow artists.

The Contemporary Situation for the Lighting Designer

Professional lighting designers have much the same working conditions as those described for the scenic designer. It is not uncommon to find lighting designers for road shows and Off-Broadway productions working with startlingly antiquated materials and instruments. However, lighting designers are also a creative and resourceful group, using giant Edison bulbs, Christmas lights, tube lighting, hand-held lights, and much more to create effects. At the highest levels, lighting design in the United States is as good as it gets anywhere in the world.

In the educational or avocational theatre, lighting designers rarely specialize to the exclusion of other related activities. In a university theatre, lighting designers often hold professorial rank, with all its resulting implications; that is, they usually teach courses in addition to designing, and only in the largest of programs do they teach only lighting. Their professional lives may also include academic committee assignments, community service, external professional design work, and academic research and publication. Smaller colleges and secondary schools rarely have stage lighting specialists. More commonly the general theatre technician must attend to a wide range of technical responsibilities, including lighting. Community theatres often press into service anyone with a basic understanding of electrical circuitry, although good design work can be found in many community theatres.

The formation of the United States Institute of Theatre Technology (USITT), with its journal, *Theatre Design and Technology*, and the increasing circulation of *Entertainment Design* magazine (formerly *Theatre Crafts* and *TCI*), a publication devoted almost exclusively to matters of design and technology, have helped upgrade the status of nonprofessional designers and technicians.

Hand-held, battery-powered lights here create a personal and striking effect in the Catawba College production of *Godspell*. Lighting by Caleb Garner, scenery by David Pulliam. *Sean Meyers Photography*

Creative Procedures for the Lighting Designer

Steps in a lighting design include the following:

1. Script analysis
2. Creation of a light plot and cue sheets
3. Light hang and focus
4. Paper tech and cue-to-cue
5. Technical and dress rehearsals
6. Light check

1. SCRIPT ANALYSIS

Faced with a new production, the lighting designer proceeds at first much like other designers, becoming familiar with the script and then meeting with the director to analyze the specific demands and style sought in the intended production.

2. CREATION OF A LIGHT PLOT AND CUE SHEETS

After the first step, however, the lighting designer proceeds differently. Obtaining a ground-plan from the scenic designer and attending at least one run-through of the production, the lighting designer begins drafting a light plot. This plot must take into account where and when any actor stands or moves during the show, and indicates where the designer plans to position the lighting instruments.

3. LIGHT HANG AND FOCUS

Then the lighting designer, often in conjunction with the master electrician (ME), plans the instrument circuitry for the control board, and lights are hung and focused.

4. CUE SHEETS

The designer then executes a rough cue sheet, listing what lighting changes will occur during the performance. Computers have made the role of the board operators (board ops—the people who operate the light board) much simpler, since instrument choice, as well as length and speed of fade, are built into the cues. However, the board ops usually revise and refine this cue sheet many times before the show opens. Since lighting design is a function of time and space, dependent on what so many other people do, such changes are nearly inevitable.

5. PAPER TECH AND CUE-TO-CUE

Sometimes the director, designers, and stage manager have a paper tech, in which they go over all the cues in advance. Nearly always, the company then holds a or "cue-to-cue" rehearsal, during which the director and designers set the intensities or levels of illumination, correct the focusing if necessary, check colors, and run the show from change to change, or cue to cue. Often the company has to go over each cue multiple times to get the timing just right.

6. TECHNICAL AND DRESS REHEARSALS

Full-scale technical rehearsals traditionally constitute the next step, with all the production elements approximating performance conditions, though subject to change or refinement. At this point, lights, sound, and (if used) projections tend to be the focus—especially of the first few technical rehearsals. If these are successful and efficient, it is because of the coordinating and organizational skills of the stage manager, the director, and the designers, as well as the preparation of the designers and crews. Once into dress rehearsals (which include costumes), the entire show is run, but the stage manager may stop and have the actors repeat a segment until the technical elements coordinate smoothly.

You are probably used to seeing audience spaces at their least cluttered. Tech brings out tables, computers, paperwork, and snacks for long days of setting cues and rehearsing. *T. Charles Erikson*

Eventually all technical matters smooth out; the operators grow accustomed to their jobs, and after several uninterrupted dress rehearsals in which all the elements function very much as planned for performance, the production can open to the public.

7. LIGHT CHECK

Because mechanical devices wear out and malfunction, lamps burn out, dimmers corrode, and gels fade, technicians must make periodic light checks during the run of the show to prevent malfunction during performance. This procedure varies widely from theatre to theatre. Some technicians use lamp charts to record how many hours a particular lamp has burned. Because manufacturers list the life expectancy for each type of lamp, light crews can replace them before they burn out. In less-organized operations, the light crew simply hopes the lamps won't burn out during a performance, evidently on the flawed premise that all will go well.

Evaluating the Lighting Designer's Contribution

Stage lighting facilitates the audience's seeing, recognizing, and appreciating the action portrayed on the stage. We have touched on some of these in "The Lighting Designer's

Alternatives and Restrictions," so you should be getting familiar with the lighting designer's concerns. As you evaluate how well a designer achieved the production's goals, take these things into consideration:

1. Illumination
2. Source/direction
3. Mood
4. Enhancement

1. ILLUMINATION

Obviously the audience must perceive the work of the actors and the other theatre artists. Scenes rarely take place in total darkness except for special effects, such as in *Black Comedy*. The practice of darkening the auditorium and lighting just the stage originated only a little over a century ago. Lighting only the acting area facilitates audience concentration, and audience decorum has changed markedly as a secondary benefit.

The lighting designer's first responsibility is to illuminate the human face and form—something especially crucial (and tricky) in plays with wide-open spaces and no walls off of which to bounce light. Designers also seek to make the action visible to the degree appropriate to the production. Some theatre people feel that comedy calls for brighter lighting than serious drama, but in any genre, an underlit stage strains the audience's concentration, and the actors seem much harder to hear and understand in dim light.

2. SOURCE/DIRECTION

In realistic staging the light should seem to come from recognizable sources, such as torches, the sun or moon, fireplaces, windows, or household lamps. Each of these apparent sources emits light of a different quality and amount, and the lighting designer usually attempts to match the amount and quality of the stage illumination with the apparent source. Sunlight and moonlight for exterior scenes vary widely with the hour, climate, locale, and surroundings. The light at high noon on the Acropolis varies considerably (in both intensity and color) from that in New York's Times Square. Designers seek to increase credulity and verisimilitude with their designs of exterior as well as interior scenes.

Recognition also implies the use of form-revealing light, which employs the artistic principles of chiaroscuro. Painters have long noted that the most form-revealing light falls from above and to one side of an object, approximately forty-five degrees in elevation and forty-five degrees to the side. Sunlight most commonly strikes objects in that way; we have thus grown accustomed to perceiving forms under these conditions. Different gel colors placed in lights coming from opposing directions (e.g., amber on the warm side, blue or lavender on the cool side) can also indicate light and shadow, and thereby help define form.

3. MOOD

Look around the room you are in. How do the lights in the room affect your mood? Glaring fluorescents make a room feel antiseptic and sterile. Incandescent lamps with shades can give a room a feeling of warmth and comfort. A sunny day can make us a bit happier; a dark, rainy day may make us sad or just sleepy. An extreme version of this sensitivity, seasonal affective disorder (SAD), is a winter mood disorder believed to be caused by lack of light. Most of us aren't affected that strongly, but all of us emotionally respond on some level to light. Thus the lighting designer observes and uses those effects to help support the emotional environment, or mood, of each production.

Modern lighting practices have blurred the distinction between stage lighting and scenery. Beams of light, made visible by smoke, vapor, or dust particles in the air, can function as important visual elements. But even in a traditional production—one in which light does not seek to call attention to itself—the amount, color, and quality of stage lighting subliminally affect the audience and its reception of the work presented. In the last century, as stage lighting developed and playwrights grew more aware of its enormous potential, the stage directions included in published scripts often grew quite explicit about light. The final scene of Jean Anouilh's *The Waltz of the Toreadors*, for example, calls for a slowly fading sunset as the general's hopes similarly fade. Shakespeare had no opportunity for lighting control at the Globe Theatre, but one need read only the opening scenes of *Hamlet, Macbeth,* or *The Tempest* to imagine what a lighting designer can add to a production of any of his plays.

One of the main tasks of stage lighting is to illuminate and draw attention to the human form. Sidelight is widely used in dance to do just this. *Courtesy of Wake Forest University Theatre. Photo by Bill Ray*

4. ENHANCEMENT

Enhancing the stage action involves more relative and subjective concerns than does mere illumination. The audience must be able to see the performers' form and action, and the color, intensity, and direction of the light guides our focus by highlighting certain things and deemphasizing others.

The lighting designer seeks to predict the audience's response to a certain set of visual stimuli and to increase their appreciation by manipulating the lighting elements. It is not an easy task, as we may each react differently to the same stimuli. The basic rule is that a bright and well-lit environment raises spirits and tends to enhance funny plays or moments. Dark and shadowy lighting with high contrasts better supports serious and tragic productions. Imagine how you envision the light at the start of *Hamlet*—a cold night in Denmark—and now think of what bright pink lights would do to that scene. Similarly, think of cold, broken shards of moonlight coloring the opening scene of *Legally Blonde*. Now reverse them and you may have lights that more clearly support the mood and context of each play.

Beyond these basics, the complexity of choice and reaction is mind boggling. A designer therefore spends years paying attention to light in everyday life and watching audience reactions to various stimuli. Through these decades of experience, he or she learns what works.

The Sound Designer

Sound effects used to be treated as an afterthought on most productions and generally were handled by the properties department. Wind was created by various substances being spun in a barrel. Thunder was created by shaking large sheets of metal. If the production company was lucky, they might actually have had a small band or musical ensemble to produce incidental music for the play, and actors who could play musical instruments were especially valuable.

The Sound Designer's Alternatives and Restrictions

With today's advances in digital sound technology and a seemingly ever-growing desire on the part of audience members for more, sound has become a legitimate design area in theatres around the world. Sound equipment is cheaper and better today than ever before, and it is well within the range of even the smallest production company.

Sound designs can be broken down into three different elements:

1. Sound effects
2. Recorded music
3. Reinforcement of sounds

1. SOUND EFFECTS

Sound effects can, through the creation of an audio environment, help define the context of a play. We know a place or time of day not only by what we see but also by what we hear. Lapping waves tell us that we are at a seashore. Softly chirping birds may establish a pastoral setting. Gunshots, automobile sounds, and thunderstorms are frequent requests in scripts that sometimes help punctuate action or establish a mood. With the improved quality of computer hardware and software, sound effects can create a stunningly realistic setting.

Sound effects can also create new worlds and imaginary creatures. In José Rivera's *Maricela de la Luz Lights the World*, the playwright requests such things as the screams of a mythical beast called a hydra. In Anton Chekhov's *The Cherry Orchard*, he calls for the sound "of a breaking string," which may symbolize the end of an entire era. When the Broadway sound designer for *Angels in America* was asked, "What do you hear when you go to heaven?" he answered with a mix of Wagner's music, 1940s radio sequences, a voiceover discussing the Chernobyl nuclear disaster, and power plant rumbles dropped to half speed. Sound designers are limited only by their imaginations.

2. RECORDED MUSIC

Recorded music is a growing addition to live theatre, before and after scenes, and even as underscoring. Possibly due to television and film's constant reliance on music to help maintain the action, theatre designers and directors are beginning to do the same. Certainly musical theatre has been a major success for decades. However, the persistent use of music for nonmusical plays is a rather recent occurrence. Recorded music can, like light, help establish mood, setting, and time of day, supporting the rest of the production choices. Equally, it is a choice *not* to use such underscoring.

3. REINFORCEMENT OF SOUNDS

Reinforcement of sounds with microphones in theatrical endeavors is also becoming more common. Wireless microphones (worn on the actor's bodies), as well as area microphones, can help the actors fill a large hall, especially when their voices are competing with a full orchestra in a musical. Microphones can also be patched through digital processors that distort voices with effects, possibly creating the voice of an angry god or adding an echo effect to a flashback scene.

Types of Sound Effects

Sound design requires conception, selection, and clever execution as a part of the total production. Directors and sound designers confer to decide what they will use, as well

Microphones are generally hidden from view. Body mics have battery packs that reside in the actors' costumes. A wire runs to the mic, which is either taped to the actor's cheek or hidden in the actor's hair. Sometimes, though, a working stand mic is what you want, both for the look and sound of the show. *City of Angels,* **directed by Cindy Gendrich, sound design by Isabella Curry.** *Courtesy of Wake Forest University Theatre. Photo by Bill Ray*

as how many of the sound effects will be executed as live effects and how many will be recorded. Live effects usually work better for such items as offstage doors, single gunshots, falling bodies, doorbells, and telephones. Recorded sound plays better for such effects as explosions, trains, cars, parades, crowds, rocket launchings, and thunder. Designers may rely on sound effects websites (such as sounddogs.com) or return to archival collections of professionally produced CDs. Other designers prefer to field-record their own effects.

Deenda Kaye and James Lebrecht note that music and sound effects fall into the following categories in theatre:

1. Framing effects
2. Underscoring
3. Transitional sound/music
4. Specific/practical cues

1. FRAMING EFFECTS

These cues help to frame the entire production. They cue the audience when the show begins (referred to as preshow sound/music), when intermission happens, and also when the show is over (curtain call). In addition to structuring the audience's sense of beginning, middle, and end, these cues can set the mood for what is about to happen or comment upon what has been seen.

2. UNDERSCORING

This is music or sound that accompanies the action onstage but is rarely acknowledged by the characters. This kind of sound may be referred to as background sound because the speakers are often placed literally in the background of the set so as not to draw too much focus over the actors.

3. TRANSITIONAL SOUND/MUSIC

These effects help to transition from one scene or moment to the next. They can often mark a change in place or time. Again, the characters do not usually notice these effects because we consider them outside the action.

4. SPECIFIC/PRACTICAL CUES

The characters are aware of and rely on these cues. Whether it be a gunshot, a train whistle, or a doorbell, the actor needs these internal cues to help move the action of the plot. The location of the speakers for these cues is important because the cue must often come from a specific direction or place (a teakettle whistles from the kitchen, a doorbell comes from the door, etc.).

Requisites for Excellence in Sound Design

1. Wide experience in the theatre
2. Aural sensitivity
3. Appreciation of musical styles and music history
4. Sensitivity to mood
5. Control of source/direction
6. Awareness of context (time period/geographical location)
7. Enhancement

1. WIDE EXPERIENCE IN THE THEATRE

By now, you should be familiar with the idea that people who work in the theatre should understand how jobs other than their own operate. As we read more scripts and see more productions, we see how the practitioners' choices help or hurt a given theatrical experience. Sound designers therefore need to have analytical skills, a practical understanding of how productions flow when they're working well, and a sensitivity to directing and acting choices, as well as a good collaborative relationship with lighting and projection designers—with whom they tend to work most closely.

2. AURAL SENSITIVITY

Sound designers obviously need to be great listeners, sensitive to differences in musical styles, pitch, volume, and pace.

3. APPRECIATION OF MUSICAL STYLES AND MUSIC HISTORY

Any good sound designer will have an intense curiosity about musical styles and different periods in music history. Sound designers end up designing everything from Shakespeare to Soyinka. A sound designer with a limited musical vocabulary can, unfortunately, ruin a perfectly good production by choosing music that is inappropriate to the period, inappropriate to the specific social circumstances of the characters, and/or inappropriate to the mood.

A few years ago, we saw a student production of a 1940s thriller that was beautifully paced and well acted, designed meticulously with furniture, costumes, hairstyles, and makeup appropriate to the period. Then, as the lights went down on this rather satisfying production, for no reason anyone in the audience could understand, the song "Seasons of Love" from the 1990s musical *Rent* began to play. This jarring choice destroyed the spooky mood, the careful attention to stylistic elements from the 1940s, and the audience's final emotional response to the play. Later, the director, who had done her own sound design, revealed that she hadn't bothered to research music from the 1940s and "just liked the lyrics of the song." Not only did this ignore the role of creating mood, but it also serves as a great example of how a little music history could have helped the play *sound* authentic as well as *look* authentic. It also demonstrates how one bad choice can undermine an otherwise successful production. Such laziness is particularly hard to understand now, when so much great music from every time period is readily available online.

4. SENSITIVITY TO MOOD

As you undoubtedly know from your own life, sound stimulates feelings—whether we're talking about the sound of a dentist's drill or your favorite song being played at a party. Sound helps us understand the mood of a play through pace, rhythm, tone, harmonies and dissonance, volume, and instrumentation.

Music, in particular, is quite subjective, so designers must be careful when choosing modern songs. One audience member may, for instance, associate positive memories with a Justin Timberlake song, while others may have experienced the worst night of their lives while listening to the same song. It is often better to choose less recognizable songs, unless you can be sure that the audience is likely to have similar associations. Lyrics are another tricky element in modern music. They are not a reliable way to suggest mood or idea, since audiences are sometimes quite noisy and rarely listen to song lyrics. However, if music is played at a very quiet part of a production (e.g., in a transition or at the end of the show), a designer should make sure that the lyrics do not detract from the mood and ideas of the play. The "Seasons of Love" choice in the previous section is a good example of a terribly confusing choice.

The sound designer's job is to create a design that supports the production's mood. Sometimes this means choosing music as *counterpoint*—for instance, a very minimalist piece of music in the midst of chaos or an upbeat sound coming from a television or radio in the midst of a sad scene. Instead of simply underscoring what is happening in the scene, music or sounds can intensify the audience's reaction to the dramatic action through contrast. However, this requires walking a difficult line between effective counterpoint and confusing dissonance, so designers must choose carefully.

Mood may also be created with sound effects. A coyote howling in the distance or an owl hooting can create a sense of isolation and loneliness. A loud clock ticking can highlight the silences between two characters in a room together. Or a chaotic combination of horns honking, people yelling, sirens screaming by, and cars accelerating can tell us we're in an urban environment and also create an anxious mood.

5. CONTROL OF SOURCE/DIRECTION

Like light, sound may have directionality. When this directionality is ignored, it can be confusing and jarring to the audience. If we're watching a realistic play, for instance, and a radio is playing onstage yet the sound comes from speakers located behind the audience in the rear of the theatre, our sense of realism is shaken. Not all plays conform to realistic conventions, so this choice could be fine in a highly theatrical work. However, the choice should make sense for the production.

6. AWARENESS OF CONTEXT (TIME PERIOD/GEOGRAPHICAL LOCATION)

Here, again, our "Seasons of Love" example comes in handy. A play written in the 1940s, carefully produced in all other ways to maintain that original context, should probably have music from that period instead of a music-theatre song from 1996. Productions that combine modern and historical elements, as *Hamilton* does, embrace their historical fluidity in the design choices. Yet if one chooses to do this, it is not license to be haphazard or lazy. In fact, it may demand double the work, as you'll need (a) knowledge of both of the periods being mixed and (b) sensitivity to how the music may work with the other time period(s). When done well (as it is in *Hamilton*) this can create great counterpoint and a wonderful bridge between eras.

Along with time period, sound can also help define geography. A song sung by Édith Piaf can transport us to a smoky club in Paris circa 1939 more fully than any line of dialogue could. The sound of a djembe drum being played can quickly tell us we're in West Africa. Even sound effects can be specific to time and place. For instance, telephones haven't sounded the same everywhere in the world since their invention. A phone ringing in Australia in the 1960s, for instance, did not sound like your grandmother's land line does today. Crows cawing in Japan don't (strangely enough) sound like the crows in the United States. The examples are endless, and sound designers must continually educate themselves about the relationship of sound to time and place.

7. ENHANCEMENT

The sound designer, like everyone else, must make choices that are consistent with the goals of the production. Sound can support the flow, mood, style, and context of a play or destroy all of the above. Audiences may be unaware that sound is helping define these things, but as you pay attention to this design element, you may be surprised at how much it shapes your theatrical experiences.

Creative Procedures for the Sound Designer

The creative procedures for a sound designer in theatre can be as varied as any other designer's and depend greatly on the skills and background of the designer. Amateur or student productions often employ sound designers who use only prerecorded and readily available material on a prewired sound system. But a professional designer goes far beyond that rudimentary process.

COMPOSITION

Often, when we hear of a sound designer composing for a production, we think of the process of writing music to underscore scenes. Certainly some productions employ composers who create original music, and that person may or may not be the sound designer. They might also use the phrase "original music by."

More often, sound designers have to compose practical sound cues for a production. Here composition refers more accurately to the process of creating a sound that is recorded in a studio and then readied for implementation in the theatre space. Say, for example, you are producing August Wilson's *The Piano Lesson*. The script calls for chilling supernatural moments as ghosts haunt a brother and sister fighting over their family's ancestral piano. Short of finding and employing real ghosts, the sound designer must compose sounds that allow the audience to imagine that the family's ghosts are actually haunting their house.

Just as with any other design, no one sound design will fit any and all productions of the same play. No ready-made sound-effects CD fits the bill in all situations. However, original music composed for the premieres of certain plays is occasionally available at the same time that scripts are purchased and royalties are paid.

Similar to what in film and television is called a "Foley artist," a sound designer in theatre has a studio with a host of equipment (now mostly computers) and digital recorders that can be taken out to create field recordings. A sound designer usually also maintains a large sound-effects and music library.

A designer for *The Piano Lesson* may then pull a prerecording of the sound of howling wind, as well as use equipment to record human voices or even various musical instruments. The designer will then take those sounds into digital editing software and mix them into the effect that suits the particular production.

INSTALLATION

Now that the cues are ready, they can be deployed in the theatre space. A sound designer may install the design or hire a sound engineer, often a highly specialized person who understands the science of acoustics, the physics of sound wave movement, and the technical specifics of the theatre building itself.

One installation issue that must be worked out in this process is whether the sound will be in stereo or in digital surround sound. Stereo sound uses two signals so that you can have variation between one side of the stage and the other, basically splitting the space into right and left channels. Many theatres are only equipped to deal with stereo signals.

Increasingly, though, and probably due to ubiquitous home theatre setups for DVD and high-definition television, many theatres are moving to surround-sound setups. Surround sound uses at least six different channels or signals that can carry the same, similar, or different sound tracks. In a six-channel setup, the channels consist of a front right, a front left, and a center channel, which send sound from the stage area in front of the audience. Two other channels also send sound from right and left but usually from behind the audience, creating a wraparound effect. The remaining channel is a subwoofer, which produces incredibly low pitches that are usually more felt in the body than heard in the ears. When you are at the cinema watching an action movie, that rumble in your seat during explosions is coming from the subwoofers.

Types of Speakers by Frequency or Pitch

There are four types of speakers, each of which is able to produce sounds at different decibels, the unit that measures the volume (not the frequency or pitch) of the unit's production:

- *Tweeter.* Named after the high-pitched sound of birds, a tweeter handles high-pitched sounds between 2,000 hertz (the base unit of frequency, abbreviated Hz) and 20,000 Hz, the upper limit of the human ear.
- *Midrange.* Sits between the tweeter and the woofer, about 300 to 5,000 Hz.
- *Woofers.* Named after the low-pitched bark of a dog, a woofer handles between 40 Hz and about a kilohertz (1,000 Hz, abbreviated kHz).
- *Subwoofer.* A type of woofer that handles super-low sounds, between 50 Hz and 150 Hz.

The advantage of using surround sound is the ability to move the sound around the audience at will. In director Robert Wilson's production of Henrik Ibsen's play *When We Dead Awaken*, sound designer Hans-Peter Kuhn created a complex sound-scape of barking dogs, notes from a piano, and human whistling that floated around the audience and supported Wilson's surreal and dreamlike production choices.

The advent of wireless speakers has, in recent years, also been a boon for sound designers, allowing them much more flexibility in placement.

The Contemporary Situation for the Sound Designer

Some years ago, an actor was playing the title role in Archibald MacLeish's *J.B.*, a modernized version of the Book of Job. He writhed in torment center stage and cried out, "Show me my sin, O God!" The script calls for God to answer, and God's voice had been recorded and processed to add a special electronic effect. When the tape deck failed because of faulty maintenance, the actor's faith in God, the theatre, and electronics shriveled visibly. A quick-witted technician snatched up a script and thundered out the lines, substituting for Jehovah, and the scene went on.

Sound technicians share the same terrors as others in the theatre. The missed cue, the equipment failure, the inept technician—all can undermine the work created by dozens of people laboring for months.

The possibilities for sound designers today are growing exponentially. MFA programs have been added to many theatre departments, and most well-trained sound designers have no trouble finding work. If the designer knows how to compose original music for plays, all the better, and most MFA programs do require sound design students to take at least beginning composition classes.

Since *Jesus Christ Superstar* sound designer Abe Jacob, the first self-identified sound designer on Broadway, sound design has come a long way. Computer software has made digital editing much easier, and computers can now execute cues. Sound can wrap around the audience and create never-before-heard effects in live theatre—for example, the helicopter landing in *Miss Saigon* or the complicated "soundscapes" created for any number of companies, from De La Guarda (a New York City company) to Dumb Type (a Kyoto-based performance collective). And in recognition of the importance of sound to even the most mainstream theatres, the first-ever Tony for Best Sound Design was awarded in 2008.

The Projection Designer

As modern theatre has tended away from traditional scenery, it has also given increased respect to technical and design elements. Modern theatre artists attempt to combine all the visual and aural elements into an organic, unified production concept. That doesn't mean that every new technology must be wildly incorporated into every production, but it does mean that we continue to be inspired by new tools and possibilities. This section of the chapter simply provides an introduction to a burgeoning field of theatrical design: projections. Straddling the border between scenic and lighting design, projections help define place, mood, and style and enhance the visual world of the play. Refer to our earlier discussions about the ways that scenery and lighting do this, and you will see how projections compare.

Though we think of projections as "new" technology, the fact is that they have been around since "magic lanterns" (or *laterna magica*) were invented in 1650. A concave mirror behind a candle sent light through a painted piece of glass and onto a lens at the front of the "lantern" and then onto a white wall or piece of fabric. These were the earliest projectors.

With the creation and evolution of cameras and projectors, theatre artists began to see the possibilities of projected words and images to enhance their work. During the twentieth century, epic theatre creator Erwin Piscator used projections widely, as did designers in the West End (London) and the great American scenic and lighting designer Jo Mielziner—who even specifically designed at least one theatre (the Ring Theatre at Wake Forest University) to encourage their use. During the 1970s and 1980s, experimental artists like Ping Chong, the Wooster Group, and others also began using video and projections. By 1979, mainstream theatre began to embrace them as well. That year, Wendall K. Harrington (called "the godmother of projection design") created projections for a production of *They're Playing Our Song* that were bright, colorful, and included animation. However, her work on *The Who's Tommy*

Machine Play,* by Janice Fuller, was developed using devising techniques and incorporated projections throughout. Directed by Elizabeth Homan. Catawba College. *Sean Meyers Photography

(1992) is often cited as *the* breakthrough moment in projection design, as her projections took us into the world of pinball games in a way nothing else quite could.

Today, projector technology is advancing quickly, and projections are used almost ubiquitously. Images can wrap around 3-D objects, as you may have seen at Disney World or in online videos. The Opening Ceremonies of the 2016 Rio Olympics seemed to be using every projector in the world to transform the space into oceans, forests, favelas, and more. Projections can change space in an instant, and they are not limited by genre. As David Barbour recently remarked, they can

> make trenchant dramatic points or frothy, frivolous décor. In the recent Broadway revival of *The Normal Heart*, Larry Kramer's AIDS-epidemic jeremiad was compounded by the ever expanding list of the dead [projected] on the upstage wall. In *Priscilla: Queen of the Desert*, the title character is a broken-down van, covered with tens of thousands of LEDs, that serves as a mobile projection surface for giddily colorful animations that contribute mightily to that production's aura of drag-queen fabulousness.

However, Barbour, Harrington, and others note that projections are not the solution for everything. They can dwarf human beings, look too sterile and perfect, be too dim or too bright, interfere with lighting, or be just plain distracting. When they work, they can transform space, add vibrancy, and support the mood and ideas of the play, but they can also be used frivolously or out of laziness. Projecting an image of bookcases and windows to say "This is a living room" might seem like a smart solution, but more often than not, it is simply an ill-advised shortcut. Stories abound of distracting moving images that have dampened audience response to the actors, of overly literal choices that stunt audience imagination, and of projection choices that seem at odds with the rest of the production's design. How we incorporate projections into our productions should therefore be done with real intentionality and not just a desire to use "the cool new toy."

That said, not everyone can afford to buy these "toys." The kinds of projectors used professionally are still prohibitively expensive for many colleges and small theatre companies, often costing $30,000 or more. However, as with all technology, the price

Wendall Harrington's stunning projection designs for *Don Giovanni* at Der Jyske Opera, Denmark. *Courtesy of Wendall Harrington*

will eventually come down. Software will also become more streamlined and easier to deal with, which is a good thing, since it is currently time-consuming to work with. The cueing of projections is more like working with film than with still images, so editing and running the cues is as time-intensive as dealing with long sound cues. The learning curve for coordinating these cues with conventional lighting can be steep, as well, and if your projectors are not high quality or can't be positioned well because of the idiosyncrasies of a theatre's architecture, you may end up spending a lot of time on something that you're not happy with the look of.

However, when used wisely, projections can lift a production to new visual heights. Harrington, who has been designing with projections for over thirty-five years, says, "Projection has been a part of theatrical language since the early 20th century. I like to think of it as the poetic part of that language." Take note of the image from *Don Giovanni*, and you can see the kind of impact such poetry can make. The flames echo the stage composition, as both people and fire surround Giovanni, and their size and intensity maximize his fear and suffering.

Our assessment of the strengths and weaknesses of projection design will grow as more critics write about their use and as more knowledgeable practitioners enter the field. Harrington runs the projection design MFA program at Yale, and the faculty at Carnegie Mellon have created a similar program. In this new generation of students, we can look forward to finding designers who skillfully incorporate projections as another layer in an overall design aesthetic. MFA programs at other schools will undoubtedly pop up in the coming years, teaching designers not only *how* to work with projections but also *when* to use them to help tell stories more eloquently.

Conclusions

The temporal designs of lighting, sound, and—sometimes—projection designers contribute to our experiences in the theatre in ways that we often don't notice. Rhythm, mood, and the simple ability to see and hear the action of the play are deeply affected by what these designers do. The complicated technical understanding required to do these jobs well must be matched by the same drive that all theatre artists have: a desire and ability to tell stories in ways that communicate clearly and move us emotionally.

Key Terms

Appia, Adolphe (1862–1928) Swiss scenic and lighting designer whose innovations revolutionized stage production in Europe and America.

batten A pipe suspended from the fly space to which technicians may attach scenery and lighting equipment to facilitate shifting.

chiaroscuro A term from the graphic arts indicating the depiction of a subject in such a way as to give the impression of three dimensions. A useful concept in lighting design.

cue A signal for a technician or an actor. An actor's cue to enter the stage setting, for example, is often a line from another actor; the cue for a lighting technician to adjust stage lighting may be an actor's touching a light switch.

decibel A basic unit of measure of volume in sound.

dimmer A device connected to stage lights allowing technicians to vary the intensity of stage illumination.

Fresnel A widely used stage lighting instrument, named after the inventor of the stepped lens common to such instruments. It casts a pool of light with soft edges that can easily blend with the light of other instruments.

gel, gelatin A term used for any color filter placed over stage lighting instruments. These filters were formerly made of rolled gelatin, hence the use of these terms for any such filter.

Harrington, Wendall K. The "godmother of projection design." Professional projection designer and founder of the projection design MFA program at Yale.

hertz (Hz) A basic unit of measure for frequency or pitch in sound.

International Alliance of Theatrical Stage Employees (www.iatse.net) A union for many stage technicians.

LED (light-emitting diode) For our purposes, LEDs are used in an increasingly popular kind of lighting system. They are lightweight, portable, and very flexible but as of 2016 still had limitations in intensity and dimming.

leko A common lighting instrument found in theatres for more exact lighting distribution, otherwise known as an ellipsoidal reflector spotlight.

lumen A basic unit of measure for intensity or output of light.

midrange A type of speaker that produces pitches between tweeters and woofers.

PAR (parabolic aluminized reflector) lights, PARcans Lighting instruments for general light distribution or washes on the stage.

scoop A lighting instrument named after its ice-cream-scoop shape and used for general lighting.

tweeter A type of speaker that produces the highest-pitch sounds.

United States Institute for Theatre Technology (www.usitt.org) An organization for those concerned with the technical theatre at any level of production. Publishes *Theatre Design and Technology* quarterly.

woofer, subwoofer A type of speaker that produces the lowest-pitch sounds.

Discussion Questions

1. Compare and contrast the roles of lighting designer, sound designer, and projection designer. What goals and procedures do they share? What is different about their jobs?

2. Select a couple of pieces of music for one of the plays you've read in class. Specify exactly where in the production these pieces would be played. Now discuss these choices. What does each choice convey? What visual choices might be stylistically congruent with these musical choices?

3. Choose two of your favorite movies that contrast in mood. Now look at the lighting in each, and describe the choices that helped create that mood. Do the same with the sound.

4. Again using one of the plays that you've read, imagine the quality of light for a specific scene of the play. How bright (intense) would the light be? What colors of gels would be appropriate? Do you envision directional lights in this scene? Gobos? Practicals? Be ready to discuss your choices.

5. Talk about the role of projections in the theatre. How do you suppose this is different from just projecting a movie onstage? How might they be used to enhance the production of a play you've seen or one you've read in class?

Suggested Readings

Gibbs, Tony. *The Fundamentals of Sonic Arts and Sound Design.* London: AVA Publishing, 2007. Covers a variety of issues and ideas as well as applications (theatre, film, television, art installations).

Kaye, Deena, and James Lebrecht. *Sound and Music for the Theatre.* New York: Back Stage Books, 1992. A superb mix of the conceptual and the technical makes this text a must for all sound designers.

Gillette, J. Michael. *Designing with Light.* 5th ed. New York: McGraw-Hill, 2007. An up-to-date introductory text, lavishly illustrated.

Leonard, John A. *Theatre Sound.* New York: Theatre Arts Books, 2001. Covers all of the basics of the use of sound in theatre practice.

Shelley, Steven Louis. *A Practical Guide to Stage Lighting.* St. Louis, MO: Focal Press, 1999. Covers the concepts of basic lighting design and implementation.

Swift, Charles. *Introduction to Stage Lighting: The Fundamentals of Theatre Lighting Design.* Colorado Springs, CO: Meriwether, 2004. A basic introduction to stage lighting.

Talbot-Smith, Michael. *Sound Engineering Explained.* 2nd ed. St. Louis, MO: Focal Press, 2001. Covers the physics as well as the electronics of sound design application.

Part IV

THEATRE SCHOLARSHIP

The idea of condensing all of theatre history, theory, and dramaturgy into one short chapter is, admittedly, absurd. Thousands of books have been written on the subject, with volumes often devoted to a single production, designer, director, playwright, performer, historical period, or idea.

However, you will have certainly noticed that our focus in this text is on the practitioners. So, though we can only give you a brief overview of the topics with which some theatre scholars concern themselves, we believe such an overview will give you a sense of who they are, what they do, and why.

CHAPTER 9

The Historian, the Theorist, and the Dramaturg

*Theatre is a clear window into the mind, the soul, the heart of hu-
mankind—the study of which should be the aim of higher education.
Theatre brings life to learning.*

—Jane Alexander

A substantial body of work exists concerning the history and theory of the theatre.
Although this text examines the theatre as a contemporary process, students can gain
considerable insight into that process by examining the theatre's evolution and heritage.

The Theatre Historian

Over the past century, scholars have found value in examining theatre history as a way
to delve into the nature of the art form and the nature of the times in which it took
place. Whatever its context, the theatre must appeal to a significant section of society;
if it does not, it ceases to exist. By analyzing and examining what appealed to a specific
audience and how, scholars can deduce much about that audience.

Most college and university theatre departments include courses in dramatic
literature, history, and criticism, especially at the graduate and upper-undergraduate
levels. Theatre departments hire specialists in theatre scholarship to teach such courses.
These professors research various theatrical topics and frequently publish their work
as books or as articles in scholarly journals, such as *Theatre Survey*, *Theatre Journal*,
Nineteenth-Century Theatre Research, and *Theatre History Studies*, among many others.

Professors find another outlet for theatre scholarship in theatre associations that
meet regularly at state, regional, national, and international levels. Typically, writers
submit abstracts for papers to committees of scholars, who then select the best of these
and arrange the program for the conference. Participation in such conferences, along
with publication and other factors, may weigh heavily when professors apply for pro-
motion or tenure at their institutions. The Association for Theatre in Higher Education

(ATHE), the American Society for Theatre Research (ASTR), state and regional groups, and similar organizations in other countries organize such programs.

Many theatre professionals have been students of theatre history. Edwin Booth (1833–1896), one of America's greatest actors, maintained a large personal library, which he donated to The Players in New York. Group Theatre founder Lee Strasberg's (1901–1982) private theatrical library was more comprehensive than the theatrical collections of many university libraries.

Scholars from other fields frequently find value in theatre research and scholarship. Scholars of history, popular culture, philosophy, aesthetics, psychology, economics, languages, English, communication, and other fields have investigated the theatre (even as the theatre has investigated them), creating an immense body of theatre and interdisciplinary literature. In fact, the literature is so comprehensive that we have made no attempt in this chapter's suggested readings to even outline it. Go to your library for both surveys and individual topics.

An Overview of Theatre History

Historical study is valuable for many reasons, not the least of which is its ability to illuminate the present and prepare us for the future. You may therefore find it helpful to know what historical eras have been particularly fruitful for theatre historians. Remember, however, that what are considered "important" areas of study change continually, and the information provided here is limited by space and scope. This, then, is not an exhaustive discussion of topics and "golden ages" but is, instead, a representative list that gives some sense of the historical and cultural breadth of theatrical experience.

ANCIENT EGYPT

Theatrical studies of Egypt from 3000 BCE to 1000 BCE have focused on religious myths and rituals. Often called "pyramid texts," Egyptian drama physicalized in ritual form the complex symbolism of Egyptian philosophy, theology, sociology, and politics. The legends of Osiris and Isis were the most frequent subjects of these rituals, which focused on concepts of birth and death and contained dialogue, enactment, and enough dramatic conventions for us to consider the Egyptians as having the oldest drama in the world.

ANCIENT GREECE

Fifth-century-BCE Athens has generated an enormous body of scholarship. Western acting as we know it, tragedy and comedy, and dramatic theory and criticism all have their roots in ancient Greece. Tragic playwrights Aeschylus (c. 525–456 BCE), Sophocles (c. 496–406 BCE), and Euripides (c. 485–406 BCE) wrote during this

Greek "golden age." Comic playwright Aristophanes (active 427–after 388 BCE) is considered the greatest writer of Greek "old comedy."

Like Egyptian drama, Greek drama was an enactment of rituals and forms from mythology. Legends like those of King Oedipus (who mistakenly killed his father and married his mother) and Medea (who vengefully murdered her own children) were popular subject matter to the Greek crowds of up to seventeen thousand spectators per play. Most Greeks already knew the stories from oral tradition and came to see the skill of the actors and hear the language of the playwrights. Though Greek comedy is still well respected, it is the Greek tragedies that have attracted the most attention. Music and dancing also played significant parts in Greek drama in its original form and in contemporary productions. Ethical issues and powerful conflicts continue to make such plays as *Antigone* and *The Trojan Women* exciting theatre for contemporary audiences worldwide.

The philosopher Aristotle wrote extensively on the forms of drama he saw enacted at the large city festivals where Greek drama was produced. His *Poetics* is still an important basis for conversation about the nature of tragedy and the basics of dramatic art.

Lysistrata, the most produced ancient Greek comedy, focuses on Aristophanes's concept of the "happy idea." The women of Sparta and Corinth deny sex to their husbands until the men stop their war with one another. Directed by John Friedenberg. *Courtesy of Wake Forest University Theatre. Photo by Bill Ray*

THE ROMAN REPUBLIC AND EMPIRE

Roman drama began around 240 BCE. Plautus (254–184 BCE) was the most popular of Roman comic writers and was quite prolific, penning at least forty-five plays. Terence (c. 185–159 BCE), less popular than Plautus but still very influential, emphasized character and language. His high moral tone was later picked up by medieval and Renaissance writers. These plays, along with others of the time, were performed by male actors in masks and were attended by members of both sexes and all social classes. Rome's major writer of tragedy, Seneca (4 BCE–65 CE), also influenced future writers. Though his plays were probably never performed in Rome, their five-act structure, moral themes, supernatural scenes, and theatrical conventions, as well as their violence, are echoed in works by Shakespeare and other Elizabethan writers.

Roman gladiatorial contests, wild animal fights, and staged sea battles also developed increasing popularity during the Roman Empire. More heavily attended than tragedy and comedy, these entertainments were sometimes bloody spectacles involving human deaths. Romans also enjoyed watching acrobats, dancers, musicians, tightrope walkers, and the like. They were also famous for building huge amphitheatres with richly ornamented pillars, statues, and other architectural details.

CHINA

China's theatrical tradition goes as far back as the ceremonial dance rituals of the Chou dynasty (1122–255 BCE). At the same time that Europeans forbade women from performing, both sexes were allowed onstage in Chinese theatres. China, of course, extends over a very large territory, and its tradition is quite old, so its history includes a wide variety of theatrical styles and practices too numerous and varied to mention here. Puppet shows, open-air dramas, farces, religious plays, and "elegant dramas" all found audiences. Two distinctive features of Chinese performance are the emphasis traditionally placed on physical skill and the presence of music to underscore or provide counterpoint to the onstage action. As mentioned in chapter 6, China was also home to one of the earliest schools of acting, the Pear Garden, in the eighth century.

The best known of Chinese theatrical styles is Beijing opera, which came to popularity in the nineteenth century. Virtually unrelated to Western opera, Beijing opera includes acrobatics and dance-related movement accompanied by sung or intoned words with (of course) musical accompaniment. Each gesture has particular meaning, as do the elaborate costumes and makeup worn by the rigorously trained Beijing opera performers, many of whom begin theatrical education at the age of seven or eight. Beijing opera's stage designs tend toward the simple, since the focus is on the performers. Many other opera forms exist in China, as well, with local and regional versions retaining their own individual conventions and traditional texts.

Despite a twentieth-century influx of Western theatre practices into China, traditional forms continue to form the basis of most Western theatrical study of China.

Twentieth-century playwright and theorist Bertolt Brecht was only one of the many Westerners influenced by Chinese theatrical tradition.

JAPAN

Evidence exists that Japanese theatre may have begun as early as 350 BCE. The classical forms of Japanese traditional theatre include Noh, Kabuki, and Bunraku.

- Noh theatre offers a complex blend of music, singing, and theatre. Noh actors wear traditional dress and intricate masks and sing their story accompanied by live musicians. Actor movements are highly symbolic and communicate a wide range of emotion and story detail.
- A more popular form of Japanese theatre is Kabuki. The masks of the Noh characters are here replaced by colorful and striking facial makeup and brightly colored costumes. Much of the emphasis in Kabuki is on the spectacle of the story. Live music also accompanies Kabuki plays.
- In Bunraku, or puppet theatre, the narrator tells the story and speaks for all the characters, while several puppeteers control each puppet. Learning to puppeteer traditionally takes at least ten years to perfect because the body language of the puppets is so intricate and precisely detailed to allow for the most expressive movement.

Chinese opera in Shanghai. *Courtesy of David Phillips*

Many contemporary productions borrow from the best elements of both East and West. For example, Chicago's Wisdom Bridge Theatre Company produced a hybrid Shakespeare and Kabuki *Macbeth* in the 1980s. Even commonplace conventions used in the West, such as having stagehands dress in completely black so that they seem invisible, come from the East.

Questions of cultural appropriation are worth considering in these kinds of intercultural productions. Please see the sidebar on this important topic, and also bear in mind that it is possible—and even important—for those of us in the theatre to figure out ways to create bridges between cultures, to help us learn from each other and empathize with each other. Cultural *exchange*, in which cultures share mutually, is very different from cultural *appropriation*, in which the borrowing trivializes the culture in question. The power dynamics of such "bridging" must, therefore, be a part of the conversation, lest we actually do damage to our connections.

Cultural Appropriation and Cultural Exchange

In the theatre, the differences between cultural appropriation and cultural exchange can be hard to pin down.

Cultural appropriation. To kick-start a conversation about cultural appropriation, we thought we would remind you of a recent controversy: the debate over the mascot and name of the Washington Redskins. On the side of retaining the Redskins name and mascot, people suggest opponents are overly sensitive, that they are disregarding the team's traditions, and that it will be too expensive to change the name. They sometimes say the name is "a tribute to the Indians." You should feel free to debate this point. On the other, perhaps less obvious, side are arguments that we hope reveal the problem of cultural appropriation—which is fundamentally a problem of privilege. So what's the big deal?

1. *Uneven power.* In the case of the Redskins, the use of the name and image shows an uneven power dynamic. The white people who own the team make the choice about the name, the image, and its use. So they get to say whether it is offensive or not and use the name and the image as they like. If it is upsetting to Native Americans, it does not matter from a legal perspective, since the legal system endows the team owners with the power to use or misuse it as they see fit. Within cultural appropriation, the question of who has the power is always important.

2. *Trivialization of suffering.* Culturally appropriated images like this one can trivialize the oppression of native people. It may surprise you to know that the term "redskin" comes from a practice by white settlers of scalping (and even sometimes taking genitalia) to prove to colonial and state governments that Native Americans had been killed—something settlers were actually paid to do. The "red skins" of native people were handed over as proof of government-sanctioned murder. You can probably see why this doesn't feel like a tribute to people whose great grandparents were killed this way. In the theatre, as in sports, we run the risk of trivializing and offending people if we use shorthand we don't fully understand—especially when that shorthand is about something deeply painful.

3. *Money.* The owners of the Redskins team profit from an image taken from Native American culture without responsibility to that culture. The reservations some of our native people live on are some of the poorest places in the United States. Meanwhile, the owners of the team are making millions of dollars from the image of an indigenous person. Using someone else's culture/image without permission, without profit sharing, and without cultural investment or remuneration is another element of cultural appropriation.

4. *Lies and half-truths instead of nuanced stories.* Using oversimplified, fictionalized, or selectively negative elements of a culture can spread lies about that culture. The Atlanta Braves, who do a "tomahawk chop" to cheer on their team may feel that it's all in good fun, but the image conveyed is that Native Americans were a group of vicious scalpers. Of course a good "mascot" needs to have some simple traits, so you can't tell a nuanced story of Native American life with such a figure. Perhaps, then, choosing such a figure is no more appropriate than a generic black man or a generic Japanese woman as a mascot. In the theatre, we have been guilty of stereotyping since the beginning. Note how many two-dimensional foreigners, prostitutes, and sassy black maids show up in plays. Though the last half century has brought great progress, the point is to remain aware of what we are doing and saying in our choices of images and narratives.

Cultural exchange. So is there a way to connect cultures in a way that is responsible? When, in choosing a setting for a Shakespeare play, we decide to swap in another culture's look, movement style, or other cultural elements, we must investigate whether we are making this choice to perpetuate stereotypes or to get an "exotic" look. Or are we doing it because the new context allows us to tell the story in a better and more inclusive or nuanced way? If we set *Romeo and Juliet* in Afghanistan, are there good reasons to do so? If so, will the director be from there or know a great deal about the country and its history? Will Afghanis be cast? Will designers have cultural competence? Will the team do the necessary research to understand how cultural history might help illuminate the play's themes and also speak to audiences? Does the choice lead to empathy and not "othering"? This is one way to look at *cultural exchange*, as opposed to cultural appropriation.

However, this is not a monolithic argument. In defense of playing people of different genders and cultures, Anna Deavere Smith, the playwright/performer of important solo plays *Twilight: Los Angeles, 1992* and *Fires in the Mirror*, once said,

> If only a man can speak for a man, a woman for a woman, a Black person for all Black people, then we, once again, inhibit the *spirit* of theater, which lives in the *bridge* that makes unlikely aspects *seem* connected. The bridge doesn't make them the same, it merely *displays* how two unlikely *aspects* are *related*. These relationships of the *unlikely*, these connections of things that don't fit together are crucial to American theater and culture if theater and culture are to help us assemble our obvious differences.

The solution, then, is not completely clear, but respect, an awareness of power, a sense of what is being communicated, what stories are being told, who is profiting, and whether we are learning from each other rather than dominating, all seem crucial if one is to embrace cultural exchange and avoid cultural appropriation. But of course this is the rule of good art, as well: know *what* you're doing and *why*, so that you can decide *how* to proceed.

INDIA

India also has a very old theatrical tradition, dating back to puppet theatre and Sanskrit drama (c. 100 BCE). Bharata's *Natyasastra*, the Indian book of dramaturgy, is comparable to Aristotle's *Poetics* and was written sometime between 200 BCE and 200 CE. Along with the *Ramayana*, the *Mahabharata* (the Great Poem of the Bharatas) is one of the great Hindu epics. Now divided into eighteen books, it is the story of two great rival families.

Dance-drama is also an important part of the Indian theatrical tradition. Kathakali, popularized in the seventeenth century, is one of the best-known forms of Indian dance-drama. In Kathakali, the performers wear elaborate costumes, headgear, and makeup. The dialogue is sung and is accompanied by intricate foot, hand, and facial movement. The beauty of Kathakali has long been admired in the West, and contemporary French director Ariane Mnouchkine has found intriguing ways to weave Kathakali elements into her productions—though again she has not been immune to critiques about cultural appropriation.

While theatre education is uncommon in India, governmental funding has allowed at least limited study of traditional and modern Indian theatrical practices. In contemporary India, theatre is richly influenced by amateur companies. Calcutta, for instance, has about three thousand amateur performing groups, and Mumbai (Bombay) has more than four hundred. These groups do both political works that examine social and governmental problems and less controversial comedies and melodramas.

Along with theatre and dance scholars, religious scholars have also spent a great deal of time studying Indian dance-drama. You may therefore find some interesting material on Indian theatre in the religion section of your library.

AFRICA AND THE MIDDLE EAST

Over the course of many centuries, storytelling, jesters, shadow puppets, and dance-pantomimes became popular in various regions of Africa and the Middle East. Traditions in the region are obviously very old, dating back to ancient Egypt (see earlier), and Turkish shadow puppets were recorded as far back as 1050–1123 CE. However, theatrical traditions here have probably attracted the least Western scholarship of any in the world. Tribal African storytelling traditions are long-lived and varied. But censorship and the unstable nature of political life in the Middle East and in sub-Saharan Africa have also made theatre production difficult and—when the drama has had political aims—dangerous.

In the West, the best-known contemporary African playwrights are South African Athol Fugard and the Nobel Prize–winning Nigerian writer Wole Soyinka. Fugard's plays, such as *Master Harold and the Boys* and *The Road to Mecca*, dramatize the ways that apartheid and other social/political systems have affected South Africans. Soyinka, who is generally recognized as the greatest living African playwright, was partially educated in England. He writes in English, but his plays are infused with the mythology of his Yoruba culture. Soyinka has had experiences as both a political prisoner and an exile from his native Nigeria, and these exemplify the problems of working in the theatre under oppressive political regimes. Nevertheless, his plays are courageous explorations of political, cultural, and gender conflicts. Such works as *Death and the King's Horseman*, *Strong Breed*, and *The Lion and the Jewel* theatrically heighten these issues with the use of dance, song, dense language, and vivid visual images.

INDONESIA

Masked dance theatre and puppet theatre have flourished for centuries in Indonesia and most of Southeast Asia. One of the most striking forms comes from the island of Java (Malaysia) and is called *wayang kulit*. Usually performed at night, *wayang kulit* uses flat puppets made of leather to cast shadows upon a screen. Masked and unmasked performers also do dance dramas (*wayang topeng*, which are masked, and *wayang orang*, which are unmasked). The stories performed throughout the islands are based in Indian and Indonesian mythology and are full of intrigue, death, demons, and animal characters. Traditional performances may have no written text, and music is not totally preplanned, so the performances are really structured improvisations. Gamelan music (literally, "gong chime orchestra") usually accompanies the performances, which are often very long, and may last into the early hours of the morning.

Trance dances, folk performances, and traditional court dramas of well-known stories are also common theatrical forms in Indonesia. In addition, professional urban drama has cropped up in Malaysia, East Java, Sumatra, and other places and is also heavily reliant on an improvisational tradition.

WESTERN THEATRE SINCE THE FALL OF ROME

Medieval Drama (c. 900 to c. 1500 CE)

After the fall of the Roman Empire, the Roman Catholic Church plunged European theatre into a nearly five-hundred-year ban. However, dance, acrobatics, and mime seem to have persisted, though we have no written evidence of how widespread their activities were.

Ironically, it was the Church that would spawn the reconstitution of drama. During the medieval period, the Church began to act out particular Bible passages. These dramatizations grew into staged Christmas and Easter stories so that the illiterate masses could understand the Latin liturgy. Regions in France, Germany, and England showed the most activity of liturgical drama. Eventually these dramas became so elaborate and so dangerously similar to previous, non-Christian forms of drama that the Church moved these performances into the town squares and churchyards. Cycles of plays with biblical themes spread throughout Europe. As these dramas became more complex, they also began to be performed in the vernacular language and not Latin.

However, it would be incorrect to conclude that secular, nonreligious forms emerged directly from liturgical drama. Instead, the secular dramas, including farces, folk drama, and morality plays, existed alongside the liturgical dramas in countries like France. These would lead to the first secular plays of the Renaissance.

Italian Renaissance

A swell of interest in the Greek and Roman periods due to the discovery of important classical texts by Horace, Seneca, Plautus, and others would lead to a rebirth of high artistic expression on the Italian peninsula. With the invention of the printing press in 1440, wide distribution of these classic texts—and, indeed, of all written works—for the first time became possible. During what is called the Neoclassic Age, the Italian Renaissance artists sought to mimic the greatest artwork of antiquity from classical Greece and Rome. The publication of a book by Vitruvius on ancient theatres, called *De Architectura*, was quickly followed by Italian works like Serlio's *Dell'Architettura*, which focused on stage effects and settings. As a result, sixteenth- and seventeenth-century Italy are known today for many advancements in the areas of theatrical design. Perspective painting and complex stage machinery (together known as Italianate scenery) transformed the previously actor-focused stages into lavish, spectacle-oriented affairs.

Largely subsidized and attended by wealthy aristocracy, the serious drama of the period focused heavily on reason and social order. What the Greeks and Romans had written as descriptions of artistic expression in their time were taken as strict guidelines

The Globe Theatre. ©ThinkStock

for how artists must work. For some, Aristotle's *Poetics* assumed the status of near law instead of a treatise on Greek theatre of his day.

A form of theatre called commedia dell'arte also emerged in Italy during this period. Performed by professional companies in open town squares and in streets, commedia was a farcical, improvisational, and highly physical style of theatre that relied on a collection of stock characters. Most of the actors wore half-masks and specific types of costumes to identify their characters, and almost all were excellent acrobats, mimics, and comedians. The plays they performed were simply scenarios or plot summaries that actors improvised around. Similar types of stock characters can be found even today, especially in television sitcoms and in the improvisational work on such television shows as *Saturday Night Live.*

Elizabethan England

Because of political conflicts and wars, the Renaissance came late to England. The English Renaissance, also called the Elizabethan Age because of the immense influence of Queen Elizabeth I, remains one of the most prolific and influential periods of drama the world has ever seen. The period produced such powerful playwrights as Christopher Marlowe, Ben Jonson, and of course William Shakespeare.

Though often denounced as sinful enterprises of the day, the public theatres of London offered a diverse range of dramatic styles from exciting tragedies (Thomas Kyd's *The Spanish Tragedy*) to well-crafted comedies (Shakespeare's *Twelfth Night*), as

Hamlet at Illinois Wesleyan University, Bloomington. *Courtesy of Pete Guither*

well as powerful histories (Marlowe's *Edward II*). Many plays of the period still hold up well in contemporary production. John Ford's *'Tis Pity She's a Whore* and John Webster's *The Duchess of Malfi* appear regularly in university and professional production seasons. And an entire industry based on the plays and life of William Shakespeare still flourishes in both the Americas and in England. A reconstruction of the Globe Theatre has been built in London and has become a major tourist attraction. And, as mentioned earlier, Shakespeare festivals in Canada and the United States are popular and important to the communities they serve.

Seventeenth-Century France

The seventeenth-century French theatre drew upon and popularized many of the innovations of the Italian Renaissance. Though most companies performed in converted tennis courts, some moved into impressive theatres and incorporated elaborate Italian-style (Italianate) scenery. During this time, talented French actresses (e.g., Mlle Du Parc, 1633–1668; Marie Champmeslé, 1642–1698; and Madeleine Béjart, 1618–1672) also made their presence felt through the production of plays by influential playwright Jean Racine (1639–1699) and playwright/actor Molière (Jean-Baptiste Poquelin, 1622–1673). Racine's tightly constructed neoclassic tragedies, such as

The Théâtre du Châtelet in Paris, France, is a theatre and opera house that seats twenty-five hundred. It took two years to construct and opened in 1862.
©ThinkStock

Phaedra, reflect the French near-obsession during this time with strict rules about form and content, while Molière's comedies fused commedia dell'arte elements with this neoclassic bent.

Another landmark event during this time was the founding of the Comédie-Française in 1680. It still exists and is the oldest European theatre company. Actors in the company, who continue to perform plays written by Molière, still sometimes use staging and comic business originated more than three hundred years ago.

The Spanish Golden Age

Emerging from nearly five hundred years of Muslim (referred to as Moorish) rule, Spanish theatre was different in tone from the rest of European Renaissance theatre, even though liturgical drama was popular and existed productively alongside secular drama. Playwrights, such as the prolific Lope de Vega (who, by some estimations, wrote more than eight hundred plays) and Pedro Calderón de la Barca, wrote numerous secular and religious plays. These plays were performed in restructured courtyards known as *corrales*.

The Spanish theatre was truly national in flavor. It was a theatre for the masses; all social classes were welcome, and theatre was well attended, partly because of its outdoor, public nature. Its greatness lasted approximately seventy-five years, from 1575 to 1650, for by 1650, all the great authors (except Calderón) were dead. The Spanish theatre created a monumental playwright in Lope de Vega, whom Cervantes called "a prodigy of nature." A theatre of royal patronage (having been supported by Philip II, Philip III, and especially Philip IV) and one often opposed by the Church, the Spanish theatre retained the didactic flavor of its liturgical parentage for centuries.

Restoration and Eighteenth-Century English Theatre

The term "Restoration" refers to the restoration of the monarchy in Great Britain. From 1642 to 1660, theatre was officially banned by the Puritans, who had taken over the English government. With the return in 1660 of King Charles II, who had escaped to France to save his life, came important innovations in British theatre. For the first time in England, actresses were allowed onstage. Also in direct reaction against the Puritan repression, the content of the plays became scandalously sexual and full of complex repartee. Titles of popular Restoration plays communicate much about the period: *The Rover*, *London Cuckolds*, *Marriage à la Mode*, *Love in a Tub*, and *She Would If She Could* were all concerned with sexual intrigue and invariably revolved around carefree, witty lovers. Important playwrights of the period include William Wycherley (1640–1715), William Congreve (1670–1729), and Aphra Behn (1640–1689), the first woman to make her living as a professional playwright.

Though Charles II died in 1685, the Restoration period is usually said to last from 1660 to 1700. By 1700, the government had become more sympathetic to the rising mercantile class, who on the whole seem to have agreed with Puritan condemnations of the immorality of London plays and players. British theatre for much of the eighteenth century was, therefore, sentimental and domestic, though a number of very

Richard Brinsley Sheridan's 1777 play about gossip still has a lot of relevance today, as seen in this fierce pose from the Rutgers University Theatre production in 2015. *T. Charles Erikson*

fine actors, including David Garrick (1717–1779) and Anne Oldfield (1683–1730), made their careers at this time. By the end of the 1700s, laughing comedy found its voice in such writers as Richard Brinsley Sheridan and Oliver Goldsmith (c. 1730–1774). Laughing comedy, like Restoration comedy, was full of sparkling, witty dialogue, but it was ultimately less cynical in tone.

Russian Theatre

Early forms of Russian entertainment, including religious plays, puppetry, and ballet, were supported by the Russian czars and nobility, who often used serfs as performers. By the late nineteenth century, Russian theatre had begun to examine the human condition of the common folk. Great writers, such as Gogol (*The Inspector General*) and Tolstoy (*The Power of Darkness*), wrote for and about hardy Russian people.

At the same time, two major theatrical centers emerged: Moscow and Saint Petersburg. Georg II, Duke of Saxe-Meiningen (1826–1914), visited Moscow in 1885 and 1890, sending shockwaves through the theatre world and emerging as the world's first credited stage director. Influenced by the gifted actress Ellen Franz and by his stage manager and assistant Ludwig Chronegk, Georg II became renowned for his ability to stage historically accurate productions under a unified, singular-vision production concept. No longer were actors, sets, and costumes totally separate; all worked together as an artistic whole.

Gilbert and Sullivan's *H.M.S. Pinafore* (1878) still delights audiences with its combination of elevated language; song; and low, silly dances. Directed by James Dodding, with Jonathan Horvath, Natalie Cordone, and Aaron Bokros. *Courtesy of Wake Forest University Theatre. Photo by Bill Ray*

The Independent Theatre Movement, which began in the late nineteenth century in France, spread to Germany, England, and Russia, and emerged in 1897 as the Moscow Art Theatre (MAT). As mentioned in chapters 4 and 6 on playwriting and acting, the MAT embraced the idea of the ensemble company and focused primarily on realistic drama. Meanwhile, a nonrealistic movement emerged, reflected in the work of Vsevolod Meyerhold (1874–1940). Meyerhold, the first real auteur director, experimented with concepts of actor physicality and audience perception. He created a system of acting he called biomechanics, which focused on improving actor precision and efficiency and linked internal motivation to acrobatics. After the rise of the Soviet Union, Meyerhold's work was labeled formalist and intolerable to the government. Meyerhold died in 1940 in a Soviet labor camp, a "nonperson."

Despite such oppression, Soviet and Russian theatre maintained its hold on the people's imagination. Though Socialist realism, a government-supported, propaganda-driven style of plays, took over the Soviet theatre during Stalin's rule, after his death came a thaw in censorship and the emergence of government support of the theatre. Such support continues today.

The Development of U.S. Theatre

Theatre on this continent began with Native American rituals that combined animal imitations, dancing, music, and comedic elements. These date at least as far back as the sixteenth-century Aztecs.

With the establishment of European settlers came Western drama and an influx of amateur theatricals, as well as the occasional professional performance, the first of which was recorded in 1665. Plagued by censorship from religious groups—especially the Puritans—until the late eighteenth and early nineteenth century, American theatre was not much more than a venue for British actors in need of extra income. As the United States struggled to form a national identity separate from England, so too did the American theatre struggle for a new identity. Forceful American-born actors such as Edwin Forrest (1806–1872) and Charlotte Cushman (1816–1876) eventually gained popularity and became emblematic of the driven and energetic country that was emerging. American actors soon vied with British transplants for jobs in resident stock companies, and by the latter half of the nineteenth century, American-born stars were not quite so uncommon.

Despite the success of such women as Charlotte Cushman, gender and racial equality were, as in society, not one of the strengths of early American theatre. In fact, African American tragedian Ira Aldridge (1807–1867), who would become renowned for his work in Shakespearean roles in Europe, left the United States at least in part because of lack of work for African American actors. And while white women were able to carve a place for themselves in the theatre, few black women were, and even white women's role was a conflicted one. Though progress has been made, such problems were not really resolved in the twentieth century.

Throughout the nineteenth century, melodrama, operettas, popular entertainments, and Shakespeare existed side by side. The theatre centers of Boston, New York, and Philadelphia still drew heavily on English models but not without acknowledging the conflict between American and European ideals. Popular plays celebrated the American individualist and romanticized closeness to nature, and Anna Cora Mowatt's play *Fashion* (1845) mocked the pretensions of American bumpkins trying to copy European fashion. Augustin Daly's spectacular productions, such as *Under the Gaslight* (1867), showed off the country's fascination with visual effects. Touring was also big business. Every major star toured, and certain shows also developed huge followings. Nothing better demonstrated this than the many treatments of Harriet Beecher Stowe's popular novel *Uncle Tom's Cabin* that toured the country throughout the second half of the century.

By the end of the 1800s, American theatre was dominated by a group of businessmen called the Theatrical Syndicate, who were, through their monopoly of theatrical interests, able to censor plays that they believed wouldn't sell. As a result, European theatrical innovations, especially in realism, took much longer to come to the United States. Eventually the Syndicate's hold was broken, and small American theatres emerged, becoming part of the Little Theatre movement that flourished between the two world wars. Perhaps the most influential group to develop out of this movement was the Provincetown Players, whose members included Nobel Prize–winning playwright Eugene O'Neill (1888–1953) and Pulitzer Prize–winning playwright Susan Glaspell (1876–1948).

American Musical Theatre

Music has been a part of theatre from the very beginning, but musical theatre as we know it evolved through opera, operetta, and variety entertainments. Musical comedies of the late nineteenth and early twentieth centuries tended to be composed of loose plotlines devised as an excuse for upbeat song and dance numbers. Operettas and comic operas were also popular.

The 1927 musical *Showboat*, by Jerome Kern, was a serious play with music and so helped break ground for the serious musicals of the 1940s and 1950s. The 1943 Richard Rodgers and Oscar Hammerstein Broadway hit *Oklahoma!* is usually seen as the most influential musical of its day. Its "dream ballet" furthered the plot rather than simply provided diversion, and it had serious subject matter, including an onstage murder. To today's audiences, *Oklahoma!* may seem tame and even a bit saccharine, but without it we would not have *Les Misérables,* the 1988 hit based on a Victor Hugo novel, and *Ragtime,* based on the E. L. Doctorow novel, which explores racial and class issues at the turn of the twentieth century.

Since *Oklahoma!* musicals have gone through a number of incarnations. The 1950s saw the continuing popularity of Rodgers and Hammerstein musicals, including

Musicians have always been an important part of American musical theatre. However, professional orchestras can be expensive, and many smaller theatre companies are turning to recorded tracks. Volume is obviously easier to control with recordings, but the responsiveness of the instrumental performers and the singers is lost, as is the warmth of sound that comes from a live group of musicians. *Courtesy of Wake Forest University Theatre. Photo by Bill Ray*

The King and I and *The Sound of Music*. Musicals based on serious dramatic works also became popular. For instance, George Bernard Shaw's *Pygmalion* was adapted into the musical *My Fair Lady*, and *Romeo and Juliet* became *West Side Story* at the hands of Leonard Bernstein, Arthur Laurents, Stephen Sondheim, and Jerome Robbins.

Experimentation with subject matter and style continued through the 1960s with *Cabaret*, set in the decadent Berlin of the 1930s, and with the advent of rock music and nudity in 1968's *Hair*. Choreographer/directors Bob Fosse (*Pippin*, *Chicago*) and Michael Bennett (*A Chorus Line*) prospered during the 1970s. Meanwhile, Stephen Sondheim and his producer/director Harold Prince popularized "concept musicals"— musicals focused on an idea rather than a plot. *Company*, *A Little Night Music*, *Into the Woods*, and *Sunday in the Park with George* were a few of Sondheim's hits.

Revivals of popular musicals, as well as import musicals from Great Britain, including the aforementioned *Les Misérables*, *Cats*, *Phantom of the Opera*, and *Miss Saigon*, were also hits in Great Britain before they came to the United States for successful runs. Revivals tend to be the safest investments, since in principle what was popular before could be popular again.

During the 1990s, the youthful passion of *Rent*, the emotional and visual impact of *Ragtime*, and Julie Taymor's superb direction and costume design for *The Lion King* raised hopes (and revenues) for the Broadway scene of the next century.

By the 2000s, Broadway was filled with stage musical adaptations of movies. *Hairspray* (based on the John Waters film), *Legally Blonde*, *Xanadu*, *Young Frankenstein*, *The Color Purple*, *Spamalot* (based on the movie *Monty Python and the Holy Grail*), and others made big bucks on the Great White Way. Musicals based around popular music have also been huge hits (with some misses) especially for the baby boomer generation: *Mamma Mia!* (based on the music of ABBA), *Jersey Boys* (Frankie Valli and the Four Seasons), *Lennon* (a John Lennon musical that closed quickly), and *Movin' Out* (Billy Joel).

Still, some new works did well. A few of these include *Spring Awakening* (a contemporary, musicalized version of an 1891 German play), *The Drowsy Chaperone* (a very silly bit of musical theatre nostalgia), *Urinetown* (mixing bathroom humor with political relevancy), the hilarious and irreverent *Book of Mormon*, and of course the wildly popular *Hamilton*, a mixture of hip-hop and American history that has brought new audiences to Broadway and—along with *Urinetown*, *Book of Mormon*, and *Avenue Q*—made the theatre scene more youthful than it has been in decades.

In the past few years, the musical has also been a remarkable vehicle for expanding diversity on Broadway. *The Color Purple*, *Fun Home*, and—again—*Hamilton* rely on the highly emotional and empathy-inducing properties of song to connect audiences to stories and characters from across a wide swath of American culture.

THE FUTURE

Many of the theatrical innovations of the past century have been mentioned in this chapter or elsewhere in this text. The continuing development of contemporary approaches to acting, directing, playwriting, and design; the growth of Broadway, Off-Broadway, and regional theatres; the rise of educational theatre at all levels—these developments were all part of the twentieth century. As we look to the future and as technology continues to grow, the theatre will still be a handmade product, but—as in all eras of history—it will absorb, reflect, and contribute to the values of its time.

The Theorist

Theory and criticism constitute another branch of theatre scholarship, closely allied to both literary criticism and the study of theatre history. Indeed, because a great deal of the written material we have about specific productions comes from critics, the historical study of the theatre is often a study of the history of criticism.

As noted in chapter 3, there are significant differences between reviewers and critics. Newspaper reviewers are frequent theatregoers who offer a response to a particular production on a particular evening. They almost always write these evaluations within a day or two of seeing the production, and their knowledge of the play and of theatre history and theory may or may not exceed that of the average audience member. Scholarly critics, by contrast, are almost always formally educated in theatre; they rarely write to offer a "thumbs up" or "thumbs down" review of a given production. Rather, they tend to evaluate plays, productions, and trends from various different standpoints as a way to examine, among other things: (1) how productions, playwrights, performers, directors, and designers make meaning and (2) what their social, political, dramatic, and/or historical significance may be.

As is true among historians, "hot" topics among critics change over time. This is not a comprehensive list, but as of 2016, topics of interest, all of which intersect with theatre in important ways, include:

- Critical race theory
- Globalization and neoliberalism
- Feminist theatres and theories
- Labor history and theory
- Queer theory/LGBTQ studies
- Ecology and "green" theory
- "Trans" themes: transnational, transgender, transgressive, transformation, etc.

Each of these topics is complex and provides a unique way of examining plays and performances. Annual theatre conferences, such as the Association for Theatre in Higher Education (ATHE) and the American Society for Theatre Research (ASTR), provide a time and place for sharing ideas and research. This research reflects what has already happened (or is happening) in theatre, but it can also influence practitioners, providing a foundation for making choices in the theatre that can lead to surprising, exciting choices.

The Dramaturg

In many cases, historical facts and critical thinking are synthesized into a performance through the work of an insightful and resourceful theatre artist/scholar called the dramaturg. Many theatre practitioners have some background in history and criticism, but how much such study is used in practice varies from person to person. Dramaturgs use such research as the very basis of their work.

Even dramaturgs themselves disagree about their exact role, but no matter the definition, they are becoming a more commonly acknowledged part of the theatrical process. Dramaturg C. J. Gianakaris notes that "the function, if not the actual profession, of the dramaturg has been with us probably from the beginning of the theatrical enterprise." Their most basic functions are as literary experts and advisors to the director. Dramaturgs may also:

1. Help select a company's repertoire
2. Translate, adapt, and/or edit texts
3. Clarify and explain cultural, social, and political aspects of a given play
4. Contribute to the content and design of posters, programs, press releases, and other interactions with the media
5. Collaborate with the director in casting
6. Advise designers
7. Work with playwrights
8. Provide a valuable second set of eyes and ears for the director to help keep a production on track once it is in rehearsal

Sometimes known as literary managers, dramaturgs were often isolated from production and regarded as researchers or out-of-touch intellectuals. They have fought this reduction, however, and have in many cases expanded their roles to include the duties outlined here. They are valuable members of the production team because they can focus closely on the way that each production element interacts with the literary text. Unencumbered by the material concerns of building the show, a good dramaturg's exceptional knowledge of the theatre and careful text analysis can make him or her a superb advisor to producers, playwrights, designers, directors, and actors. With such help, productions can communicate to audiences better and be more historically accurate, dramatically valid, and conceptually sound.

Conclusions

Audience members do not have to know all the details of Elizabethan life to understand one of Shakespeare's plays. However, art is often enhanced by thorough understanding of its historical, social, political, and cultural context. New perspectives can also be gained through rigorous critical and theoretical study. In short, theatre can be more deeply satisfying when you are able to pick up subtle nuances from a script, a design, or the work of performers and directors.

Hopefully your study and exploration of the theatre will not end here. Theatre has added richness to the lives of millions of theatregoers, and as productions become increasingly diverse, there will surely be something to appeal to everyone who enjoys a connection to live performers onstage. But even if you never attend a play again, we encourage you to remember the tradition, passion, and hard work of theatre artists of all kinds.

Key Terms

Aeschylus (525–456 BCE) Greek dramatist, said to have written ninety plays, only seven of which are extant; the best known is the Oresteia trilogy (*Agamemnon, Choephoroi,* and *Eumenides*).

Anouilh, Jean (1910–1987) French dramatist, two of whose best-known works are *Antigone* and *The Waltz of the Toreadors.*

Aristophanes (c. 448–380 BCE) Greek dramatist and one of the outstanding comic playwrights of all time. Among his best-known works is *Lysistrata.*

Aristotle (384–322 BCE) Greek philosopher and scientist. His analysis of tragedy in *The Poetics* influenced drama for centuries and is still studied by modern scholars.

Beijing opera A form of theatre in China characterized by acrobatics and dance-related movement accompanied by sung or intoned words and musical instruments.

Bunraku A form of Japanese theatre in which puppeteers control intricate puppets while a narrator tells the story and speaks for all the characters.

commedia dell'arte A form of Italian folk theatre that flourished from the sixteenth to the eighteenth centuries. The commedia performers usually improvised their dialogue and business from a scenario rather than adhered to a written script.

Dionysus The Greek god of nature, fertility, and wine, equivalent to the Roman deity Bacchus. Dramatic contests, which began in 534 BCE, evolved in Greece from the Dionysian festivals.

dithyrambs Choral hymns of praise to Dionysus, thought by some scholars to be one of the main factors in the rise of drama in Greece.

dramaturg An individual who functions as a literary expert and adviser to the director.

Elizabethan Age The period of the reign of Elizabeth I of England (1558–1603), during which time Shakespeare, Jonson, and Marlowe led English dramatists to an unequaled dramatic excellence. Although the reign of James I (1603–1625) is called the Jacobean Age and the reign of Charles I (1625–1642) the Carolinian, some historians refer loosely to all three reigns as the Elizabethan Age.

Euripides (484–406/7 BCE) One of the three great Athenian writers of tragedy. His best-known plays include *The Trojan Women, The Bacchae,* and *Medea.*

existentialism Modern philosophy associated in drama with the Theatre of the Absurd. It varies widely among its many proponents, chief among whom were Albert Camus (1913–1960) and Jean-Paul Sartre (1905–1980).

Feydeau, Georges (1862–1921) French dramatist who specialized in farces, the best known being *A Flea in Her Ear.*

Globe Theatre (www.shakespeares-globe.org) The Elizabethan public theatre with which Shakespeare is most commonly associated. Built on the south bank of the Thames River in London in 1599, the theatre burned and was replaced in 1613 and was finally razed in 1644. A functioning replica has been built in London again; it runs Shakespeare productions all summer long—a highly successful tourist attraction.

Goethe, Johann Wolfgang von (1749–1832) Germany's greatest literary figure and a major playwright, especially noted for *Faust*. A man of many talents and interests, Goethe also addressed himself lucidly to problems of aesthetics and dramatic theory.

Jonson, Ben (1572–1637) English playwright, a contemporary of Shakespeare, especially esteemed as a comic writer. His most admired script is *Volpone*.

Kabuki A form of Japanese theatre in which actors wear colorful and striking facial makeup and brightly colored costumes.

Lope de Vega, Félix (1562–1635) Spanish playwright and the most prolific of all dramatists, credited by some with over two thousand scripts. Of the more than four hundred extant scripts, the best known are *The Sheep Well* and *The Mayor of Zalamea*.

Molière (1622–1673) Stage name of Jean-Baptiste Poquelin, a French actor/manager/dramatist usually regarded as one of the greatest comic geniuses of all time. *Tartuffe* and *The Miser* are among his better-known scripts.

Moscow Art Theatre A famous Russian theatre, still in operation, founded in 1898 by Stanislavsky and V. I. Nemirovich-Danchenko, and the site for the major premieres of most of Anton Chekhov's plays. Stanislavsky made his major theatrical contributions during his tenure there.

National Theatre (www.nationaltheatre.org.uk) The government-subsidized theatre of Great Britain, founded in 1963 with Laurence Olivier as director. Having won worldwide acclaim from the beginning, the company opened a magnificent complex of theatres on the south bank of the Thames in London.

Neoclassicism A literary and artistic philosophy that emerged during the Renaissance and spread throughout western Europe, stimulated by the rebirth of interest in Greek and Roman cultures and the lessening of ecclesiastical domination of thought. Basically humanistic, Neoclassicism found humanity's greatest hope for earthly happiness in analysis and systematic thought.

Noh A complex blend of music, singing, and movement in which actors wear traditional Japanese dress and expressive masks.

Plautus (254–184 BCE) Roman dramatist whose style was marked by a coarse wit, rapid action, and a considerable insight into human affairs. Plautus influenced many later playwrights. His best-known works include *The Menaechmi* (the source of Shakespeare's *Comedy of Errors*) and *The Braggart Warrior*.

Renaissance That period of time in Europe, roughly from the fourteenth to the seventeenth centuries, marked by increases in humanism, learning, and classicism.

repertory A collection of productions; more commonly, a production scheme in which several plays are alternated by a company, as opposed to the long run or stock approach to production.

Restoration, Restoration drama Literally, the restoration of the English monarchy with Charles II in 1660; in English literary history, the period following until about 1700. The drama of this period was a remarkable mixture of verbal wit and inverted moral values.

romanticism A literary or theatrical movement that emerged about 1800, extolling the virtues of natural instinct and the beauties of nature.

Royal Shakespeare Company Like the National Theatre, a government-subsidized British theatre company. The RSC, which tends to be somewhat more experimental than the National Theatre, operates theatres in London and Stratford-upon-Avon.

Sheridan, Richard Brinsley (1751–1816) British dramatist and manager. His best-known plays are *The School for Scandal* and *The Rivals.*

Sophocles (496–406 BCE) Greek dramatist who presumably wrote over a hundred scripts, of which only seven are extant, including *Oedipus Rex* and *Antigone.*

Terence (c. 190–159 BCE) One of the two Roman comic dramatists whose works are partially extant, the other being Plautus. Terence had a more sophisticated and literary style than Plautus and thus had greater influence on Renaissance scholars and playwrights.

Thespis A legendary Greek poet and actor of the sixth century BCE, traditionally considered the first actor and the founder of drama. He won first prize at the earliest recorded drama festival in Athens in 534 BCE.

Voltaire (1694–1778) Pseudonym of François Marie Arouet, a French man of letters and philosopher whose several plays and staging reforms had important effects on the French stage.

Discussion Questions

1. How does the study of theatre history and criticism fit into the study of theatre as an art form?
2. Do you have a favorite historical period? How does theatre of that period reflect the personal and cultural lives of the people who lived then? Can theatre offer a different perspective on that historical period than more traditional historical approaches do?
3. What similarities and differences are apparent in the theatre history of the different eras and geographical regions discussed?
4. What does a dramaturg do?
5. How might a dramaturg be useful in producing a particular play you have read? Of course, research is only one of many dramaturgical contributions, but you might devise a series of research questions for a play, as well as consider how an expert on the text might inform other production decisions.

6. Does theatre scholarship have relevance to the production of live theatre? If not, how do you believe the goals of the scholar differ from those of other theatre artists? If so, what particular skills and gifts do scholars contribute?
7. What other courses does your college or university offer that could further stimulate your knowledge and appreciation of theatrical practice? Which of these courses are performance based, and which are more scholarship based?

Suggested Readings

All of the books listed in other chapters could be valuable sources for a good dramaturg or any serious scholar of theatre history. It would be absurd to try to detail all the books that apply to the subjects described in this chapter. However, here are a few collections that could be valuable:

Brockett, Oscar G., and Franklin Hildy. *History of the Theatre*. New York: Pearson, 2012. The most widely used theatre history text on the market.

Gassner, John. *Masters of the Drama*, 3rd ed. New York: Dover, 1951. An immense compilation (890 pages), often used as a reference work or a text in theatre history classes.

McConachie, Bruce, Tobin Nellhaus, Carol Fisher Sorgenfrei, and Tamara Underiner. *Theatre Histories: An Introduction*. 3rd ed. New York: Routledge, 2013. A widely admired and relatively new text written by multiple theatre history scholars from a variety of backgrounds. The text explores history and historiography and the creation of metanarratives.

Nicoll, Allardyce. *World Drama from Aeschylus to Anouilh*. Rev. ed. New York: Barnes & Noble, 1976. Comparable to *Masters of the Drama*, this volume was written by one of the outstanding British scholars of theatre and drama.

Smith, Cecil, and Glenn Litton. *Musical Comedy in America*. New York: Theatre Arts Books, 1981. A descriptive history of the rise and development of musical comedy from the beginning. Excellent insights on the rehearsal process and working with actors.

Index

About the Authors

Cynthia M. Gendrich is a professor of theatre at Wake Forest University, where she teaches acting, directing, introduction to theatre, and first-year seminars. In addition, she is the director of IPLACe, the Interdisciplinary Performance and the Liberal Arts Center. Interested in acting and directing history, theory, and practice, she directs and publishes regularly. Recent productions she has directed include *Honk!, The Importance of Being Earnest, Marisol, Embers and Stars: The Story of Petr Ginz, Smash,* and *King Lear.* Some of her articles include "Another Terrain: Theatre Nohgaku's *Pine Barrens,*" in *Theatre Topics;* "Noise and Nudity: Kyoto's Dumb Type" in *Theatre Forum;* and "Straight into the Body: Handmade Technology and the Akhe Group's White Cabin,*" also in *Theatre Forum.* She has also published in *PAJ, Theatre Journal, Western European Stages,* and *Theatre Studies.*

Stephen Archer is professor emeritus of theatre history at the University of Missouri, Columbia. Among his published works are *American Actors and Acting: A Guide to Information Sources, How Theatre Happens,* and *Junius Brutus Booth: Theatrical Prometheus.* His articles and reviews have appeared in *Theatre Journal, Dramatics Magazine, Theatre History Studies,* and other journals.